A Fable of a Seeker and a Sage
Destination Happiness
20 Secrets Revealed

Books and Booklets By J.P. Vaswani

In English:
The Seven Commandments of the Bhagvad Gita
Kill Fear Before Fear Kills You
Swallow Irritation Before Irritation Swallows You
Its All A Matter of Attitude
You Can Make A Difference
101 Stories For You and Me
108 Pearls of Practical Wisdom
108 Simple Prayers of a Simple Man
108 Thoughts On Success
114 Thoughts on Love
A Child of God
A Day with Dadaji
A Mystic of Modern India
Begin the Day with God
Beloved Dadaji
Conversations with Dadaji
Dada Answers
Daily Appointment With God
Daily Inspiration
Doors of Heaven
Education: What India Needs
Feast of Love
Five Fragrant Flowers
From Darkness Into Light
From Hell to Heaven
Glimpses
Glimpses Into Great Lives
God In Quest of Man
Hinduism
How to Have Real Fun Out of Life and other Talks
How to Make Your Life A Love Story
How to Overcome Temptations
How to Overcome Tensions
I Have Need of You
I Luv U, God!
Invest in the Child
Joy Peace Pills
Laugh Your Way to Health
Life After Death
Life is A Love Story
Love and Laugh!
Nestle Now
Notes from the Master's Lute
Pictures and Parables
Positive Power of Thanksgiving
Prayers of a Pilgrim
Prophets and Patriots
Sadhu Vaswani: His Life and Teachings
Little Lamps
Secrets of Health and Happiness
Shanti Speaks
Snacks for the Soul
More Snacks for the Soul
Stories for Meditation
Stories for You and Me
Teach Me to Pray
Tear-Drops (poems)
Temple Flowers
Ten Commandents of A Successful Marriage
The Holy Man of Hyderabad
The Kingdom of Krishna
A Little Book of Life
A Little Book of Wisdom
The Little Book of Prayer
The Little Book of Service
The Little Book of Success
The Little Book of Yoga
The Little Book of Freedom From Stress
The Magic of Forgiveness
The Simple Way
The Story of a Simple Man
The Way of Abhyasa (How to Meditate)
Ticket to Heaven
Twinkle, Twinkle Tiny Star
What you would like to know about Karma
Whispers
Why Do Good People Suffer?
You Are Not Alone!
You Can Be a Smile Millionaire

In Hindi:
Ishwar Tujhe Pranaam
Prarthna Ki Shakti
Alwar Santon Ki Mahaan Gaathaayein
Atmik Jalpaan
Atmik Poshan
Bhale Logon Ke Saath Bura Kyon
Chitra Darshan
Dainik Prerna
Krodh Ko Jalayen, Swayam Ko Nahi
Mahan Purush Jeevan Darshan
Santon Ki Lila

**Published by
Sterling Publishers Private Limited**

A Fable of a Seeker and a Sage
DESTINATION HAPPINESS
20 Secrets Revealed

J. P. Vaswani

Compiled by
Dr. Prabha Sampath
and
Krishna Kumari

A Sterling Paperback

STERLING PAPERBACKS
An imprint of
Sterling Publishers (P) Ltd.
A-59, Okhla Industrial Area, Phase II, New Delhi-110020
Ph.: 26387070, 26386165 Fax: 91-11-26383788
E-mail: ghai@nde.vsnl.net.in
www.sterlingpublishers.com

Destination Happiness: 20 Secrets Revealed
© 2007, J.P. Vaswani
ISBN 81 207 3146 2

All rights are reserved. No part of this publication may be reproduced, stored in a retrieval system or transmitted, in any form or by any means, mechanical, photocopying, recording or otherwise, without prior written permission of the publisher.

Published by Sterling Publishers Pvt. Ltd., New Delhi-110020.
Lasertypeset by Vikas Compographics, New Delhi-110020.
Printed at Sterling Publishers Pvt. Ltd., New Delhi-110020.

Contents

1. There Are Many Reasons To Be Unhappy!   7
2. The Truly Happy   15
3. The Realm Of Happiness   23
   - The 1st Secret of Happiness   29
   - The 2nd Secret of Happiness   47
   - The 3rd Secret of Happiness   71
   - The 4th Secret of Happiness   81
   - The 5th Secret of Happiness   92
   - The 6th Secret of Happiness   118
   - The 7th Secret of Happiness   133
   - The 8th Secret of Happiness   150
   - The 9th Secret of Happiness   162
   - The 10th Secret of Happiness   173
   - The 11th Secret of Happiness   183
   - The 12th Secret of Happiness   194
   - The 13th Secret of Happiness   218
   - The 14th Secret of Happiness   231

The 15th Secret of Happiness	247
The 16th Secret of Happiness	259
The 17th Secret of Happiness	272
The 18th Secret of Happiness	297
The 19th Secret of Happiness	324
The 20th Secret of Happiness	342

Chapter One

There Are Many Reasons To Be Unhappy!

Ram and Neela are a devoted couple who come from a close-knit family. Ram's old parents and Neela's widowed mother live with them, and are well looked after. Their children Anil and Deepa are well behaved, intelligent and lively. Ram looks after the textile business built up by his father. He is hard working and smart, and the business is flourishing. Whenever I visit the city in North India where they live, it gives me great pleasure to meet the family and greet them with love and affection.

I was surprised when Ram and Neela came to see me in Pune, though I was delighted to see them again. But something seemed to bother them. Not wishing to assume that anything was amiss, I waited for them to open up – which they did, soon.

"Dada, we need your special blessings for our son Anil," Ram began hesitantly.

"God is sure to bless him abundantly," I assured them. "When is Anil completing his Engineering degree?"

"That's next year, Dada," said Neela eagerly. "This year, he is appearing for his GRE. Please Dada, we want him to get into a first rate American University *with* a scholarship. Please bless him, Dada, that our dreams may come true."

I smiled and said to them that an intelligent and industrious boy like Anil would find many doors opening for him. But they insisted that he should get into an American University of his choice.

God heard their prayers and Anil won a scholarship to do his M.S. in Bio-engineering at a prestigious university in the U.S.

It was several months later that I visited their hometown. The family came to see me, but their smiles were conspicuously absent. They attended the *satsang*, met me afterwards, and departed. Only Ram's old father stayed behind to talk to me.

"I hope all is well with your family, brother," I said to him gently.

"We are indeed well, Dada," said the old man. "But alas, all is not well with our Anil!"

"Why, what of dear Anil?" I enquired anxiously.

The old man cast anxious looks about him and lowered his voice. "It hurts me to have to say this Dada," he said in a whisper. "Anil has broken his mother's heart. He has let us all down!"

"Whatever has he done?"

"He... he," the old man's voice broke into a sob. "He has married a Chinese girl!"

The old man was inconsolable. Nothing that I said could comfort him. As for Neela, she could not even see me without tears. Her American dream had turned sour!

I have known Jagdish since he was a young man of twenty. Starting off as a small entrepreneur, Jagdish has built up a formidable business empire that spans three continents. Recently, he has opened an office in China.

Jagdish talked to me about the opportunities now opening up for businessmen like him in China. His firm was poised for a quantum leap with the new move. He had himself travelled to Shanghai thrice in the last year, and he found the Chinese people professional and easy to deal with.

"Only give me your blessings, Dada," he said to me earnestly. "My hard work will take care of the rest."

I wished Jagdish Godspeed.

His teenage daughter Neha was with him during the visit. She looked on sullenly as Jagdish was explaining his future plans to me. The moment Jagdish moved away from us to attend to a call on his cell phone, Neha said to me imploringly, "Dada, I don't want Papa to take his business to China!"

"Why ever not?" I asked her. "Papa has worked hard to achieve his breakthrough, and he deserves to do well in China!"

"But Dada, as it is, we hardly get to see Papa! He's always flying off to Hong Kong, Taipei, Thailand or Singapore. If he starts going to China, we will probably see him only on Deepavali day! It may make my father very happy to expand his business into China – but it's going to make me and my kid sister very, very unhappy!"

Suchitra is the only child of doting parents. Her mother is a scientist and her father is a successful architect. Suchitra was a brilliant student through school and college, and topped her class in the M.B.A. programme. Multinational companies offered her lucrative posts. The parents were delighted and proud, and began to consider the best option open to her.

Suchitra turned down fat pay packets and plum posts and decided to work with a voluntary Aid organization in Gujarat – for a meagre salary.

"Money is not enough to make me happy," she told her parents firmly. "I have set my heart on a job that will benefit my fellow human beings. My education will be wasted if I do not use it to serve those in need."

Her parents were devastated by what they perceived as her stubbornness!

Keshav was a senior executive in a successful software company. His astronomical salary, generous perks and stock options had made him a millionaire before he was fifty years old. He was made the vice president of his company in Silicon Valley, and it was rumoured that in two years, he would be the C.E.O. of the company.

On his 51st birthday Keshav quit his job. He felt that he had been running a rat race all these years. He felt that he had heard the call of the spirit, and he wanted to devote his life to *sadhana* and *abhyasa* at the feet of a spiritual master. Above all, he wanted to return to India, to the land of his ancestors...

Keshav's wife and children would not hear of it. California was their home; they would not move anywhere else!

It was a tough choice — but they had to make it. Keshav moved to India to seek his heart's desire; his family stayed on in California, where, they felt, their happiness lay.

I thought of Ram, Neela, Jagdish, Suchitra and Keshav, as I was working at my desk one evening. They had all been in quest of happiness — all of them. Moving along different pathways of life, engaged in different spheres of human activity, they were all seeking happiness in their own way.

Seeking happiness... which meant that they were not really happy with their lot in life. At times, some of them made a choice which resulted in a great deal of unhappiness for their loved ones. What was it that went wrong for them – and thousands of others like them, all over the world? Could it be that in their quest for happiness, they were moving along wrong routes?

I left my desk and decided to take a walk. We were then on a retreat at a quiet hill resort and I had time at my disposal to devote to long walks, reflection and meditation.

What is it that can make people truly happy? Money? Pleasure? Power? Position? Authority? Popularity? Fame? But then have we not known men and women who had all this – and continued to be unhappy?

I mused on these issues as I walked along a scenic mountain track. The morning sun shone brightly. A fresh breeze was blowing. Birds chirped merrily. Down below, the green valley stretched as far as the eye could see. The whole scene was so beautiful and serene that it seemed so natural to think of human happiness and happy people. How could people possibly be unhappy in such a world as this?

And yet I knew that many of them *were* actually unhappy. Worse, they did not know how to find happiness.

My eyes alighted on the book I was carrying with me. I saw the portrait of my Master, Sadhu Vaswani, on the front cover. His eyes seemed to radiate peace and joy. A heavenly smile played upon his lips.

Sadhu Vaswani was indeed one of the happiest men I knew. One day, I asked him, "You have faced many difficulties and tribulations in your life. What is it that helped you to face such situations and remain unscathed, unfettered in spirit?"

His answer had been simple. He only said, "I praise the Lord!"

I was a persistent seeker those days – I would not rest till I had found a satisfactory answer to my queries. Therefore, I asked him, "What do you do when you are ill, and your body is caught in the throes of pain?"

"I still praise the Lord!" was the answer.

"And when you are passing through the strain of suffering?"

Again he answered, "I still praise the Lord!"

In those beautiful words lay the secret of the Master's happiness. The simplest way to be happy, he taught us, was to praise the Lord in all circumstances, all situations of life.

Simple – for those who had conquered themselves! So what about the rest of us? I was anxious to address this issue, so that I might be of some help to the brothers and sisters who came to me with hurt feelings, broken hearts and lacerated spirits – seeking that elusive happiness which they longed for.

I sat down on a rocky ledge that seemed inviting. It gave me a breathtaking view of the valley – and the clear blue sky above. I took in the beauty and tranquillity of the scene; I let it enter my soul. It was time to look within, time to reflect, time to find answers to the many questions people brought to me. I had been blessed enough to be gifted a Book of Wisdom – Sadhu Vaswani's profound teachings, his wonderful precepts, his living example and the crystal-clear message that was his life itself. I would need to undertake a journey of the spirit to find answers to my questions at the Lotus Feet of the Master.

That night, as I slept, I had a powerful vision. I dreamt I was a seeker, a *jignasu*, in search of happiness – not for myself alone, but for all humanity. Could we not all be happy and contented? If there was a secret of happiness, I was determined to find it and share it with my brothers and sisters!

Chapter Two

The Truly Happy

My quest took me across the land to distant hills, remote dwellings, and amidst the crowds who thronged cities and towns. Everyone I met had questions, but alas, very few had answers! With only my Master's teachings as my constant source of guidance, comfort and inspiration, I persisted in my quest.

On a beautiful evening, when pink and orange and mauve tinted the sunset sky, I came across a quiet *ashrama,* located at the foot of a hillock, far from the haunts of men, distant from the rush of the material world. My instinct told me that I was in the vicinity of a great soul who could offer me enlightenment and provide answers to the questions I had been asking. I could *feel* the positive, holy vibrations that emanated from the *ashrama* as I walked up the path that led to the front door. I knocked at the door.

"What is it you want?" asked a voice from inside.

"Master, I have wandered long, I have sought everywhere to find just one thing," I answered. "I am in quest of happiness."

The door opened and I saw a tall man in a white robe. His eyes were luminous; his glance, compassionate. "Come in," he said, with a smile.

I entered and sat at the feet of the saint. "Tell me Master," I said, "Where is happiness? How is it people are not able to find it though they look for it with single-minded purpose? Could it be that we have missed it altogether?"

The saint said to me, "Here are two fruits which I offer, for you to choose. If you eat one, you will *know* and *understand* what happiness is, if you eat the other fruit, you will enter the realm of happiness, but not understand what happiness is. Choose any one of these fruits!"

I considered the choice for a moment. Then I said, "Master, I choose the second."

The saint said to me, "You have chosen well. For to understand what happiness is and not to have it, is to be unhappy. To enter the realm of happiness is to rise above understanding. They are truly happy who rise above the dualism of mind and speech. They do not understand; they do not speak; but they are truly happy!"

I understood that the first fruit is like the shadow shapes that we keep on chasing. Happiness, true happiness, is an inner quality. It is a state of the mind.

If your mind is at peace, you are happy. If your mind is at peace, but you have nothing else, you can be happy. If you have everything the world can give – pleasure, possessions, power – but lack peace of mind, you can *never* be happy. So it was that a holy man exclaimed, "Nothing in the morn have I; and nothing do I have at night. And yet there is none on earth happier than I."

The realisation dawned on me that happiness does not depend on outer things. Happiness is essentially an inner quality!

It was a wise man who observed, "Happiness, in itself, does not exist. It is an illusion. Only by being happy with yourself can you find it."

"Unfortunately," the saint said to me, "we are engaged in searching the entire world over for happiness. If we search until our last breath, we are not going to find happiness 'out there somewhere'. We cannot buy it; nobody can hand it over to us on a platter. It is a very personal feeling – and it must come from within!"

"Does that mean, Master, that most of us will never find happiness?" I asked him gently. "After all, very few of us ever learn to look within!"

The saint smiled. "We can all actually experience happiness," he assured me. "No matter who you are, no matter what circumstances you are placed in, you must realise that happiness is your birthright. You are entitled to happiness."

I reflected on this powerful truth: Happiness is your birthright! But happiness must come from within you!

"You cannot depend on another person to make you happy or 'give' you happiness," the saint continued. "This will place a tremendous strain on both of you. On the other hand, if you are truly happy inside yourself and allow the other person to feel the same, then both of you are truly bringing happiness to each other … without any expectations, without any pre-conditions, without any anticipations."

I thought of Aldous Huxley who said, "Happiness is a by-product of effort." In other words, it has no existence or value in itself. It is not an object, which we can pursue or possess, or attain as a prize. Rather it comes as the effect of appropriate actions – and therefore Huxley's use of the term, 'by-product'; it is almost incidental – a bonus, which we receive in the act of self-fulfilment through right thought, right attitude and right actions.

They asked a woman who had lived life to the fullest – who had drunk the cup of life "to the lees", to the very dregs: "Have you known what it is to be happy? Can you tell us at which stage of life you were really happy?"

The woman thought for a while and said, "Whenever I was not unhappy, I was happy."

Perplexed, they requested her to explain what she meant.

"Happiness is the absence of unhappiness," she said enigmatically. "Or, to put it another way, unhappiness is the absence of happiness."

Here is a couplet which gives us much to think about:

Sukh sapna, dukh budbudaa
Donon hai mehmaan
Usko aadar dhijiye
Jo bhejhey Bhagwan

Joy is a dream; sorrow is a bubble – accept with reverence, whatever God sends to you.

The Wise One broke my reverie. "You can never get happiness by what you *do* or what you *achieve*. Even the so-called spiritual practices, on their own, cannot get you happiness."

"There are people who say they are searching for God," he continued, "but they are unhappy even when they are engaged in this lofty quest.

"God is Bliss Supreme – *Sat Chit Ananda*. Is it possible for anyone to be unhappy when they are seeking Perfect Happiness?"

"That is indeed a paradox," I agreed. "Yet I know that people who claim to be seeking happiness are profoundly unhappy."

"This paradox becomes 'truth' in proof because people have forgotten their true nature," said the Wise One. "God has made us in His image. He is perfect bliss. As His image, are we not also happiness personified? *Tattwamasi!* That art Thou! You are supreme joy and you are eternal bliss. It is only when you forget this that you lose your happiness. You forget your true nature. You forget that you are an aspect of the Divine. It is this lack of self-knowledge, this *avidya* that makes you unhappy.

"With an unhappy mind, how can you look for happiness? How can you hope to find it outside, when your 'inside' is dark and clouded?"

I remembered an anecdote narrated to me by a friend. There was a businessman who led a contented, busy life. He had a comfortable home, a lovely wife and children, a reasonable income and a thriving business. He drove a large family car, made in India, and he was very fond of his car.

One day, he saw a Mercedes Benz driven by a neighbour. "What a car that is!" he thought to himself. "How I wish I could own a car like that!"

The man became restless. He moved heaven and earth, spent lakhs of rupees to get hold of a Mercedes Benz. And – he was happy!

Consider this. The man was happy to begin with. Or, to put it differently, he was not unhappy. Then he *wanted* something. He did not want *to be happy* – he wanted *a car*. He attached a great deal of value to the car, and he did everything he could to obtain the car. He got the car. He was happy – or he was no longer unhappy – in other words, he was back where he started.

We may not all want Benz cars – but we are like this businessman. We are fine; we are content; we are happy – until we want something. Our happiness is replaced by "I want something." We pay a certain price. We get what we want. We say, "I've got it." We are happy – just as we were, before we wanted something.

So ask yourself – is it the Benz, the *thing* that you wanted that brings happiness to you? Does happiness actually come from a Benz, a bungalow or a diamond necklace? By themselves, none of these things can 'generate' happiness. You create a cavity, a depression in your mind when you *want* something. When you get it, the cavity is filled. You created the hole; you fill it, and you tell yourself, "I'm happy now."

You threw your happiness away, when you created the 'want' cavity. When you don't want anything, when you rise above 'wants' you leave your original state of happiness intact.

Haven't you heard it said of great men, "He is happy because he is above wants"? This does not mean that the man has everything he needs; it only means he can do without a lot of things. He no longer wants things.

"How can we rise above wants?" I asked the Wise One.

"Don't forget your true nature!" he said simply. "If you do, you will become unhappy. You will find happiness and unhappiness rising in waves, and beating on the shores of your life. You will be lashed by disappointments, failures and frustrations. In the end, you will learn to give up and you will say, 'I've had enough. I don't want anything anymore.'

Give up wants and desires; give up everything else – and you will find God. God is true happiness!"

"O Wise One!" I said to him, "How can people find true happiness? I would like to share with countless people the wisdom you have imparted to me. Tell me how people may be happy!"

The Wise One smiled. His eyes radiated compassion and understanding. "I will take you to the realm of happiness," he said. "You can discover for yourself the secrets of happiness – which constituted a way of life in that beautiful land."

"The realm of happiness!" I exclaimed. "Is there such a land here upon our planet? Do we have to travel very far to reach it? When do we set out? Do we travel on foot…?"

"I have told you already," smiled the Wise One. "The realm of happiness is within you. Come and sit before me. Make yourself comfortable and relax your mind and body utterly. We will begin our journey – with meditation."

"Will you accompany me on this journey, Master?" I enquired as I prepared to enter into meditation. "For I do not wish to lose so valuable a guide as you on this quest."

"I will be with you all the way," the Wise One assured me. "Now, let us shut out the world and enter within… let us discover the secrets of true happiness!"

Chapter Three

The Realm Of Happiness

My inner consciousness awakened as I entered into a state of deep meditation...

The Wise One and I stood upon a vast plateau. At a distance, its gentle slopes led down to stretching plains. The plateau itself presented a rolling landscape, rising here to a hillock, falling there to a low lying valley or a hollow depression. As we stood on high ground, I was able to see a green landscape all around, dotted with trees. A gentle breeze was blowing, and the sky was flecked with clouds, reminding me of the skyscape one sees through the windows of an aeroplane. As I stood gazing, we were enveloped in a soft mist. I took a deep breath and felt the freshness and cleanness of the moist air. In a few seconds, the mist cleared, and we saw it ascend gently to the top of the hillock just ahead of us.

"Shall we move on?" said the Wise One, leading the way. We walked up a steep slope, to what appeared to be the summit of the hillock, which sloped upward in an easy curve. The peak was actually a flat table land, with a magnificent view all around. On one side I saw a clear stream running down below, in a green and silent valley. I could actually hear the gentle murmur of its waters even where I stood.

I walked across the summit to the other side. An eerie, lonely landscape met my eyes here. Wherever I turned, I saw vast ruins – bare foundations, broken walls, mere shells of dwellings and houses, pillars standing without walls and roofs, stairs and steps that led nowhere, roofless structures – and a profound silence which I imagined I could actually hear around us.

"This is like the site of an archaeological excavation," I whispered to the Wise One who had walked across with me. The silence was so pervasive, so profound, that I felt that my whisper was like a shout. "Is this really the realm of happiness?"

"What makes you doubt it?" asked the Wise One with a smile.

"It's just this – the land is deserted! The weather is salubrious, the environment is clean and unpolluted, but I see nothing but ruins, and not a soul in sight!"

The Wise One began to walk down a narrow path that led us downhill towards the ruins. "Once upon a time," he said, sighing, "this realm was a bustling, prosperous land. Thousands of people lived and worked here, and led a happy existence. As the years passed, their descendants lost touch with their way of life – with the secrets of happiness once known to their parents. They were no longer happy people – and they could not continue to live here. Fate, circumstance, character, destiny – call it what you will, it took them away from the realm of happiness. And now, as you can see, no one lives here."

"But surely, people would like to come and live here, if they know that this place exists," I said earnestly. "Someone must tell them that this land exists, and that our ancestors lived here happily long ago. Someone must guide them here, show them the place, help them settle here and rebuild this place…"

"People are free to come here anytime they wish," said the Wise One. "But they must fulfil the basic condition in order to gain the right to live here."

"And what's that?"

The Wise One smiled his enigmatic smile. "They must be happy!"

"I'm reminded of the chicken-and-egg conundrum," I said, a little heatedly. "In school we used to argue endlessly over which came first – the chicken or the egg. Some of us said that the egg surely came first – and our friends objected that there must have been a chicken to *lay* the egg in the first place. To which we would reply that *that* chicken must surely have been hatched from an egg – and so the debate went on and on."

"What makes you recall that debate now?" asked the Wise One.

"Surely, as you can see, it's the state of this place," I replied. "If people want to live here, they must know the secret of happiness. But those who lived here earlier, those who knew the secret have all passed on! The *others* moved away from here because they had forgotten how to be happy. Now, the *others* are the only ones left. Who will teach them the art, the science, the secret of happiness and bring them back here?"

"Do you want people to be happy?" the Wise One turned to ask me.

"I do, I do!" I replied emphatically. "That's why I have come in search of you. That is why I sat at your feet to learn my lesson. That is why I have followed you on this quest. Whatever truths you impart to me, I hope to share with my brothers and sisters who long to be happy."

"You have answered your own question," smiled the Wise One. "You and others like you who want people to be happy, can lead them back to the realm of happiness by teaching them the secrets of happiness, which humanity, alas, seems to have forgotten."

Walking rapidly and talking earnestly all the time, we reached the foot of the hillock. Across the path from us, I saw a gate that stood open. It led to what had once been a beautifully landscaped garden, but was now wild and overgrown. Nevertheless, multicoloured flowers still bloomed there in abundance. I walked up the path into the garden, fascinated to have come across such a place in the deserted land.

"Isn't nature marvellous, nay miraculous?" I exclaimed with delight. "See how she displays her magnificent splendours even where there is no one to see!"

We walked quietly in the overgrown garden, carefully avoiding the weeds and finding our way through what must have been well-laid walkways once upon a time.

"Is it not strange," I remarked, "the moon and the stars shine, but the heart aches when no one is out to enjoy their beauty. The breeze blows, the sun shines, the flowers bloom – but there is no one to take pleasure from the sight. What a tragic loss, what a waste of beauty and goodness! What is the earthly use of a realm of happiness if there are no people to live here happily?"

"People will surely come back to live here one day," the Wise One said to me. "They are looking for happiness, desperately, all of them. Only, they are looking in all the wrong places. When they are taught to look in the right direction, they will surely find the secrets of true happiness, and this beautiful land will ring with the sound of human laughter and glow brightly with the spirit of human endeavour!"

"How I would love to see that wonderful sight!" I exclaimed. "And perhaps, I will learn something about the secrets of true happiness while I am here, in your enlightened company."

"The secrets are all right here," said the Wise One. "As I said, you only have to look in the right place..."

As he spoke, my eyes fell on a rose bush, bursting with beautiful red roses. The bush was untrimmed and had spread out wildly in all directions. A caring and skilful gardener would have pruned and cut it to give it an artistic shape. But even in its wild, overgrown state, it had its own charm. And sticking out of the bush, somewhere in the middle, was a little board, now completely hidden by the leaves.

"There is a signboard there!" I exclaimed. "Perhaps it tells us the botanical name of this particular variety of rose."

"Why don't you see what it is?" said the Wise One, "May be you will find something interesting."

Quickly, I reached across and cleared away the thick leaves which almost hid the sign from view. It was hanging to one side, almost upside down. With an effort, I straightened it, and exclaimed in surprise as I read the words on it:

If you want to be happy, make others happy!

The 1st Secret of Happiness

If You Want To Be Happy Make Others Happy!

"This is exactly what Sadhu Vaswani taught us!" I exclaimed.

In one of his beautiful poems, Rabindranath Tagore also tells us the same truth:

> I slept and dreamt that life was happiness.
> I awoke and saw that life was service.
> I served and found that in service, happiness was found.

Meditating upon this thought, I walked around the rose bush. "Give, Give, Give!" I heard Sadhu Vaswani's words ring in my ears.

"It is the mature, the wise, who are ever ready to give," said the Wise One. "They give of their time; they give of their energy; they give their efforts; they give away their smiles."

"You seem to read my thoughts," I said in wonder.

"Give, and you shall receive, it has been said," he continued. "We would do well to practise giving in every area of life. Give good wishes to everyone you meet. Send good thoughts, good feelings to everyone you think of. Give your considered, patient, understanding advice and suggestions when someone appeals to you for guidance. And, whenever you can, give money where it is needed, if it can help someone.

"Have we not heard that happiness cannot come to us from somewhere else? But happiness can always come *through* us; it comes through the work we do, the struggles we undertake, the love and attention we show to others. Give and you shall receive!"

Give! This was a word very dear to Sadhu Vaswani. On one occasion, he said to us, "I have but one tongue. If I had a million tongues, with every one of those tongues, I would still utter the word, give, give, give!"

"To give is to live," was the message of Sadhu Vaswani's life. How true it is that those that give, live! As for those who do not give – they are no better than dead souls!

Many of us are happy only when we receive, I reflected. We are not always prepared to give. Perhaps humanity falls into two major categories – those that give and those that receive. Let us seek, let us strive to belong to the first category. Let us give, and give, and give – and never be tired of giving. Let us give without any thought of getting something in return. Let us give freely, unconditionally – for conditional giving makes us mercenary.

Someone said to me once, "I gave that person so much – and all I received in return was ingratitude!"

Do not give to individuals! Think of the individual as an image of God. Your destination is God. Give in this spirit, and you will be abundantly blessed.

It has been said, "Happiness sought eludes; happiness given returns." Truly, happiness can come to us only indirectly, through love, service, prayer – and above all, from the happiness we give to others. For this is where real happiness dwells.

Here is a beautiful poem by Ella Wheeler Wilcox, which offers us an apt message in the context of *giving:*

> Give, and thou shalt receive. Give thoughts of cheer,
> Of courage and success, to friend and stranger.
> And from a thousand sources, far and near,
> Strength will be sent thee in thy hour of danger.
>
> Give words of comfort, of defence and hope,
> To mortals crushed by sorrow and by error.
> And though thy feet through shadowy paths may grope
> Thou shalt not walk in loneliness or terror.
>
> Give of thy gold, though small thy portion be.
> Gold rusts and shrivels in the hand that keeps it.
> It grows in one that opens wide and free.
> Who sows his harvest is the one who reaps it.
>
> Give of thy love, nor wait to know the worth
> Of what thou lovest; and ask no returning.
> And wheresoe'er thy pathway leads on earth,
> There thou shalt find the lamp of love-light burning.

When you go all out to try to get happiness, you find your efforts futile. But when you give happiness to others, you are sure to get it. It was Emerson who said that happiness is like perfume: you cannot sprinkle it on others without a lot of it being wafted back to you.

There was a spoilt young woman, who had had her own way all her life. She demanded – and got whatever she wanted. As long as these were merely things that money could buy, the going was fine. However, none of the things could make her sweet natured or good tempered or nice to be with.

She met a smart and intelligent young man at a party – and decided that she wanted to get married to him. Unfortunately for him, the young man was tempted by her wealth and consented to marry her. Soon enough, he realised her true nature – and decided that the farther away from her that he kept, the happier he would be.

The girl went to her doting parents and demanded a divorce from her husband of six months. In their eyes, their "darling child" could do no wrong, and they promptly took her to the best lawyer in town. This man was a sane, sensible, down-to-earth person. "Why do you want a divorce?" he asked her.

"I have been married to him for six months," she pouted. "And he doesn't make me happy."

"If you get another husband, are you sure he will make you happy?" the lawyer persisted.

"He *must* make me happy," the girl said with a glint in her eyes. "Otherwise, why should I marry him? Why should I marry anyone at all?"

"Indeed, why should anyone marry you?" the lawyer returned. "Unless *you* want to make *him* happy?"

The girl was nonplussed. She only knew one thing: her husband was supposed to make her happy. As for making *him* happy, she had not thought of that!

"The happiness you give to others comes back to you," said the Wise One, "for happiness moves in a circle." And he began to narrate the following story to me.

The king of Ratnapuri was dying. He had no children, and therefore, no successor to his throne. His Chancellor, a wise and learned man, advised the king to choose a successor from among his most faithful followers.

The king summoned Sher Singh and Ramdas – the two men whom he loved and trusted the most. Addressing Sher Singh first, he said, "Tell me, my faithful friend, if I nominated you as my successor, how would you rule the people?"

"Your Majesty," Sher Singh replied, "I shall do all I can to uphold the power and glory of the sovereign. I shall rule the people with an iron hand, and impose the laws of the land with the utmost severity."

Turning to Ramdas, the king said, "What about you, brother? What kind of king will you be?"

"I shall try and be a good servant to the people, your Majesty," said Ramdas. "I believe a true king is one who serves his people well. The only difference between him and the other civil servants is that he sits on a throne. And so sir, I shall continue to be to the people what I am to you now – a devoted servant."

Ramdas was chosen to be the king's successor.

Truly has Sadhu Vaswani said, "He is truly great who greatly serves."

If you would be happy, make others happy. I recently read a profoundly moving story of a man who had gone out to the beach with his family on a beautiful Sunday morning. His three children were laughing and playing happily.

"Look Papa, there's a wave as high as a tree!" exclaimed his five year old daughter.

The man turned around to look – and he could not believe his eyes! A huge sheet of water came tearing its way to the shore …

The next thing he knew, the man found himself clinging on the top of a tall coconut palm tree, several metres away from the beach. How did he get there – he could not say. And all around him on the ground was a vast expanse of water. There was no sign of the sandy beach that he had stood on, just a few seconds earlier.

It was Dec. 26, 2004… the day the infamous Tsunami struck South Asia…

Sometime later, the waters receded. The sea appeared calm and placid – but it had left behind a terrible devastation in its wake. Someone came to the rescue of the man – he could not climb down from the tree or even jump off – for it was so high. He shuddered to think of the force and power of the tidal wave that had swept him so high, and began to look for his children.

He found their lifeless bodies a few hours later.

To say that his life was shattered would be an understatement. He tells us that he and his wife mourned and wept without food or water, for three days, in their large, beautiful bungalow which they had built with great love and care for their children.

"On the third day," he recalled later, "I told my wife that we should go out and share the grief of others like us, for surely, we were not the only ones to suffer such loss."

Husband and wife made their way along the seashore, which was a site of devastation all around. Picking their way through debris of boats and fishermen's cottages and dozens of dead bodies still lying unclaimed, they reached the local school where an even greater horror met their eyes.

There were sixteen children huddled together in the roofless, wall-less, damaged school building. A grief-stricken couple who were looking after the children told the couple that all sixteen children had been orphaned by the killer tsunami.

In retrospect, the couple found it difficult to explain exactly what went through their minds at the time – to adopt one or two of the children…to set up an orphanage to care for them and others like them… or else to find foster homes for them all…

It is next to impossible to analyse the workings of the human mind. The couple looked at each other, and the decision was made almost at once. There was no question of taking one or two children away; they would adopt all the sixteen…

"It is we who have to be grateful to the children, not the other way around," the man said to his friends later on. "We thought we had lost everything including the reason to live. They gave us a new meaning, a new purpose to live."

Yes, the very first secret of happiness is – if you would be happy, make others happy!

It was Charles Kingsley who said, "Make it a rule never, if possible, to lie down at night without being able to say, "I have made one human being at least a little wiser, a little happier, or a little better this day."

There was a woman who lost her husband to cancer. She had adored him, and they had led a happy life together. She had been a happy-go-lucky person, and her husband had thought it his life's mission to fulfil her every whim and fancy. When fate snatched him away, she became a changed person. She forgot how to smile.

"Time will heal all scars," her friends said to her. "You have got to get on with your life. You cannot mourn forever!"

"I will not be able to smile," she told them, "for as long as I live. I shall just exist till my time comes – and I'm praying for that blessed moment to come to me as soon as possible."

She lived a life of loneliness, desolation and despair. For her, life had lost all meaning and purpose.

Months passed. Early one morning, she was awakened by the noise of firecrackers and laughter and celebrations. Startled, she got up from bed and looked out of her window.

She had forgotten all about it – but it was the sacred day of Deepavali. People were celebrating the festival of lights with fun and laughter and a happy sense of togetherness.

Her eyes fell on two children – a little boy and a girl – in the street below. Their feet were bare and they were shabbily dressed. They had no firecrackers to play with, but they were watching others and enjoying the fun.

On an impulse, she went down to them and brought them inside her home. She shared breakfast with them and asked them what they were doing all alone on Deepavali day. "Where are your parents?" she wanted to know.

"We have no parents," they said to her. "We are orphans," they added, as if to help her understand.

She felt a lump rising in her throat. "How do you… who looks after you?" she asked them.

"Our neighbours give us something to eat, whenever they can spare it," the boy explained. "We try not to trouble them. The temple priest gives us *prasad* – and that is how we survive."

As she listened to the children, the wealthy woman forgot her own sorrow and misery. "I, too, am an orphan like you," she said to them, through tears. "I think we should celebrate Deepavali together, don't you?"

She took them to a huge department store and bought new clothes for them. The children insisted that she should also have new clothes, and helped her to choose them. She found her spirits lifting, and she urged the children to buy all they wanted – toys, games, eats, whatever took their fancy.

At first the children hesitated, for they had never had such an experience ever before. But because she encouraged them to take everything they wanted, they allowed her to indulge them. How their faces sparkled with joy! How their eyes lit up – reflecting the glow, in the woman's eyes too!

Their joy and laughter stole into her heart, and she forgot her loss and grief. As they laughed and chatted and ate together she realised that life was too precious to be spent in sorrow and misery – it was meant to serve those in need.

Who was it that said, "If you are depressed, it is time for you to open a service station"? I agree with him one hundred percent. For when you look around you, you see that the world is sad, is broken, is torn with tragedy, is smitten with suffering. Living in such a world, we must help as many as we can to lift the load on the rough road of life.

I love to recall the wonderful words of Sadhu Vaswani:

Did you meet him on the road?
Did you leave him with the load?

On the long, hard, tough road of life, there are many who go about carrying heavy loads. These loads are not always physical. There are many people who carry in their hearts the terrible burdens of worry, care, anxiety and fear. Lighten their loads! Be a burden-bearer! The day on which we have not helped a brother here, or a sister there, a bird here or an animal there – for birds and animals, too, are God's children and man's younger brothers and sisters in the one family of creation – the day on which we have not helped someone in need is a lost day indeed!

Life fulfils itself in service. There is no joy greater than the joy of those who spend themselves in serving those in suffering and pain.

William Gladstone was, one day, preparing a speech to be delivered in Parliament the following day. In the midst of this work, he was called upon by the parents of a sick boy, who urgently entreated him to visit their son. The little boy, who was suffering from a critical illness, had expressed the desire to meet the British Prime Minister. The fond parents had rushed to the P.M's office with this request – and Gladstone did not disappoint them.

Hours later, he returned to his office to tackle the unfinished speech. As he got back to work, he remarked to a friend, "This speech may fail or not, the empire may fall or not, but in helping that boy I have tasted exquisite joy!"

The true religion of humanity is the religion of service. So, I urge my friends all the time, let us do as much good as we can, to as many as we can, on as many occasions as we can.

Do you know, that for several years, psychologists would not admit to the existence of that human impulse which we call altruism? Altruism simply means giving of ourselves to another for no other reason than to help the other person. Psychologists believed for a long time that the only reason we would ever help others would be indirectly to help ourselves – because, as they say, there was something in it for *us*.

Thus, if you come out of a pastry shop, and saw a poor woman begging and gave her a ten-rupee note – the psychologists would say that you did it only to avoid feeling guilty. In other words, you were indirectly helping yourself by being charitable to the poor woman.

I am glad to say that this attitude is changing now. Behavioural scientists and researchers now agree that helping others actually makes people healthy and happy. It may even extend our life, so we are told. The well-known physician, Dr. Dean Ornish, actually encourages his heart patients to help others, care for others, as an antidote to their unhealthy tendencies.

Psychologists have also altered their earlier attitude to altruism. They agree that some people do things specifically, solely and exclusively to benefit others – and not just to help themselves. They also agree that such people who give of themselves selflessly, find great joy in living.

Of course, experts do not call this impulse by its old fashioned name, altruism. They have given it a 'technical' name – *pro-social behaviour*.

Pro-social behaviour it shall be! After all, a rose by any other name still smells sweet! Let us cultivate the spirit of altruism, in whichever name we choose to describe it.

Having accepted that this tendency exists in people, research scientists have now set out to 'study' it thoroughly in the United States. Some of these studies looking at 'pro-social behaviour' asked volunteers a very interesting question: *How do you feel when you help someone?*

The answers were truly revealing:
- "I feel high! I feel great!"
- "I feel stronger and more energetic."
- "I feel warm all over."
- "I feel calmer and much less depressed."
- "I feel better about myself."

So don't be surprised if your doctor starts advising you to eat nutritiously, exercise regularly, sleep restfully – *and* give of yourself to others unselfishly!

Have you read St. Paul's first Epistle to the Corinthians? It is part of the New Testament – but to my mind, it belongs to the religion of humanity. I regard it as one of the most inspiring passages which outlines the essential virtues for a happy and useful life. Here is a gist of that beautiful letter which the saint wrote to his loyal and devout followers:

> Love, kindness, charity, doing things for others – these are the essential qualities. Love never fails. Other things fade and pass away, but love endures. Faith, hope and love – these three endure. And the greatest of these is love.

Loving and giving – these have been regarded as the highest virtues. Let us remember too, Khalil Gibran's words: "You give but little when you give of your possessions. It is when you give of yourself that you truly give."

Dr. W. Beran Wolfe was a young psychiatrist. Many men and women, who came to him for treatment – bitter, frightened, paranoid, anguished and frustrated – had been desperately unhappy, expecting him to provide a miracle cure which would help them achieve a tranquil adjustment to life.

Dr. Wolfe's compassion went out to those anguished people who had come to him for help. Young as he was, he realized that many of his patients were unhappy because they were obsessed with themselves. They had one trait in common: a totally selfish concept of life. Selfishly absorbed in their own interests and concerns, they had failed in human relationships; they had created their own unhappiness.

Dr. Wolfe realised that he had to make people understand that true happiness could not be found in *being* or *having* – but rather in *doing* – doing things with and for others. Thus was born his wonderful book, *How To Be Happy Though Human*. Let me quote a few lines from his book:

> For those who seek the larger happiness and the greater effectiveness open to human beings, there can be but one philosophy of life, the philosophy of constructive altruism…the good life demands a working philosophy of active philanthropy as an orientating map of conduct. This is the golden way of life. This is the satisfying life. This is the way to be happy, though human.

Epictetus was a slave in Nero's Rome. Lame and poor, he was nevertheless content, and his words are respected and admired along with the writings of the great philosophers of the ancient world. "If a man is unhappy," Epictetus wrote, "remember that his unhappiness is his own fault; for God had made all men to be happy."

True happiness is not to be found in being someone, having something or getting all that we want. It is to be found in giving, going out of ourselves, thinking of others and doing something for them. J.B. Priestly expresses this truth in his characteristically blunt manner:

> To me, there is in happiness, an element of self-forgetfulness. You lose yourself in something outside yourself when you are happy; just as when you are desperately miserable, you are intensely conscious of yourself, and like a solid little lump of ego weighing a ton.

So the choice is yours. What would you rather be? Light and liberated and truly happy, living for others – or "a solid little lump of ego weighing a ton"?

A recent survey in the US found that strong marriages, secure family relationships and friendship were essential to happiness. Many people also said that spirituality and self-esteem were important in order to be happy. Above all, people felt that one must have the feeling "that life has a meaning".

How can we give meaning to our lives? The survey gives us the answer: "Helping people to be a little happier can jump-start a process that will lead to stronger relationships, renewed hope, and a general upward spiralling of happiness."

What we *give*, more than what we *get*, makes us happy. Think of how you can make someone happy today: perhaps it's as simple as making a visit, or even a phone-call; perhaps it's a kind smile or a simple gift. Promote others' happiness – and you will find you become happy. Goodness will come to you when you seek the good of others; happiness will be yours when you make others happy.

> Not what we have, but what we give
> Not what we see, but how we live –
> These are the things that build and bless
> That lead to human happiness.

"My friend, you seem to be in a deep reverie," said the Wise One to me, after a prolonged period when we had been walking, each reflecting on the powerful words that we had read: *If you want to be happy, make others happy!*

"I have been here only for a short while, in the realm of happiness," I said. "And you have led me to my first secret of happiness. I am eager to learn more!"

"So you shall, so you shall," asserted the Wise One. "But look, here we are on the banks of a stream. Let us have a wash and a drink of water, and rest a while on its grassy banks."

We washed our hands and faces, and drank the clear, cold, sweet water. "This is heavenly," I sighed, as we sank down on the grass, taking the weight off our weary feet.

I leaned against a nearby boulder, which seemed to offer a perfect head rest. When I was about to put my head upon it, my eyes fell on the words which were engraved upon it:

Appreciate everyone you meet!

The 2nd Secret of Happiness

Appreciate Everyone You Meet!

"I have found the second secret!" I exclaimed in delight.

"So you have, so you have," smiled the Wise One. "Has it not been said to us – seek and you shall find? Seek – keep on seeking, and you will surely find what you are looking for!"

"Appreciate everyone you meet," I repeated. "How wonderful the world would be if only we appreciated one another as we should…"

The American philosopher William James, tells us: "The deepest principle of human nature is the craving to be appreciated."

"Human relationships thrive on caring, sharing and mutual appreciation," the Wise One remarked. "We rely on our loved ones, our friends and those closest to us, for moral support and encouragement, don't we?"

"The amazing thing is that appreciation costs us nothing," I added. "It requires hardly any effort. A smile, a warm gesture, a word of praise is all it takes; and yet we are so reluctant to offer it to others."

"No one knows who originally wrote or said these lines," the Wise One said thoughtfully, "but all of us have read these lines and been inspired by them. I'm sure you have heard them too…" and he began to quote them in his deep powerful voice:

> I shall pass through this world but once. Any good, therefore, that I can do, or any kindness that I can show to any human being, let me do it now. Let me not defer nor neglect it, for I shall not pass this way again.

Any kindness that I can show to any human being…

The popular writer, Dale Carnegie, calls this one of the basic requirements for happiness in life. "Cut out this quotation and put it where you will see it every morning!" he tells us.

Is it not true that all of us feel happy when we are appreciated? In this, as in other things, what we send out comes back to us. For life is like a boomerang: what we are, what we do, comes back to us. When we give our best to the world, when we send out warmth, love and appreciation – it all comes back to us.

Of a great English poet, I read that he never spoke a word of appreciation to his wife. As long as she lived he criticised her and found fault with everything that she did. Suddenly, the wife died. The poet was grief-stricken. He was ashamed that he had failed to write poems in appreciation of her, when she had been alive. "If only I had known," he lamented. "If only I had known…"

Truly it has been said, life is too short to be small. Let us not be small-minded. Let us be generous with praise, appreciation and encouragement.

The great artist of the Renaissance, Leonardo da Vinci said: "Never reprove a friend in public. Always praise him in front of others."

When you appreciate others, you help to draw out the best in them. This leads to happiness all around.

There are very many occasions in life which call for celebration – special events like a birth or a wedding in the family, birthdays, promotions, a new home and so on. But let us not forget that each and everyday is filled with numerous things which deserve our appreciation and gratitude. If only we would pause, reflect and consider life's countless blessings, we would realize how much there is to be appreciated in life!

"Appreciate nature!" said the Wise One. "The blue sky above you, the green grass at your feet, the magnificent hills, the vast seas, life-giving, life-generating rivers and the beauty and grandeur of gardens and woods.

"Appreciate each day that comes to you out of the Spotless Hands of God. Think of all that you take for granted – your life that is a great gift, your good health, which is a blessing, your family which is precious, and the joy and love that come to you from all around. Learn to appreciate all the beauty and warmth which we so often ignore!

"Above all, appreciate people! Human relationships need to be nurtured. We often think of our friends, spouses and parents as 'pillars of strength' that are always there for our solid support. I urge you, at least occasionally, to also think of them as precious plants that need constant tending!

"When tensions are rising and troubles are mounting, it is people who are close to us that bear the brunt of our stress. We are often courteous, polite and kind to perfect strangers, but rude and brusque to our own spouses and parents."

And the Wise One began to narrate a few of his fascinating real life stories.

There was a young lady, Heena, who was strenuously climbing up the executive ladder, making her way steadily to the top of her profession. She was near-perfect in her work, always the calm, composed, cool manager at the workplace. At home, it was very different. She took her mother for granted, lost her temper often, argued, shouted, demanded to have her own way in everything, and generally made herself unpleasant.

One day, Heena had a serious difference of opinion with her immediate superior at work. Tempers frayed and angry words were exchanged.

For the first time the young woman lost her cool and gave her senior colleague a piece of her mind.

She was still shaking when she returned to her seat. She felt she had to talk to someone – and almost without thinking, dialled her home number.

Her mother picked up the phone.

"Mom, I've had a nasty tiff with Wendy," Heena said in a low voice. "I'm afraid I lost my temper and spoke too much."

"It can't have been that bad, honey," said the mother reassuringly. "I know you. You are always polite and careful with your words. I'm sure you're exaggerating the damage done."

"No mom, it's not like that," Heena persisted. "I spoke to her like – like I sometimes speak to you!"

The mother smiled, and the smile could be heard in her voice when she said softly, "Was it really that bad?"

Somewhere inside Heena, a chord was touched. "Oh Mom," she said, barely able to restrain herself, "I'm awful, aren't I? And I don't deserve you!"

"Nonsense! Of course we deserve each other – that's why God has given you to me."

"I love you, Mom," said Heena, forgetting all about the quarrel with her boss. "And I'm so glad that you are always there for me!"

Many relationships suffer from sheer neglect and indifference. It was a wise man who said, "Even love has a shelf life."

A man was trying to hang a picture on the wall, when he hurt his thumb badly with a misplaced blow from his hammer. One of the 'digits' on his thumb was cracked, and the thumb was put in plaster.

"That's too bad," said a sympathetic friend.

"It isn't actually," said the man. "I'm glad it happened, because I have begun to appreciate my thumb now. I really took it for granted – and now I'm actually able to see the hundreds of tasks for which I actually require the use of my thumb. I never realised this before – but that thumb is practically indispensable to me."

A Rabbi was offering special counselling sessions to his congregation on nurturing marital relationships. An old man came up to the Rabbi and offered his help. "I *know* the secret of marital bliss," he asserted vigorously. "It's very simple."

"What makes you so sure?" asked the Rabbi.

"I'm an expert on the subject," the old man said, gleefully. "I ought to know, because I've been married four times."

The Rabbi was taken aback, and his shock must have shown on his face. The old man laughed at the expression on his face and added, "*To the same woman.*"

He proceeded to explain that he and his wife had been married for 45 years. The first marriage was when he and his wife had been young and carefree. The second was when they had been rearing their three children. The third was when the children grew up and left home. The fourth was when they both retired.

"Each of these marriages called for different ground rules," the old man said. "We gave each other the love and appreciation and support we needed, as the situation and circumstances of our life changed. We married each other – over and over again!"

There is nothing like warmth, love and appreciation to resurrect relationships!

Mr. Saunders was an old man who took full advantage of his neighbours' kindness and helpful attitude. He was especially dependent on little Peter, the 8-year old boy who lived next door. Peter ran errands for the old man tirelessly, now fetching his mail, now buying tobacco for his pipe, now watering his garden or doing his shopping. Mr. Saunders only thanked him profusely and abundantly in *words* – never ever offering the boy even a small token, a little gift to show his gratitude.

One morning he had little Peter occupied for hours together. When the little boy returned from his fifth errand of the morning, the old man said to him complacently, "Peter, I have no words to thank you!"

Peter looked up at him and said innocently. "Mr. Saunders, I too wish I could thank you for something!"

In London, there was a taxi driver named Harry. His cab was hired by two young ladies from Spain who arrived at Heathrow Airport. They asked the cabbie to find them a good hotel for the night.

Harry drove them around all the decent and reasonably priced hotels in Central London. As luck would have it, not a single room was available anywhere, for it was the 'peak' of the tourist season.

It was nearing 10 p.m and the young ladies were upset and distressed. "What can we do?" they asked him in halting English. "Where shall we go?"

Harry thought for a minute and decided that he would take the young ladies to his own home. He told them of his plan, and called up his wife to get the attic bedroom ready for his guests.

When they arrived at the cabby's humble home in East London, his wife greeted them cheerfully. A welcoming fire was burning in the grate; there was hot cocoa and thick cheese sandwiches for the hungry guests.

The next morning, Harry drove them to the YWCA hostel, where rooms were available for the girls. They parted from him with many expressions of gratitude.

They did not forget his kindness to them. They worked for Spain's Tourism Department, and when they returned to their country, their Department invited Harry and his wife over for a free holiday. The couple were looked after as special guests wherever they went, and Spain's highest award for drivers, *The Golden Steering Wheel*, was conferred on Harry!

There are so many kindnesses and benefits we enjoy in our daily life. Let us make it a point to acknowledge them and appreciate them by words and gestures and deeds!

I am told that in the mountains of Mexico, there are multiple hot and cold water springs that gush out of the earth like many little spouts, all bunched together. The local women bring their laundry to the spot on their weekly wash day, and benefit from the use of these natural washing machines.

An American visitor saw this and remarked to one of the women, "You must consider yourself lucky to have free running hot water for all your washing!"

"Well …there is no soap," said the woman with a sour look.

The visitor became speechless!

If you keep the 'milk of human kindness' all bottled up inside you, how can you expect to enjoy the cream of life?

Mrs. Lal was a warm and hospitable hostess. Practically every weekend, she invited friends, relatives and her husband's colleagues for dinners, which she cooked and served with her own hands.

"How can you go through the bother of parties week after week?" a friend said to her. "Why don't you throw a dinner party once in six months or so, and invite everyone over? You could leave the food arrangements to the caterers, and people can entertain each other and save you a lot of trouble!"

"Oh no, I couldn't do that," Mrs. Lal replied. "I like small, intimate parties where I can look after my guests personally and talk to them individually. I enjoy my guests…and I like to make them feel special!"

She was a lady who had the gift of true appreciation!

There is a beautiful painting by the immortal artist Raphael, called *The Madonna of the Barrel.* It is displayed in a museum in Florence, Italy. When you look at it carefully, you will realize that it is not painted on canvas, but on the lid of a barrel, which is of course now tastefully framed.

How did "The Madonna of the Barrel" come about? We are told that Raphael was one day walking through the busy market of Florence when his eyes fell on a poor woman sitting in a street corner, feeding the child at her breast. Her clothes were in tatters – but on her face was the divine expression of motherly love. Raphael was so moved by the sight that he was determined to capture her in his painting then and there. He had colours and brushes in his pocket – but there was no canvas.

He saw the lid of an old barrel lying nearby, and he painted on the barrel head, the masterpiece which people admire even today, as a divine expression of motherly love.

Raphael was a great artist because he had the great capacity to appreciate the beautiful and the romantic in ordinary people and everyday situations!

"If only we look around us," the Wise One remarked, " if only we see and listen with care, we will never complain that life is boring and dull! When you learn to appreciate the world and its people you will find the grass greener; you will see that the moon shines brighter; and the dreariness of life will disappear, leaving fresh colours and fragrances behind!"

I thought of John Ruskin, the distinguished Victorian writer, who remarked, " I am not surprised at what men suffer, but I am surprised at what they miss out on!"

There is a world of beauty and charm lying out there for us – and we are blind to it! We lack the quality of appreciation!

There was a distinguished American surgeon who was also kind-hearted and generous. His heart was touched by the little crippled boy at the street corner, from whom he bought his daily newspaper. He was always smiling and cheerful and the surgeon decided to operate on him and help him walk and run and play like other boys of his age.

He made arrangements with the local medical school for the boy's surgery. The hospital attached to the medical school offered all its facilities free for the operation – if the medical students would be allowed to witness the operation and learn from the great surgeon.

The surgeon explained to the boy what he planned to do, and the boy agreed happily. He thought that it would be wonderful if young medical students learnt from the surgeon – for they would be able to help many more crippled children like him.

The day of the surgery dawned. The boy was wheeled into the operation theatre and placed on the operating table before the surgeon and his assistants. A little away from the group, behind glass partitions, students were seated in rows as in a theatre to witness the procedure on closed circuit TV.

The doctor began by talking about the boy's condition and the procedure he was about to follow. When the preliminary talk was over, he turned to the little boy who lay on the table, a little anxious, a little afraid and a little excited. "Now Johnny, we are going to set your leg right," he said to the boy kindly, as the anaesthetist got ready to put him to sleep. The little boy raised his head and said in a soft, clear voice, "Doctor, I think you are a truly wonderful person. I pray that God may bless you for your kindness to me."

The doctor's eyes were filled with tears as he whispered, "Thank you, my boy!"

The operation was successful. When the students surrounded the surgeon for a question–answer session outside the theatre, he said to them, " I have operated on VIPs and multimillionaires who have paid a fortune to be treated by me. But nothing has moved me so much, given me greater happiness than the words of appreciation uttered by that young lad."

Appreciate others!

Express your appreciation in words and deeds. This will make your life fresh and interesting!

A working woman returned home late one day, worried and anxious that her husband would be back home, hungry and impatient, while a dirty kitchen with a sink full of unwashed dishes would be awaiting her arrival. When she let herself inside the flat, she rushed to the kitchen, and to her amazement, it was scrubbed clean, and the tiles were sparkling and the dishes had been washed and dried and put away in place.

Her husband had never been one to lend a helping hand with housework. How had this 'miracle' come about? She found the answer on a note that had been pinned to the refrigerator door.

Darling,
I tried to make myself a cup of coffee, and the milk boiled over.
I made toast and burnt the bread slices.
I switched on the deep fryer to fry potatoes and the pan caught fire. I doused the flames, but spilt all the oil on the floor.
I now realise what you must be going through to produce all those delicious meals for me – on the dot, even before I get really hungry.

I have scrubbed and tidied the kitchen and I'm rushing out to buy some food so that you don't have to start cooking when you return home, tired and hungry.
I love you – and I want you to know how much I appreciate all that you are doing for me – for us!

Need I say that the wife was moved to the point of tears?

Appreciate another person – and you will make two people happy – him and you!

President and Mrs. Woodrow Wilson were on a tour of the U.S. by train. Their train stopped at a small town in Montana, and the First Couple went out on to the observation platform of their special carriage to greet the people who gathered to meet them.

Local leaders and VIPs thronged to shake hands with the First Couple. Mrs. Wilson saw two little boys who had wriggled their way through the waiting crowds, and were eagerly reaching out to touch the President's hands. She drew her husband's attention to the boys and he graciously held out his hand to them.

One of the boys shook his hands warmly, and gave the great leader the American flag he had been waving all the while.

The President accepted the gift thanking him warmly, and handed it to Mrs. Wilson.

The other little boy stood still for a minute, for he had nothing to offer to the President. Then he put his hand into his pocket and after a fast check, came out with a dime – the lowest denomination coin of those days. Straining upward, he held it out to the President. Mr. Wilson accepted the coin, thanking the boy for his gift.

Several years later, when President Wilson died, Mrs. Wilson was amazed to find the dime carefully wrapped in a piece of paper, and kept in his wallet. The little boy's impulsive gift had been so appreciated by the President that he had carried it with him all those years!

Mr. Thomas was a man of culture, who had become very lonely since his wife's death. He was delighted when his son came to live near his house, and he gladly took up the charge of baby-sitting his grandchild whenever his daughter-in-law wanted him to. He enjoyed being with the baby so much that he began to offer to baby-sit for his other neighbours too.

"Except for Saturday and Sunday evenings, I'm always free," he said to Carol, the girl next door who brought over a freshly baked cake for him. "If ever you need me to baby-sit for you, just ask, and I'll be glad to do it for you."

"Thank you, uncle," said Carol, smiling mischievously. "But my daughter has two grandfathers who are willing to baby-sit for free!"

"For free?" exclaimed old Mr. Thomas. "I *pay* to look after those dear little angels!"

Old people appreciate children more – but stressed and harried parents often find children and childcare demanding and tough. It is obviously because they have not learnt to appreciate the great joy that children can bring!

Radha and Raghu were a young couple who lived and worked in Mumbai. Returning from a holiday in Delhi, they were travelling by train in a relatively uncrowded carriage. Opposite them were an old couple who sat silently, staring into vacant space, not moving, not uttering a word, not even stretching out to relax.

Radha, who was kind hearted and warm, could not bear to see the old people so miserable. She offered them a few biscuits; she invited them to stretch out comfortably; she gave them magazines to read. When nothing worked, she held on to the old lady's hands and said to her, " Ma, you must tell me why you are so unhappy. I can't bear to see you both like this!"

The old lady quietly withdrew her hands and refused to reply. "Take no notice of us," said the old man. "You have a long life ahead. Be happy, and don't take on our problems."

"But how can I be happy if you are so sad?" Radha persisted.

"What is it to you?" said the old lady sharply. "What are *we* to you?" Mind your own business!"

"I'll tell you what you are to me," said Radha, not at all put off by the sudden outburst. "Both my husband and I have lost our parents. We know what it is to have loving, caring elders in the family – and we miss them terribly! You remind me of my parents, and that's why I cannot bear to see you so sad. Does that answer your question?"

On hearing her answer, the old man closed his eyes as if in deep despair, and the old lady began to sob gently.

Their story came out of them slowly – in broken sentences, with tears and sighs. They had been driven out of their son's home by a cruel and bitter daughter-in-law who did not want them to live with her. Their son, who ought to have known better, did not want to displease his wife. And so the old couple were sent packing. They were travelling to Mumbai, because someone had told them of a charitable old age home which would be willing to take them in.

Radha and Raghu were now sitting on either side of the old couple, comforting them, holding their hands, wiping away their tears!

"Radha, I know what we must do," Raghu exclaimed. "We shall adopt Mama and Papa!"

The old man laughed out aloud. "Nobody adopts old people," he said to Raghu. "You adopt babies and young children!"

"Well, we can have babies of our own," said Radha. "But we can't have our parents back. So we are going to adopt you. If you don't think that's right – well, its simple, *you* must adopt us!"

Radha and Raghu knew what it was to have loving, caring elders at home. They were able to appreciate the treasure that a thoughtless young couple had thrown away so carelessly and heartlessly!

"Take time to live – because the world has so much to give!" proclaimed the caption of a beautiful picture which I saw in a friend's house. All of us need to take time to live – to appreciate all the good things and wonderful people around us. This is sure to bring us – and them – a great deal of happiness!

Vidya was an earnest and dedicated teacher, just fresh from a College of Education where she had obtained her B.Ed.degree. Luckily for her, she got a job offer just as soon as her results were declared. Her professor told her about a local school, whose Headmistress had appealed to him to recommend one of his students to take up a teaching assignment with them. One of their teachers had married and left in the middle of the term – and they urgently needed a replacement. The professor gave Vidya an excellent reference, and Vidya was taken on the very next day!

However, her first-few weeks were beset with problems. The students, who loved their former teacher, were unhappy and disgruntled about her departure, and treated Vidya with suspicion and antipathy. They were noisy and indisciplined in class;

they jeered and laughed at her movements and gestures; they refused to do their homework. When Vidya disciplined and dealt with them strictly, they complained to their parents that the new teacher was harsh. One of the parents actually lodged a protest with the headmistress: the children did not like Vidya. Could they have another teacher?

The next day, the headmistress sent for Vidya.

Now Vidya was not only sincere and dedicated. She was also smart and alert. She knew what was happening; she had heard that the parents were beginning to complain about her. And when the headmistress sent for her, she felt a little sad and discouraged.

When she was seated before the headmistress, the lady looked straight into her eyes and said, "Vidya, first and foremost, I would like you to know how happy I am with your work. Your work plans and weekly reports have been really impressive, and I think you are doing a terrific job!"

Vidya could not believe her ears! She had come into the office fully expecting to be pulled up, warned, perhaps even shown the door. But this was really unexpected.

The headmistress was a wise, kind and experienced lady. She had understood the problem very well right from the beginning. When the parent had come to her with a complaint about Vidya, she had explained the whole situation, and asked the anxious mother to give the new teacher a fair chance.

Her words of encouragement and appreciation made a world of difference. Vidya became determined to win the children over. The parents, on their part, urged their children to be better behaved, and the 'problem' had a happy solution all around!

"How easy it sounds when we talk about appreciating others," I remarked. "And yet people find it so difficult to put this simple suggestion into practice!"

"Appreciation is like expensive perfume," said the Wise One. "If you don't use it regularly, it just evaporates, dries up. I'm afraid people have forgotten what it is to appreciate – and what it is to express their appreciation!"

"That is a timely reminder for me," I said to him. "May I tell you how deeply I appreciate the pleasure and privilege of your company on this quest? I'm learning so much from this journey with you—and I wish to assure you that everything I learn, every insight I gather, will be shared with my fellow-seekers."

"Well, it's time to move on," said the Wise One. "Dusk seems to be falling. We must find our way to a shelter before darkness sets in."

We rose from the banks of the stream and began to walk on. The evening sky was tinted with the myriad hues of the setting sun, as if a master artist had been mixing his paints on a magical palette.

"All this beauty, this tremendous sense of serenity and peace touches the very core of my soul," I remarked. "But my heart yearns for the presence of my fellow human beings here! What a pity it is that such a beautiful land should lie bare and uninhabited, a waste land devoid of human habitation!"

The Wise One nodded, his eyes filled with compassion. "This is a beautiful, pleasant, fertile land," he pointed out. "But you used the term *waste land*, which is not, strictly speaking, accurate. And yet I know you meant it in the sense that all this beauty and goodness seem to be wasted without human occupancy."

"I can't understand how people could ever have left this beautiful land behind them, never to return," I remarked. "We now have the technical know-how and the means to reclaim fallow lands and even barren, unfertile lands into productive habitats —and yet people have turned their back on this pleasant realm. Why, oh why?"

"You need a special visa to live here," smiled the Wise One. "A special 'entry permit' as some nations describe it."

"A special entry permit? But we got here as quickly as thought could take us!" I exclaimed. "No one stopped us to ask for a visa!"

"I said it was a very special visa, didn't I?" the Wise One replied. "Alas, not a lot of people can claim that visa: *it is the will to be happy!* It is the attitude that makes you believe that happiness is your birthright, and you must seek to claim it by every right means that you can adopt! In other words, you must claim your right to live in this realm, for no one can transport you here without your own active involvement."

By now, a mauve and deep blue darkness was beginning to fall on us like a translucent veil. The Wise One pointed to a rocky formation that lay ahead of us, an outcrop of smooth sandstone shaped like one of those wayside pavilions built by kings in ancient India for the benefit of weary travellers. "We have found our shelter for the night," he remarked with a smile.

"How lucky we are!" I exclaimed with delight. "It's so long since I slept under the stars. I shall treasure this experience – oh, ouch!"

In my enthusiasm, I had not noticed a sharp brier that lay on our path. Its thorns had brushed against my feet, causing sharp pain.

"Easy, easy now," said the Wise One anxiously, as he led me limping towards the rocky pavilion. "Here is a raised part. Sit down on it while I attend to your feet."

Gently, he wiped the blood away, where the thorn had torn into my flesh, pressing a piece of cloth to arrest the flow of blood.

"Does it hurt very much?" he enquired kindly.

"Not much," I replied truthfully. "I'm so overwhelmed by your kindness and concern, that I don't feel the pain at all."

"Let me remove this bramble from the path," he said, carefully lifting the deadly growth. "I'm not going to throw it anywhere here, lest it should hurt another creature! I will take it away and dispose of it carefully, and find something for us to eat. I want you to rest here quietly till I return."

Such was my absolute faith in the Wise One that it did not in the least occur to me to ask him, "Something to eat? What can you hope to find here?" I just knew that he meant what he said, just as I was certain that he would return with something for us to eat.

I was right. He returned a while later, his arms laden with luscious fruits and berries. We shared a delicious repast, and I felt well enough to walk down to the stream, which still flowed close to where we were, for a drink of water.

As we returned to the rocky pavilion, the Wise One remarked, "There are many people who cast thorns and briers on the pathways of life, unaware, uncaring that they might be causing pain and injury to the others. What can we do about such people?"

"There is only one thing we can do," I sighed. "We must forgive them and hope that they will learn to be better!"

The Wise One nodded approvingly. As we sat on the cool floor of the pavilion, he drew my attention to the words which had been inscribed on the rocky wall to my side. They were bright green in colour, and shone like fluorescent paint – obviously from fast dyes drawn from special herbs and leaves.

Forgive Before Forgiveness Is Asked

The 3rd Secret of Happiness

Forgive Before Forgiveness Is Asked

"Forgive Before Forgiveness Is Asked," I read aloud. "Why, the words were taken out of my mouth!" I exclaimed. "Can I take it that this is the next secret?"

"Forgive and forget – for forgiveness is divine!" said the Wise One. "And, remember, forgiveness does you good! For while we are on this earth-plane, forgiveness contributes to our own inner well-being."

"No one who clings to his resentments can ever hope to be happy," he continued. "In fact, by refusing to forgive and forget, he will harm himself irreparably, walking the way of spiritual death. On the other hand, the person who forgives, enters a new life of gentle peace and quiet inner joy. I always emphasise that forgiveness is its own reward: it is the *forgiver* rather than the forgiven, who receives the greater benefit.

"If you have not forgiven someone who has harmed you, if you are harbouring resentment in the heart within, let me say to you: you have not experienced the most sublime joy of life. And let us forgive one another here and now – today! For, a day may come when the opportunity to forgive will be taken away from us.

"No negative emotion is ever appeased by indulgence – it demands more and more until it consumes you. So it is with anger, revenge and retaliation. The more you feed them, the more they will destroy your peace of mind."

I nodded, in complete agreement with his words.

"For every minute you remain angry," Emerson writes, "you give up sixty seconds of peace of mind."

Dr. Richard Johnson lists the following benefits of forgiveness:

- It stimulates our spiritual growth, which is stunted by an unforgiving nature.
- It releases us from the terrible burden of resentment and allows us to channelise our spiritual energy into constructive activities.
- It restores our zeal and zest for life, giving us back our *joie de vivre* – the joy of living.
- It brings peace and harmony back into our lives.
- It allows us to lead a fuller, more abundant life, with our minds uncluttered and our hearts unburdened.

"Forgiveness is the cement that binds families together," I said aloud. "It is a known fact that we are most hurt by those who are nearest and dearest to us. The pain and hurt caused by others can be brushed aside or even ignored; but when someone you have loved, someone who you have grown up with, someone you have eaten with, laughed with and played with hurts you – it's very painful indeed!"

"But even this pain can be healed with the soothing balm of forgiveness, can it not?" asked the Wise One. "Let me tell you another story …"

There was a woman who suffered from severe rheumatic pains in her knee joints. No treatment was of any avail. The pain became unbearable. Losing faith in medicine, she sought the blessings of a holy man to help her out of her misery.

The holy man listened to her complaints. Then he asked her gently, "Do you hold a grudge against anyone?"

For a split second, she hesitated: then she answered, "My mind is seething with resentment against my own sister, who has hurt me grievously."

The holy man said to her, "Your pain will disappear only when you forgive her and make peace with her."

The woman could not bring herself to do so. However, she had great respect for the holy man, and was firmly resolved to do as he said. With a tremendous effort of will, she went out to meet her estranged sister. She held her hands quietly for a while and then embraced her. The sister was astonished but returned her warm embrace. The woman said to her, "Let bygones be bygones. Let us begin anew!"

To her amazement she found her pains disappeared without a trace, very soon thereafter.

"When we hold resentment against someone, we may or may not harm them – but we are sure to harm ourselves," the Wise One concluded.

I reflected on the story he had narrated. How true it is that negative emotions harm us – and yet so many of us continue to harbour envy, jealousy and hatred against people!

It is a sad fact of life that the greatest souls born among us cannot always escape the slander and calumny of the envious.

Thus it was, that an editor of a newspaper in Hyderabad-Sind, began to heap slander and abuse on Sadhu Vaswani. Deeply resentful of Sadhu Vaswani's good name and his saintly reputation, the editor published several false reports against him and his *satsang*, and had his newspaper distributed free in each and every house.

Deeply saddened by this unprovoked malice, some of the devotees spoke of it to Sadhu Vaswani – but he smiled, and did not take it to his heart. He would not hear a word against the editor who had slandered him so viciously.

A few days passed, and the editor was beset with personal problems. He faced great difficulties and hardships, and knew not where to turn for help.

When Sadhu Vaswani came to know of this, he visited the man in his home, and spoke to him in love and kindness. He also did his best to redress the man's difficulties.

Overwhelmed by the goodness and sympathy that Sadhu Vaswani offered him so generously, the editor fell at his feet and began to weep tears of repentance. Sadhu Vaswani picked him up and embraced him lovingly.

How kind, compassionate and ever forgiving are the saints of the Lord! They return love and blessings to us in place of our negativism and dark deeds.

"Love, love, love thine enemies," said Sadhu Vaswani. "And though they hate thee as a thorn, thou wilt blossom as a rose."

A holy man was invited to be present at a council of village elders. The council was to sit in judgement over a wrong-doer and decide on his punishment.

The holy man was extremely reluctant to join the council. However, on the appointed day, the President of the council sent him a message saying, "We are all assembled, and await your arrival. Do kindly join us!"

The holy man came to the council dragging behind him a basket full of holes, filled with sand. He left a trail of sand behind him as he walked into the council chamber.

"What is this that you are dragging behind you?" the elders asked him.

He said, "Like this sand, my sins are running out behind me. I do not see them, and today, I come to judge the sins of another!"

The words went home to the hearts of the elders. And the wrong-doer was pardoned and allowed to go.

Forgiveness sets us free – free from remaining victims of the past, free from anger and hatred; above all it frees us from the burden of expectation, of wanting anything in return for what we have had to go through.

Forgiveness is not weakness, or passivity. It requires spiritual strength. So far from leaving us weak and vulnerable, it actually empowers us to lead a more meaningful life. It helps us to overcome the vicious cycle of resentment and revenge and enter the realms of unity, peace and harmony.

Psychiatrists tell us that when people refuse to forgive and forget, their life takes a definite turn for the worse – a downturn. They become bitter; they wallow in self-pity; they even develop disorders like paranoia and persecution complex. They stop seeking the company of positive, optimistic cheerful people who give them good counsel; instead, they lock themselves up in a self-made prison of isolation and alienation. Some even take to excessive drinking; thus begins the spiral downwards…

The fact of the matter is, if you are unable to forgive and forget, you pay the price in physical and emotional terms. What form this emotional, physical deprivation may take, it is difficult to predict.

A husband and wife once came to see me. They had been married happily for fifteen years. Suddenly, something seemed to have gone wrong with their relationship.

The husband noticed that his wife had become aloof. She often withdrew into herself, and was sad and depressed. At times, he would find her sitting in a silent corner, shedding tears.

The atmosphere of their home grew dull and gloomy. The husband tried to reach out to his wife, to talk to her, to bring her out of her self-imposed gloom – but there was no response on her part.

The wife came to meet me, and I understood that a terrible load of guilt weighed on her mind. Something that she had done in the past obsessed her, and she could not condone her guilt. And so it was that she had become aloof and estranged from her loving husband.

I said to her, "God is the greatest Forgiver. He forgives us generously. But we must learn to accept His forgiveness, and feel that we are forgiven. We must learn to forgive ourselves!"

She was a great devotee of Sri Krishna. I advised her, "When you are alone at home, go and sit at the Lotus Feet of Lord Krishna and actually describe to Him all that has happened. It will not do merely to tell Him, 'Lord, You are the All-knowing One! You already know what has happened.' Actually recount, in detail, the things which you feel you should not have done, then ask for forgiveness – and then, what is very important, forget all about it!"

"Will Sri Krishna forgive me all that I have done?" she asked me, with tear-stricken eyes.

I said to her, "Krishna forgives our sins; by His power, sins are taken away and we can be free!"

For is this not the promise that Sri Krishna makes to us in the Bhagavad Gita? *"Come unto Me for single refuge, and I shall liberate you from all bondage to sin and suffering. Of this have no doubt!"*

She did as she was told. After some days, the couple met me again, and I rejoiced to find a radiant smile on the face of the wife; she said to me, "It's gone! It's gone!"

The Wise One broke my reverie. "If we wish to be happy, we must learn to live in the present," he observed. "This effectively means burying the disappointments and hurts of the past. Life, after all, is too precious to be spent in nursing grievances. The past, we must realise, is dead and gone, and we must realise it – rather, we must release ourselves from clinging to it."

I recalled the lovely story told to us of Clara Barton, the founder of the American Red Cross Society. One day she met an old friend after a long interval of several years. As they exchanged reminiscences, the friend reminded Clara of a nasty incident – a friend's cruel betrayal that had hurt and upset Clara long ago. However, Clara could not recall the incident.

"How come you don't remember it?" asked the friend in surprise. "Try and recall…"

"No," came the reply. "I distinctly remember forgetting it."

Forgiving others is not a favour you confer upon them; it is a freedom that you permit yourself, so that you may be free and easy in your own mind.

I often ask my friends to try a small exercise. I tell them to think of two people who have hurt them, insulted them or let them down in the recent past – two people with whom they are still angry.

I urge them to ask themselves: "What is my anger doing to me? Am I happy nursing my resentment, holding on to it? Does it help me in any way? Does it improve my sleep? Is my life better, richer, more meaningful because of my resentment? Am I happier holding on to my animosity?"

If the answer to all the above questions is *NO* – then they must take a courageous decision – to let go of the bitterness and disappointment, to forgive and forget – and be happy!

"The 'F' of forgiveness is freedom," said the Wise One, as if reading my thoughts. "Forgiveness sets us free from the hurts which otherwise would continue to afflict us, for as long as memory lasts."

We sat up long into the night, reflecting, exchanging views. I do not know when we slipped into sleep: all I know is that when I awakened next morning, I felt cheerful, energetic and ready to go – not in the least like someone who had slept on a hard, rocky floor all night!

"This place is invigorating and energising," I said to the Wise One as we continued our journey in the realm of happiness. We had had a refreshing wash in the clear, cold waters of the stream, and eaten a few more of those delicious fruits. "We have slept out in the open and we have eaten nothing but sun-cooked food – and I feel fresh as fresh can be!"

"Freshness, energy and well-being are as much a matter of the mind as of the body," the Wise One replied. "When the mind is open and positive, weariness cannot affect you."

We were now passing through what appeared to be a village, with rows of roofless huts on either side, their thatched roofs having fallen off and dried up with age. As we turned a corner, I caught sight of what appeared to be a road-sign. I went closer to have a look. It was indeed a sign – a sign for the road of life:

Don't Hold Grudges Against Anyone In Your Heart.

The 4ᵗʰ Secret of Happiness

Don't Hold Grudges Against Anyone In Your Heart

"Isn't this a little difficult?" I said to the Wise One. "It is easy for great souls and holy men of God to keep their hearts free of resentment. But how about lesser mortals – ordinary people?"

"Aren't you underestimating ordinary people?" he asked me with a smile.

"No," I assured him. "It is just that people often tell me, 'I am not Mahatma Gandhi,' or 'I am not a saint,' when I urge them to forgive and forget."

"The blame game does us no good," said the Wise One. "Let me tell you about Dipen Chacha…"

Dipen Chacha lived in an old people's home, with several others like himself. It was one of those rare places, run by people with hearts – whose aim was to care for the elders as well as they could, to treat them with love and care and respect, and give them peace and security in the winter of their lives.

One day, a young girl of eighteen, called Mira, came to the Home to offer her services as a volunteer.

She had a little spare time to offer each day, and she wished to spend it with the old people. "I can do whatever you want me to do," she said to the Manager of the Home. "I can read to the old folks; I can take them out for a walk if they wish; I can even cook and clean if you are short of help!"

"That's really kind of you," said the Manager, Mrs. Narayan. "We need all the help we can get from spirited volunteers like you. Since this is your first day here, why don't you go and talk to the old people and introduce yourself to them? May be they themselves will tell you what you can do for them."

"What a splendid idea!" said Mira brightly. "I'll do it right away!'

It was about ten in the morning, and as was their custom, the old people were starting their day's activities after breakfast. The Home did not have a rigid routine, and gave its inmates considerable freedom. Some were out walking in the shady garden; some were in the reading room; a few were in the lounge, chatting to their friends; there was a lady reading aloud from the Gita and quite a few had gathered around her to listen to her melodious recitation.

Mira found one man sitting in a corner, all alone.

His back was hunched; he stared down at the ground without looking up even once. When he heard someone laughing aloud nearby, he flinched as if it made him angry.

Mira pulled up a chair and sat next to him. "Hello Baba," she said, "I'm Mira. Can I sit here with you for sometime?"

To her shock, the old man looked up at her, and started screaming. "Go away, go away," he said. "I don't want to see anyone. I don't want to talk to anyone. Get out from here! I say, get out! Did I ask you to come and talk to me? Did I ask you for anything? Why can't you leave me alone? Why are you harassing me?"

Mira recoiled with horror, terrified that she had unwittingly upset the old man. An old lady came up to her hastily, and led her away gently by the hand.

"Uh.. I'm so sorry!" Mira stammered. "That was very careless of me! I must have upset him, going to him like that without a proper introduction..."

"You're a sweet young girl, and it's not your fault," said the little old lady briskly. "That Dipen – he's a hard nut. Don't you take any notice of him. We love it when young people like you come to the Home and spend time with us. You must not think that we are all like him."

"But what's wrong with him?" said Mira. "I can't help thinking that it is he who needs help most. As for the rest of you – you are all so cheerful and normal..."

"You're right, there *is* something wrong with him," nodded the lady. "He is suffering from an incurable condition."

"Oh, the poor soul," sighed Mira, overcome with pity. She glanced back at the old man furtively. "Is it... is it cancer? Or is it some mental condition causing severe depression?"

"No, no, it's none of those," said the old lady, leading Mira to a comfortable garden seat. "He's got severe *grudgitis*."

"Grudgitis?" asked Mira puzzled. "What's that?"

"He's got a grudge against everyone," said the old lady. "He thinks the whole world is to blame for making him unhappy – and *he* is the wretched victim."

"Aunty," said Mira, "aren't you being a little unkind?"

"Why should I be unkind to him? I came here because of him," said the old lady. "He is my husband, you see!"

Mira was ready to faint. "I... I don't understand," she said weakly. "You are his *wife?* You brought him here? Can you please explain?"

Sita Aunty – for that was her name – began to tell Mira her story. Like all old people, she loved to tell stories, especially to sympathetic, interested listeners like Mira.

Dipen and Sita had been married for over fifty years. Dipen had always had a massive chip on his shoulder – life had dealt him a raw deal; fate had been cruel to him. His parents had not left him enough money; his superiors at work did not appreciate him; Sita's parents had not given him enough dowry; his sons were not smart; daughters-in-law were not cultured; his grand children were noisy, selfish brats…

"I tell you dear, my sons are good boys, devoted to us and hard working," said Sita aunty. "As for my daughters-in-law, they are such sweet, kind girls…"

"Surely Aunty," Mira interrupted her. "If they are as *kind* and *sweet* and *good* as you say, they wouldn't allow you to live in a home like this!"

"That's where you and everyone else are mistaken," Sita aunty said triumphantly. "They did not send us here; *I* insisted on bringing him here, because he was making everyone miserable with his grudgitis. He did not have a single kind word to say to my sons – he only found fault with everything they did. He constantly criticised our daughters-in-law – and worst of all, he bullied the grandchildren too! 'Don't play in the house – don't run about – don't laugh loudly – don't talk' – it was *don't, don't* all the time!"

"I'm married to him, so I had to take it all. Why should my poor children suffer? So I decided we would move into this home. My sons and their wives would not hear of it – but I stayed firm. And I'm very glad I came here too! I have such good company of people who are my age – and my friends here do not allow Dipen to bully me. He's now left alone to make himself miserable. Of course he complains and frets and fumes all the time – but no one pays any attention to him!"

The Wise One smiled. "It is futile to blame others for our setbacks and difficulties," he said. "Mean, petty minded people always blame others for their misfortunes. But in reality, it is we who are to blame for our own attitudes."

I agreed with him whole-heartedly. I have always thought that the unwise blame others; the partially wise blame themselves; while the truly wise blame nothing and no one. Dipen Chacha was indeed an unwise man, who had thrown away the loving kindness of his family and chosen to inflict misery on himself.

"If you are mature, you realise that the impulse to blame someone is foolish," the Wise One said, after a pause. "There is nothing to be gained by blaming and resentment."

"True," I agreed. I was reminded of the words of Epictetus:

> One of the signs of the dawning of moral progress is the gradual extinguishing of blame. We see the futility of pointing. The more we examine ourselves, the less we are apt to be swept away by stormy emotional reactions in which we seek easy explanations for unbidden events.

"No shame, no blame," said the Wise One, as if he could read my thoughts.

"How should we react to people like Dipen Chacha?" I asked him. "Don't they deserve our sympathy and understanding?"

"I don't think you can demonstrate your kindness or friendship to them by indulging their negative feelings," said the Wise One. "You do them a great service by remaining detached and not allowing their negative feelings to overwhelm you."

I thought it over, and I realised he was right. When we come across a friend who is downhearted, or a grieving parent, we must not allow ourselves to be overcome by their misfortune. The same applies to our own disappointments too! The event, the occurrence is not to be blamed; there are people who can take on the situation and face it bravely. What hurts us and makes us unhappy is the response we adopt – by blaming others, carrying a grudge and resenting those around us.

"We should learn to appreciate the sunshine and the roses," observed the Wise One, "instead of looking at the clouds and thorns."

How true, I thought to myself. We win half the battle when we make up our minds to take events as they come. It is a great obstacle to happiness to expect too much! It was Sir John Lubbock who said, "The world would be better and brighter if our teachers would dwell on the duty of happiness, as well as on the happiness of duty."

"The *duty of happiness*," I said, thinking aloud. "What do you make of that?"

"We have a duty of happiness," said the Wise One. "We owe it to ourselves, to others, and above all to God, to make ourselves happy – and this is not done by blaming others or bearing a grudge."

I recalled the story of Oliver Wendell Holmes, who, in his old age, remembered the nurse of his childhood with profound gratitude. She had taught him to ignore unpleasant incidents. If he stubbed his toe or skinned his knee or bumped his nose, his nurse would never permit him to dwell upon the pain and misery. Rather, she would divert his attention to some interesting object, amusing story or happy memory. "To her," he said, "I am indebted for the sunshine of a long life."

The nurse had taught him not to bear a grudge; not to harbour bitterness or resentment about people and events.

It was a wise man who said that in looking at life, we are looking at our own consciousness. If life seems cruel, bitter, oppressive, intolerable – then the bitterness, the oppression and the intolerance lie within us, in our tendency to bear a grudge. Therefore, it is far better to stop 'wrestling' with conditions and blaming others for what happens to us – it is far better to change our consciousness. By doing this, we overcome that which is negative within us and outside us by our own positive thoughts and attitudes.

"This wonderful universe and everything in it is good," said the Wise One. "All is for the best in this best of all possible worlds. Why should we set out to change the universe or anything in God's creation? Far better it were, to change ourselves. When we bear a grudge, when we blame others, we are perceiving the world through our own distorted ideas. The distortion is in our perception.

"Many people go around with the notion that they have enemies everywhere. Their colleagues, their neighbours, their business rivals, their bankers, their lawyers, their employees – everyone seems to be an 'enemy' who is out to get them.

"We cannot hope to 'convert' so many enemies! The easier and quicker option would be to change our attitude to our so-called enemies. We must replace grudge with generosity; we must replace bitterness with sweetness; we must substitute hate with love…"

I thought of Abraham Lincoln. Shortly after the Civil War in America, an indignant, near-hysterical woman had accused Lincoln of "loving the rebels". Confronting him with anger, she had screamed, "You should do away with them! Remember, they are your enemies!"

"I agree that my enemy should be done away with," Lincoln had replied. "But I think loving them is the surest way of doing away with one's enemies."

When you adopt this attitude, you pave the way for your own happiness and peace of mind. The change that we demand, the change that we long to see, actually takes place *inside* us, when we replace grudges and resentment with love and understanding.

I opened the book I was carrying in my pocket, and Sadhu Vaswani's words sprang to life, almost as if I could hear him speaking them in his mellifluous voice:

> Are you easily offended? Are you suspicious? Are you upset when others speak ill of you? Have you a secret desire to be popular? Are you unkind to the poor? Are you dictatorial in your talk and your conduct? Are you irritable, artificial, ostentatious, complicated in your life? Are you overbearing to those who are socially your inferiors?
>
> The cause is lack of humility. The humble are simple, straightforward, gentle, kind, reverent. "Except ye be as little children," said Jesus, "ye cannot enter the Kingdom of Heaven."
>
> ...Life, not lip belief is the real test of my religion. Oh let us *live* religion, not talk of it: let us grow in humility...

"We must think of solutions, not problems," said the Wise One, breaking the silence. "We must not make problems and grudges the centre of our thinking. We must not blame people or circumstances for our condition.

"When people say to themselves again and again, 'I am unhappy', 'I am miserable', 'People are against me', 'Conditions are against me', they are gripped by a misery of their own making from which there can be no release except through their own effort. They imagine that they are injured beyond repair, and they simply cannot rise above their grudges.

"Instead, they must affirm to themselves, 'I was born to be happy', 'Happiness is my birthright', 'God created me to be happy'. As their conscious and unconscious thinking changes, conditions and people will also change miraculously. Thought by thought, step by step, as their minds change, the world will also change."

We had reached what appeared to be a huge, yawning pit. I glanced inside, and it seemed to be a sort of garbage dump, filled with all kinds of waste material.

My eyes fell on a signboard that stood nearby. It was covered in a grey cloth which I lifted. The fifth 'message' read loud and clear:

Cleanse Your Mind: Unclutter Your Thoughts.

The 5th Secret of Happiness

Cleanse Your Mind: Unclutter Your Thoughts

"How appropriate that this sign should stand next to a dump!" I remarked to the Wise One. "It seems to tell us symbolically to dump all our negative feelings and emotions right here, doesn't it?"

"You are right," said the Wise One. "Talk to any housewife. She will tell you she 'turns out' all her cupboards and shelves periodically and 'spring cleans' the whole house at least twice a year. Don't we need to 'turn out' our tired, negative thoughts and spring clean the mind as often as we can?"

In my mind's eye, a familiar vision was unfolding... It was a sight I had seen, an event I had participated in, year after year...

... The night was bitterly cold. But there was joy and serenity writ on the faces of the large group which had gathered together round a blazing fire in the forecourt of the Sadhu Vaswani Mission campus. A band of volunteers stood at strategic spots, preventing the people, especially the children, from getting too close to the fire.

It was the night of *Lal Loi* which is celebrated with fervour in India on the night before *Makar Sankaranti*. On the night of *Lal Loi*, fires are lit in every *mohalla*, every community, and people throw old and useless things into the fire, to signify the new beginning on the morrow, when the sun enters the *Uttarayana* – the northern sphere of the zodiac. In the South, this is called the *Bhogi* festival, and there too, people 'cast out' old things, to signify fresh, new beginnings!

"At the Sadhu Vaswani Mission, we observe *Lal Loi* with a difference," I said, sharing my thoughts with the Wise One. "People are urged to cast out their negative traits, negative tendencies, bad habits and bad thoughts, so that these may be destroyed in the fire of truth and purity. I feel that the symbolic gesture of consciously witnessing the fire, enables people to deal effectively with their own negative forces. For people who like a more physical demonstration, I encourage them to actually write out their negative traits on a piece of paper, and throw it into the blazing fire with their own hands!"

"Admirable!" said the Wise One. "We need to tell people again and again: *Cleanse your mind! Unclutter your mind.* Our minds are full of negative thoughts and negative ideas. With all these joy-killers inside us, how can we ever hope to be happy?"

I thought of the sage who remarked, "That man is happy, who thinks the happiest thoughts." I have always said to my friends: thoughts are things, thoughts are forces, thoughts are the building blocks of life. Therefore we must keep our thoughts clean.

Household encyclopaedias urge you to 'spring clean' your house every six months – if not, at least every year. In spare rooms, attics, balconies and garages, people accumulate unwanted stuff – old newspapers, buckets without handles, broken machines, rickety stools and chairs which they don't want to throw away, unused sheets, children's bicycles and what not. All of it is useless clutter that is getting in the way, occupying valuable space.

Give it all away while it is still in working condition, experts advise housewives. Don't wait for your children's toys and old clothes to become moth-eaten and useless; don't let cushions and pillows and blankets disintegrate; give it all away to the needy. As the clutter disappears, order and neatness will return to every corner of your home, and you will find space created for things you actually need!

There is a sister who is a college professor. The shelves and tables in her tiny flat overflowed with books, papers and research articles that she had used in the last several years. When she was about fifty years old, she decided to build a small cottage for herself in the suburbs. Space was going to be severely limited in the new house. The lady realised that she could not carry all her 'stuff' to the new house.

One night, she sat up to sort all her books and papers. She brought down books from the lofts. She unpacked books which had been put away in cartons; she opened dozens of files and folders overflowing with papers. She went through all her material systematically.

To her amazement she found that over 75% of the accumulated material was outdated, out of use and not really needed at all! As a conscientious teacher, she was always reading new books and referring to new material to incorporate into her lectures. She was certainly not one of those lecturers who recycled the same notes year after year. And the frontiers of knowledge were always expanding – and there was much that had become useless and outdated. Even libraries and students would not want some of those books, if she were to give them away free. She realised that she simply had to get rid of most of the stuff!

If you wish to be happy, you too, must unclutter your 'house' – the house of your heart. You must throw out all the joy-killers, the negative thoughts of greed, ill will, jealousy, malice and envy. But throwing these out is not enough – you must fill your mind with happy thoughts – thoughts of purity, prayer, sympathy, service and sacrifice, love and kindness, prosperity and peace, success and victory.

You are a precious and unique being! Your life has a purpose and a meaning. How can you allow your life to be weighed down by joy-killers?

One of my friends from the U.S. told me about a contest that he saw on television. It was a chilli-eating contest! The participants had to eat hot, jalapeno pepper-chillies one after the other, and the one who ate the most was declared the 'winner'. Men and women stood earnestly at a table gulping chillies as fast as they could – and when the contest ended, winners and losers collapsed with streaming eyes and burning tongues!

My friend told me that there were hamburger-eating contests, hot-dog eating contests, beer and coke drinking contests. Contestants often 'prepared' for these events by regularly eating/drinking vast amounts of these unhealthy 'junk' foods.

To what end? What earthly purpose could be served by such 'contests'? What possible benefits would the contestants get out it – except ulcers, acidity and indigestion?

In our days, we had different kinds of contests – we wrote down the *Mahamantra*, as many times as we could:

Hare Ram, Hare Ram, Ram Ram Hare Hare
Hare Krishna, Hare Krishna, Krishna Krishna Hare Hare!

The boy or girl who had written the *Mahamantra* the maximum number of times was awarded a prize or a certificate. We also had Gita recitation contests;

we had *Man Prabodh* contests. People participated eagerly, and everyone benefited from the purifying, cleansing effects of the exercise.

I am told that people in the South write *Sri Rama Jayam* at least 108 times a day, as an exercise to focus their minds on God and cleanse their thoughts. What could be better than *nam japa* or *likit japa* to cleanse the mind and purify the heart of all impurities?

We had been walking as I reflected on these matters and we had now reached up to a clear and beautiful fountain. All around were seats, and we sat down to gaze at the bubbling water as it flowed freely.

"Even water is useless, unless it is pure," said the Wise One. "Therefore, we must live a clean and chaste life. We must rid the mind of all its accumulated impurities by a systematic process of cleansing and uncluttering. What better way to do this than by uttering the Name Divine?"

"The Name Divine is pure: it is the purest of the pure," I agreed. "But there are people who come to me and ask: How may I, who am impure, sing the Name which is so immaculate and clean? I am unclean and dirty: how may I sing this most pure Name of God? I try again and again, to keep my mind pure: yet, again and again, it gets soiled, it becomes unclean. How then may I sing the Name Divine?"

"And how do you reassure them?" the Wise One asked me.

"There is a beautiful text in *Sukhmani,* the great Sikh Scripture, which rolled out of the heart of Guru Arjan Dev," I said to him. " It says:

> Holy, holy, holy, is the Name of God:
> It purifies him who meditates on it,
> With all the love of his mind and soul!

"The Great Guru says that in itself, the Name of God is pure, and it also purifies those who recite it or sing it. In those words is the message of hope. The Guru tells us not to despair, nor be disheartened. Even though we are not pure, if we will but sing the Name of God, we shall be purified. Let us keep on singing the Name Divine and, one blessed day, we, too, under the grace of God, shall become pure as the snow on mountain-heights, pure as the waters of the river Ganga."

We sat in silence, gazing on the fountain.

Purity is needed, I reflected. I remembered a story I had read, concerning a merchant, an old man and a little girl who met by the side of a fountain of clear, sparkling waters. On the fountain was an inscription which read: "Learn of me!" The merchant said that he learnt a great lesson from the fountain. It started as a trickle of water but as it wended its way to the sea, it was joined by streams and brooks and creeks and, in due course, became a roaring river. We should do our work likewise – start with small beginnings and soon develop big business centers.

The old man said that the lesson he learnt from the fountain was to be useful to as many as he could.

The little girl said that the lesson she learnt was that water is useless unless it is pure. Even animals reject turbid water. Therefore, we should live a clean and chaste life.

The Wise One had indeed spoken the truth. Purity is needed. And what purifies is the Name Divine. Repeat the Name of God, again and again, repeat it with deep love and longing of the heart, and you will feel purified.

The Name of God is like the waters of the Ganga. The river Ganga is like a mother: Ganga Ma! Ganga Ma! It purifies those that bathe in it. As you come out of the waters of the river Ganga, you will feel cleansed, washed, purified. Impure thoughts and sinful impulses wake up in the mind, again and again. Never yield to them, but sing the Name of God – not in a mechanical way, but with deep feeling and emotion of the heart. Pour into the unclean mind, the purifying Ganga of the Name Divine. Purity is needed. Whenever an unclean thought comes to you, immediately, in that very instant, say to yourself, "I was made for greater, nobler, loftier things: I shall not be a bundle of unclean, impure desires," and start repeating the pure Name of God.

"The Name of God is at once pure and purifying," said the Wise One, "It purifies those that sing it with deep love and longing of the heart. Let us together sing the Holy Name, shall we?"

Together, we chanted softly, the hymn that is dear to the heart of all Indians:

Ishwar Allah tero Naam
Sabh ko Sanmati dey Bhagwan
Raghupati Raghava Raja Ram
Patit Pavan Sita Ram
Ram, Ram, Ram, Ram, Ram,
Ram, Ram, Ram,
Ram, Ram, Ram, Sita Ram,
Ram, Ram.

"That was beautiful," I said. "We are so obsessed about external cleanliness, that we tend to neglect what's on the inside, don't we? And what is inside is far more important, isn't it?"

The Wise One smiled and said, "Let me tell you a story about why the inside matters more than the outside…"

A little black boy who was at a country fair was watching a man fill multicoloured balloons with helium gas and send them up. The balloons rose higher and higher, filled with a gas that was lighter than air.

"I bet the black balloons will not go up as high as the white ones," said the boy wistfully.

"Watch now, son," said the kind man. He blew up a black balloon and filled it with helium and let it go. It soared up just as higher as the others.

"It isn't the colour of the balloon that matters," he said to the boy. "It's what's *inside* the balloon that really matters."

"When your mind and heart are uncluttered," the Wise One observed, "when they are filled with light, joy-giving thoughts, your spirit too, can soar high!"

Scientists tell us that a magnetised piece of steel can lift up iron particles that weigh several times its weight; but if the same piece of steel is demagnetised, it cannot even lift so much as a feather's weight. When you unclutter your mind and cleanse your thoughts, you are magnetising your mind. You will find that confidence, hope and optimism fill your mind and you will achieve success and happiness.

When your mind is filled with negative emotions, you become insecure and fearful. You are overcome by negative thought patterns; "I may fail," or "I may lose my money," or "People may laugh at me," and so on.

This kind of thinking weighs you down. You let opportunities and chances slip by; you are afraid to make bold moves; you begin to stagnate...

Fill your mind with positive thoughts! But remember, positive thoughts cannot dwell in a cluttered mind, any more than a delicate plant can thrive in a closed, dark jar in a dry and dusty corner. Therefore, begin to believe in God, in the goodness of the heart, in the beauty and the order of the vast universe. Believe in the eternal truths and values upheld by our ancient scriptures – the values of *satya*, *dharma* and *ahimsa*. Such thoughts will help your consciousness to expand. The doors and windows of your mind will be opened, and you will feel the joyous winds of liberation blowing within!

If you wish to be happy, get rid of the joy killers! Gautama Buddha called them, "the three evils of the mind" – lust, hatred and greed. Hatred and happiness can never go together, even as light and darkness can never dwell together! And the Buddha also taught us how to conquer hatred – eliminate it from our lives: "Hatred ceaseth not by hatred; hatred ceaseth by love!"

When a thought of hatred enters your mind, stamp it out at once! Extinguish it – and replace it consciously with a thought of love and good-will.

A newly married girl came to seek my help. With tear-filled eyes, she said, "No matter how hard I try, I cannot please my mother-in-law! She makes my life miserable! I can't stand it anymore! I'm thinking of returning home to my parents. I can't sleep at night; sometimes I can't even breathe, I feel suffocated with her criticism and bitterness!"

I advised her to breathe out thoughts of prayer and good will towards her mother-in-law. The young woman was beginning to be weighed down by her unspoken resentment and ill-will towards the older woman. Now, it was not in her power to reason with her mother-in-law. But she could, however, unclutter her mind of all the ill-will that had been building up inside. I urged her to consciously say, "God bless my mother-in-law," or "I wish her well," whenever she felt gloomy and depressed.

Whenever a thought of hatred or malice comes into your mind, trample it underfoot and breathe out a thought of blessing and love!

The great historian, Arnold Toynbee, had profound insights to offer us on the course of human civilisation. He was of the opinion that as the world progressed in material and technological terms, man had gained several comforts and benefits – but he had to pay a terrible price for the same. The price he paid was his own peace of mind.

Is it not true my friends? Our material comforts have increased beyond our wildest imagination. We keep out the heat and dust of summer with central air-conditioning; we fly to the four corners of the earth in a matter of hours; we keep in touch with our family and friends through mobile phones wherever we are; we transfer vast quantities of information electronically, in seconds...

"As we have 'progressed' technologically, peace of mind has become a vanishing quality!" the Wise One observed.

"You seem to read my thoughts," I said.

"Negative emotions are like the toothache," said the Wise One. "Can you ever be at peace with a toothache? Let me tell you a story..."

A man was suffering from severe toothache, due to a cavity in one of his teeth. He came to the dentist, who first put him on antibiotics to reduce the severe infection. Then he began to clean the cavity. As he was probing the cavity with his drill, he was shocked when the end of the delicate dental drilling instrument broke off. With great care, he thoroughly cleaned the patient's mouth until all particles were removed. The cavity was then filled, and the man went away; on subsequent visits to the dentist, he reported that he was now free from pain. The toothache and the cavity were happily forgotten.

About three years later, the man began to complain of severe pain in his neck. The doctors examined him thoroughly, but could not find the cause. They had to treat his symptoms and let him go.

Six years later, he began to feel terrible pain in the shoulders. Once again, no diagnosis was possible. The doctors put him on a course of 'pain-management' and helped him come through somehow.

Twelve years later, the man came back to his doctor with pain in his arm – and this time, the X-ray revealed a small foreign substance. When this was surgically removed, it was found to be a tiny fragment of the dentist's drill, which had been lodged in his system, and which had been causing him intermittent pain for twelve long years!

"We too, may have some fear, hatred, jealousy, envy or resentment lurking in our consciousness," said the Wise One thoughtfully. "If we wish to be happy, we must eliminate the joy-killers."

I thought of one of the worst joy-killers I knew: the habit of thinking and talking negatively. I read of a businessman who always carried a little card in his wallet. Every now and then, he would open the wallet and take a look at the card, before he put it away.

Noticing this, a friend asked him what was written on the card. The man drew the card out and showed it to his friend. On it was written:

> I shall not speak any negative words today. I shall not think any negative thoughts today.

Every morning, the businessman would take a new card and write the words afresh. He found that his conversation and his mind were gradually cleared of all negatives! He found his life becoming happier, more content and more peaceful!

When you have driven out the negative thoughts, fill your heart with love – love of God, love of your fellow-men, love of brother birds and animals, love of nature, love of yourself. Where there is love, there is joy.

I read of a dying miner, trapped in a coal-mine. Before he died, he scribbled a few words to his wife. He wrote: "I love you more than words can tell. I love you more than you will ever know. Take care of our children. Raise them to be good human beings who love God. I am clinging to His Lotus Feet right now, and I know He will receive me in His infinite love and mercy. I die a happy man. There is peace in my heart and I'm not afraid of death!"

When rescue workers reached the victim a week after the accident, they found the note attached carefully to his safety-lamp. He had probably died within a few hours of the crash in the mine. The brief message, written in the dark underground cavern which was to be his death-chamber, was an eloquent tribute to his great capacity for love and faith. He was a man not only happy in life – but also happy in death! Even in those terrifying moments, as he faced death alone in the dark, he had had the courage to write: "I die a happy man." His heart had been filled with positives – with the love of God, love of his wife and children, and hope for the future of his loved ones. He had eliminated the joy-killers!

A Samurai maxim tells us: "Control your emotion – or it will control you." I would alter this maxim just a little: *Control your negative emotions – or they will control you.*

In fact, I would go one step further: don't just control them; defeat them; eliminate them from your system; unclutter your mind of all negative thoughts and emotions! They are the joy-killers, and they will never let you enjoy real happiness!

Hatred is self-destructive. An asked to depict hatred in personif hatred as an old man shrivelled up a. clutching in his claw-like fingers lighte wriggling serpents, and cruelly tearing out. heart with black, decaying teeth. People were a at the sight of the painting. They begged the painte to explain its symbolism.

The artist said, "I have made hatred an old man because it is as ancient as mankind. It is pale because he who hates, destroys himself and lives a tragic life. His fingers are claws, because hatred is ruthless and unmerciful. The lighted flames and serpents symbolise discord and destructiveness. And he is tearing out his own heart because his hatred will eventually destroy him."

Occasionally, I feel saddened by the number of young people who tell me that they are troubled by violent dreams, and unable to sleep peacefully at night. "Why do we get these bad dreams, Dada?" they ask me.

This is a psychological problem and there can be no easy answer to their question. But this much I know: the reason why we get violent dreams is because our days are spent in stress and tension. All that stress and tension accumulates in the subconscious self – and it is thrown out at night in the form of violent dreams.

Another negative influence on our life is TV – endless hours of watching 'action' movies and scenes of violence. This violence too, has its impact on our subconscious. Therefore, I urge my friends to be careful about everything they watch, everything they read, everything they see and hear, and everything they take in. If these negative tendencies are stored up in the subconscious, they will disturb our peace until they find an outlet – either in dreams, or through unexpected words and actions.

How can you unclutter your mind with these tendencies weighing you down? How can you avoid nightmares and violent dreams?

I have a simple suggestion to offer: as you are about to slip into sleep, carry in your mind a line from a favourite *mantra*, a line from a prayer you say often, or a saying of a great one, a Saint of God or *satpurkha*. Repeat the words over and over again, as you enter the realm of sleep. Or, take with yourself the gracious form of your *gurudeva*, or your *ishta devta*. Feel that you are at His Lotus Feet – and you will enjoy a peaceful night's sleep, and be blessed with wonderful dreams.

Depression is another joy-killer. I always tell my friends that it is the cruel, ruthless spirit of competition that prevails in modern times, which drags many people to depression. Psychiatrists tell us that there are various causes for depression –

tension, anxiety, competition, struggle, failure, frustration, disappointment and a guilty conscience.

How can we overcome depression?

We must remember that even the deepest depression is a temporary phase. Just as the sun sinks below the horizon every night, but rises brightly the next morning, depression will also disappear, eventually. Therefore, affirm to yourself again and again: *This too shall pass away!*

Take care to see that stress and tension do not accumulate and clutter your mind. Therefore, make it a point to practise relaxation everyday, and learn to take your troubles to God.

Find someone to whom you can unburden yourself. Open your heart to a spouse, a parent or a loving friend. Understanding and patient listeners can help you unburden yourself – and this will have a magical effect on your mind.

It was John Milton who wrote:

> The mind is its own place; and in itself
> Can make a Heaven of Hell, a Hell of Heaven.

Significantly, the lines come from his immortal epic, *Paradise Lost*. When your mind makes itself a veritable hell, filled, cluttered with undesirable, negative thoughts, you lose the paradise of happiness which is your birthright!

"Did you say something?" I asked the Wise One, breaking out of my reverie.

"No, I did not say anything," he smiled. "But you are listening to your own inner voice, and that is the source of the best wisdom! The mind is one of God's most amazing gifts to man. Scientists tell us that at any given time, we are using less than one-fiftieth of the brain power available to us. When we train our minds – and ourselves – to use this fabulous power in the right way, we can make our lives beautiful and positive. Therefore, let us take care of our thoughts.

"The human brain has been described as a 'fabulous mechanism'. We are told that it is about the size of half a grape-fruit – but its powers are amazing! It is capable of recording eight hundred memories per second for seventy five years without exhausting itself. It is a storehouse capable of keeping between ten billion and one hundred billion 'pieces' of information. Till recently, even the most powerful computers in the world could not match the brain's power of access, association and random memory. We may not need to recall much of the information stored in the brain – but everything we have seen or heard and taken in, is on a permanent file in our brain.

"How can we allow this magnificent filing system to become cluttered with useless, destructive, negative thoughts?"

"Very true, very true!" I concurred heartily. "And so I often tell my friends: Shampoo your mind!"

Shampoo your mind! Cleanse your mind! Unclutter your mind! The mind is more precious than gold and silver, greater than any asset you possess. In your mind, you have a 24-hour friend. You may be alone, afraid or in distress – but your mind is ever ready to help you and guide you to overcome any situation. It is your precious friend, your priceless asset. But keep your mind clean and uncluttered! Cleanse your mind of all negativity. Get right down into your consciousness and throw all those rotten thoughts that hold you captive, preventing you from experiencing the true joy of life – thoughts of impurity, selfishness, greed, lust and hatred.

Only when our minds are clean and uncluttered, can we hope to be truly happy. When destructive, negative thoughts darken our hearts, how can we ever hope to be in peace?

Sadhu Vaswani, when he was a young boy, used to keep a pin with himself. When he found an undesirable thought waking up within him, he would pierce the pin into his flesh until he felt acute pain. His mind would also cry out, "Forgive me, forgive me!"

I followed his example when I was studying in college. When I used to get unwanted thoughts, even if I was sitting in a classroom and the teacher was lecturing, I would immediately slap myself, hard. Friends sitting next to me would ask, "Is it a mosquito?" and I would say, "Yes, it was a mosquito."

The truth was that it was an *internal* mosquito, whose 'bite' could be far more dangerous!

Whenever you find a negative or undesirable thought waking in your mind, slap yourself immediately; stop a negative thought in its tracks.

The easiest way to unclutter the mind and quieten its disturbing tendencies is to engage in a loving and intimate conversation with God. Ask for His strength and wisdom to conquer such negative tendencies.

Here are a few ways in which you may cultivate the subconscious mind, so that negative thoughts are not generated therein:

- Always entertain positive thoughts – thoughts of love, peace and goodwill. Never harbour thoughts of ill-will and hatred.
- Do not react emotionally to events that happen to you and around you.
- Never make any negative suggestions in regard to what you want to be. Don't say, "I have a bad memory," or "I can never remember names." This will only make the problem worse. Rather say, "My memory is improving," and you will see that it does!
- Never hate or resent people. Let love and tolerance be your guiding principles in life. Hatred and resentment lead to many illnesses.
- Read books that inspire and uplift you, rather than the books that feature violence, sex, crime and such viciousness. This is particularly important for young people and children.

Inward beauty is reflected in joy and peace that prevail in a person's life. When I talk of inward beauty, I mean the order and the harmony that prevails in the mind. It is the beauty of good thoughts, high aspirations and fervent prayers. If our thoughts and aspirations are pure, our desires are also noble and beautiful. In short, we are beautiful within! Inward beauty is also reflected in our person – for the face, as they say, is the index of the mind.

We cannot take this inner beauty for granted. For impure thoughts come to us again and again. Even when we are seated in a holy place, evil desires, evil thoughts strike us unexpectedly. If we let these thoughts and emotions stay with us, they become ugly blocks and stains on our consciousness.

Socrates used to pray again and again, "God, make me beautiful within!" If you wish to keep your mind uncluttered and grow beautiful within, build your life in purity! Every impure impulse, impure thought and impure emotion, spoils your inner beauty and robs you of happiness. Therefore take the next step – pray to God constantly.

All these years, we have cluttered the mind, allowed it to wander, achieving nothing, gathering nothing. Control the mind! Unclutter the mind. Instead of allowing it to wallow in impurities, pick up a thought of a great one, a *Shloka* from the Gita, or a line from the *Gurbani*. Keep on repeating the great thought; enter into the depths of the meaning of those words. This will help you to cleanse your mind of its impurities and restore your inner beauty and bring you the true joy of life.

"The inner resources of your mind are tremendous," said the Wise One. "Deep within you, your subconscious is in touch with infinite beauty, wisdom and joy. It can bring you great power, wealth and happiness, when you use it effectively. It is up to you to uncover this power of light and beauty. It can lift you from the depths of defeat and despair and allow you to experience health, happiness and harmony. It can heal your troubled mind and broken heart.

"It is with reason that the cluttered, impure mind has been compared to a monkey. Swami Vivekananda once narrated a parable about the restless mind..."

There was a chattering, restless monkey, which was given a great quantity of wine to drink. The monkey began to wander like one possessed. In this state, a scorpion stung him – and he began to jump and prance. To complete his misery, an evil demon entered into the animal. Oh, how can we describe the uncontrollable restlessness of the pathetic creature?

The human mind too, is like the intoxicated, possessed, stung monkey. It is drunk with desires; stung by the scorpion of envy and jealousy, possessed by the demon of pride.

Cleanse the mind of these evil impulses!

"Your mind can be compared to a 'thought factory', according to a modern psychiatrist," the Wise One continued. "It is right inside you, and you are the absolute master who controls everything about it. You are the owner, you are the supervisor, you are the worker, you are the security guard. You monitor all that goes into the factory – you produce everything that comes out of it.

"What would you like to manufacture in your factory? Anxiety, worry, fear, envy, jealousy and ill-will? Or faith, love, optimism, courage and compassion? Will you pollute your inside and the environment outside with harmful effluents? Or would you produce 'goods' that everyone will benefit from?

"Keep your 'thought factory' spick and span, in perfect production conditions! It will generate a great deal of wealth and happiness for you and everyone you come into contact with!"

And the Wise One began to narrate to me the story of the Augean stables.

Greek mythology tells us of King Augeus, who owned three thousand oxen. The stables where these cattle were housed, had not been cleaned out for 30 long years. Cleaning the Augean stable was one of the 'labours' of Hercules – a task that he was commanded to carry out in a single day.

Can you imagine the condition of a stable with three thousand oxen, which had not been cleaned for thirty years? In Indian villages, peasants and farmers keep cows in their backyards, and they lovingly wash and clean the cattle and the cattle sheds everyday, even as they wash and clean their own homes. If they don't do it, they know the smell and the filth will actually begin to affect their own homes.

When Hercules saw the Augean stables, he was truly dismayed by its size, its stench and its filth. Then he noticed that the stables were situated between two mighty rivers – the Alpheus and the Peneus. With his enormous physical prowess, he managed to divert the course of the two rivers, so that they flowed through the stables. In a matter of hours, the Augean stables were washed and rinsed. The accumulated filth of years had been swept away by the floods.

To this day, the phrase 'Augean stables' in English means a state of affairs or condition which is dismal and filthy due to long neglect. When we neglect our thoughts and feelings and attitudes, our minds too, become Augean stables. We need the power of prayer, meditation and the flood of God's grace to wash them clean.

We rose from our comfortable seats and looked at the bubbling fountain.

"Let us wash our hands and faces," I said. "The water of this fountain appears to be so refreshing!"

We washed our face and hands and drank the clear cold water of the fountain. As I splashed more water on my face I caught sight of an inscription that had been engraved on the rim of the fountain:

What Matters Is Not What Has Happened, But How You Think About It.

The 6th Secret of Happiness

What Matters Is Not What Has Happened, But How You Think About It.

"Here is the next secret of happiness!" I exclaimed. "Pray tell me what you think about it!"

"There are events, incidents and circumstances of life over which we have no control," the Wise One said. "Natural disasters like floods, earthquakes and tsunami come easily to mind. But I don't only refer to catastrophes – I also include ordinary occurrences in our daily life."

"I know what you mean," I said earnestly. "I myself like to be punctual, and keep to my schedule as far as possible. But there are so many incidents and accidents that one simply cannot anticipate…"

A teacher leaves home early to get to her school on time; as luck would have it, there is a public transport strike that day. It has been called without earlier announcement. The school is 10 km away from her home, and the teacher is forced to return home, upset and uneasy about missing her class and an important staff meeting…

Lalita works hard in the kitchen all day, preparing a very special dinner for her husband's business partners who have come from U.S. At 6.30 in the evening, when everything is ready, in a state of perfection, her husband calls to say that they have missed the Mumbai-Pune flight, and will not be home for dinner. Lalita is angry and disappointed…

Raju has always believed in 'selective' studying. If there are twelve topics to be studied in a subject, he carefully selects six or seven which he studies thoroughly, two or three which he studies as a sort of stand-by, and two or three which he 'leaves out' completely. This technique has worked well for Raju, who has always passed with a First Class. In his final year of Engineering, he is caught unawares. Due to his selective technique, he is unable to attempt three out of five questions. Raju is frustrated and dejected…

I often tell my friends the story of the hard working farmer who ploughed his fields deep, sowed the best seeds, used the best fertilisers and kept away insects and pests from his crop. You would have thought he had a plentiful harvest – but no! The monsoons failed that year, and his crops dried and withered without water.

In all actions that we undertake, there is an element of *adhrishta* – this word is often mis-translated as luck, but it literally means *a + dhrishta* – that which is unseen, therefore unknown.

"The unexpected is always a possibility in life," the Wise One observed. "So what do we do when bad things, unpleasant things happen to us?

"Man cannot interfere with his *karma*. But he can surely change his attitude to life and to all that happens to him."

I thought of the teacher, Lalita, and Raju, of whom I spoke earlier. They met with disappointment; they were dejected. But they could have also have taken a more pragmatic approach. "Well, that could not be helped," they could say. "Let us therefore concentrate on what is to be done next.' Thus the teacher could call her school and explain her predicament and ask for a day off. Lalita could call her friends/neighbours over for a surprise dinner, or she could send some of the food round to her friends or family. Raju could resolve to prepare for the next examination, working hard to pass with flying colours.

"I began by saying that we have no control over certain events," the Wise One continued. "Let me add here, that we *do* have full control over our *attitude*. We have the choice to accept all that happens to us in the right spirit. Attitude is thus of utmost importance in our actions, reactions and responses.

"*As you think, so you become*, is the immutable law of nature. Fill your mind with thoughts of joy, love, peace and harmony; these aspects will be reflected in your life. Give way to fear and despair – you will sink into abject misery.

"Pessimism, the negative way of looking at life, is a thoroughly destructive attitude. It is the greatest joy-killer. It not only blights one's life, it is also an infectious disease which its 'carriers' transmit to others.

"When you allow your subconscious mind to store negative feelings and emotions, you will find it difficult to develop optimism and positive thinking. And each time you give in to despair and frustration, you will allow negative thoughts to dominate your mind. You will constantly gravitate towards pessimism and despair.

"The best way to cultivate the right attitude is to be aware of the truth that there is a meaning of God's mercy in all that happens to us. You will promote optimism when you ask God to give you the wisdom to understand all that happens to you in the right spirit.

"Here is a simple way to encounter negative situations: repeat to yourself the *mantra – This too shall pass away*. Allow your thoughts to turn to God, to dwell on His love and mercy. Such thoughts will help you to elevate your mind and energise your spirit. Do not dwell on the negative situation; but allow the love of God to flood your mind, to cleanse it of all negativism, to fill you with hope and faith and peace.

"Pessimism degrades you and defeats you. Optimism, born out of the understanding that God's Divine Plan is being worked out in your life, will set your mind at rest, and give you the courage and confidence to take on life's challenges."

I remembered a story that I had read earlier. A man was walking along the street when he saw a poor beggar, blind, hungry and shivering from the cold, crying for alms. The passers-by simply turned their faces away from him.

The man became angry and said to God, "What kind of father are You that You can allow such misery on earth? Why can't You do something about this?"

God's answer came to him, loud and clear, "I certainly did something. I made you!"

Attitude counts! Instead of blaming others, blaming ourselves or blaming God, let us face each situation squarely, and do the best we can!

Several years ago, when the Gold Control Act was promulgated in India, a jeweller who heard the news was so affected, that he had a massive cardiac arrest and passed away immediately!

Hundreds of other jewellers must have heard the news at the same time; but they decided to take it in their stride, and see how events shaped up. Their optimism was justified – after a few years, the Act was lifted, and people were back to buying and selling gold as usual.

It isn't what happens that matters; it is how we look at what happens.

Two American soldiers had been prisoners of war in Japan during World War II. Eventually, they both survived, and returned home to resume their lives. They met at a reunion fifty years later, in 1995. By now, Japan and U.S. were actually allies. Everything had changed.

One of them asked the other, "Have you forgiven those who imprisoned you?"

"No!" replied the second man vehemently. "Never, ever shall I forgive them."

"In that case," said the first man softly, "somehow, you are still their prisoner."

The Buddha's teachings in the great *Dhammapada* begins with these memorable lines:

> We are what we think.
> All that we are arises with our thoughts.
> With our thoughts we make the world.

We must always make sure that our thoughts are good and positive; and that our attitude is correct, constructive, friendly and optimistic.

Attitudes constitute a great force in the life of the individual. When William James, the philosopher, was asked, "Tell us what is the greatest discovery of our generation?" he answered: "The greatest discovery of our generation is that by changing our attitude, we can change our life!"

He spoke out of his own experience. There had been a period in his life when he suffered from acute depression. He had even toyed with the idea of committing suicide. Someone suggested to him,

"William, why don't you try and change your attitude?" so he had decided that he would change his attitude for just *one* day – to see if it really made a difference. And he found that it did! And the day came when, as a respected and distinguished philosopher, he could actually declare to the world that the greatest discovery of his generation was that by changing one's attitude, one could change one's life!

The man with the right attitude always looks at the bright side of things. He is an optimist. The pessimists are continually expecting the worst to happen. Modern management experts talk of something which they call "negative self-fulfilling prophecy". If you think you are going to fail, you most probably will; if you are afraid of poverty, disease or accident, you will, in all likelihood, encounter the same.

I love to recall the wonderful statement made by Dr. Karl Menninger, a great psychiatrist of the 20th century. He said: "Attitudes are more important than facts." The fact may be that you are ill; or that you have lost your job – but in all these situations, your attitude can make a difference. More important than the fact is how you react to the fact.

It is said that John Ruskin had a carved stone on his desk, used as a paper-weight; engraved on it was a single word: *Today*.

Live today; live in the present; live *now* – you cannot wait indefinitely for an ideal tomorrow which may or may not come.

"Too many of us wait for the perfect circumstances," said a learned man, "with the result that we do nothing, achieve nothing." Get on with your life; go ahead; start *now!* Regrets over the past or the dread of the future are futile; if we are obsessed with them, we will have nothing to show for all the decades we have lived.

A friend who visited Hong Kong found this direction for the control of the room air-conditioner in his hotel: "If you want the right temperature in your room, please control yourself."

Here are a few lines which I read somewhere:

> You are the person who has to decide
> Whether you do it or toss it aside;
> You are the person who makes up your mind
> Whether you will lead or linger behind
> Whether you'll try for the goal that's afar
> Or just be contented to stay where you are.

A distinguished statesman was visiting a forest that had been devastated by fire. After taking a tally of the trees that had been destroyed, he declared, "We must replant the cedars."

"They take two thousand years to grow to their full height!" someone remarked.

"Two thousand years?" said the statesman. "In that case, my friend, there's not a minute to lose. Let's start on the replantation drive immediately."

When Bernard Shaw was young, he suffered from a terrible sense of shyness, reserve and fear of speaking to others. What would you have done if you had such problems? Would you perhaps have chosen to remain a recluse, avoiding all contact with people?

I'll tell you what Shaw did. He went and joined a Public Speaking class. Not only did he join the class, he became so good at public speaking, that he was invited all over England to deliver lectures, especially on behalf of the Fabian Society – a group of people who believed in bringing about social change through persuasion. He went wherever people called him, accepting only his train fare, food and accommodation. And he also became one of the most impressive speakers in the land.

The first writing that Shaw attempted was a novel. He wrote not one or two but five novels, which were all rejected by the publishers. But he did not give in to despair. He became a reviewer, and kept up his writing. Eventually, he attained great fame as a dramatist, winning the Nobel Prize for Literature. Imagine what our loss would have been, if he had been discouraged and disheartened by his early failures!

Researchers in America carried out a study in which people on opposite sides of an issue were given a newspaper article to read. They were asked to give their reaction to the article.

Most of the people who read the article, felt that it was biased against them. The surprising thing was people with opposing ideologies felt that the article was attacking their position. Now this could not possibly be true! Obviously, it was not so much the content of the article which caused this reaction – but the *perception* of the people who read it.

Events in our life can have the same effect. We can see the same event positively or negatively.

Have you heard the beautiful story about the six-year old girl who found out that she was adopted by her parents, whom she loved more than anything else in the world? The child was stunned by the discovery. "I'm not your own baby, am I?" she kept asking. "You didn't *make* me, you only *took* me."

Her mother was a sensitive woman. She said to her daughter, "Well darling, people just get their own children, and they don't have a choice in the matter. But you are special because we actually *chose* you!"

In a research on working women, it was found that even among those doing the same kind of jobs, some people viewed work as a series of hassles, while others saw it as a positive experience in which they were in control of their lives. Among those who felt positive about their work, satisfaction was 30% higher.

If you would see your work only as a 'job' then it drags you down. If you see it as a calling, a vocation, then it is no longer toil or trouble. It becomes an expression of your self, a part of you.

A distinguished visitor arrived at a quarry where several poor labourers were toiling hard. He went up to a few of them and asked just one question of each man: "What are you doing?"

The first one snarled angrily, "Can't you see I am breaking stones?"

The second one wiped the sweat off his brow and replied, "I am earning a living to feed my wife and children."

The third man looked up at him and said cheerfully, "I am helping to build a beautiful temple!"

You can imagine which of these men got the most out of his work.

Whether you are at home, or in the workplace or among friends, you must exude optimism and positive thinking – and you will find it reflected right back at you!

If you are facing a challenge – trying to win a game or just finish a difficult assignment, what kind of people would you like to have with you? Pessimistic people who keep telling you that you will fail – or positive people who motivate you to succeed?

We always gravitate towards optimists who expect the best out of life. Living a happy, contented life is a great challenge – and a great achievement. It is a challenge that is best met with optimism.

Yasa was the son of a rich nobleman, and lived in a palace. Coming under the influence of the Buddha, he renounced all his wealth and comfort and accepted all the hardships of a mendicant's life. He slept on the bare ground. He ate what he received as alms from charitable people. He was happy.

One day, he got a severe attack of rheumatism. At first, he took the pain in his stride. Days passed by: the pain persisted. He could not walk with ease. At times the pain was so great that he could not even concentrate on his meditation. He felt miserable; gone was the joy of his life. His mind became sluggish; he felt weary and exhausted.

One day, as he was out begging alms, he found a little girl playing with her friends. She was a cripple; she had but one leg and was hobbling on crutches. Yet she was happy as a wave dancing on the sea! She shouted and laughed and made merry with the other children.

Seeing her, Yasa felt ashamed of himself. "This little girl who has only one leg is bright and happy," he said to himself. "And I, a disciple of the Buddha, am dejected by a little pain!" He turned over a new leaf. The pain could no longer trouble him. He was free!

Depression is not due to what happens to us: it is due to what happens *within* us.

There is a poem I read somewhere about people with a negative attitude:

> He always has something to grumble about
> He is the man with a chip on his shoulder;
> The world to the dogs is going no doubt

> To the man with a chip on his shoulder.
> The clouds are too dark, the sun is too bright,
> No matter what happens, it is never right,
> When peace is prevailing he is spoiling to fight
> The man with the chip on his shoulder.

Have you heard about the man who was gazing at a beautiful rose garden? "It's beautiful, isn't it?" his companion said to him. "Hmm," he sighed, "But it is such a pity that these roses have to have thorns."

"If I were you, I would thank the Lord," chided his friend, "for allowing these thorns to have roses."

Life has its store of 'thorns', undoubtedly. But failures, problems and difficulties only add spice to life. It is unrealistic to expect success and profits all the time – and it is foolhardy to consider life as nothing but a series of problems.

"Learn to live with life as it is," a wise man urges us. Accept life as it comes! Adjust yourself to take its ups and downs in your stride. Meet the vicissitudes of life with a smile. Bend – and you will not break!

"You don't acquire happiness," says John E. Haggai, "you assume happiness."

Happiness is a state of mind: it is stabilised by your attitude to life.

"Tell me what you think of life," said someone, "And I will tell you what you will make of it".

I am never tired of repeating the story of Thomas Alva Edison, which has always inspired me. Edison, lost over two million dollars worth of equipment and the accumulated records and results of a great deal of his life's work, when his laboratory in Edison Industries was destroyed by a raging fire in the year 1914.

Edison's son Charles rushed to look for his father in the scene of the conflagration. He found him watching the fire thoughtfully, his white hair blown by the winter wind.

Charles's heart ached for his old father.

Edison saw his son, "Where is your mother Charles?" he called out. "Bring her here at once. She will never see anything like this again as long as she lives!"

And the following morning, as he walked among the ashes of his hopes and his dreams, sixty-seven-year old Edison remarked, "There is great value in disaster. All our mistakes are burnt up. Thank God we can start anew!"

He was a great man who knew how to react to life's adversities and pitfalls!

"Shall we move on?" asked the Wise One softly. "I'm sorry to break into your reflections, but we still have so much more to see..."

"And so much more to learn!" I exclaimed, following him. "It's just that each one of these secrets is so powerful, so profound, it gives me so much to think about. I wonder how many more secrets there are!"

The Wise One laughed. "There are a hundred, a thousand ways to be happy," he observed. "Even one of these secrets can change a man's life for the better, if he followed it in letter and spirit. The more secrets he learns, the happier he will be, if he puts them into practice."

We heard something that sounded like a distant rumble. Before we could realise what it was, the sky became overcast, and a thunderstorm broke out.

"Quick, here is a tree that can shelter us," called the Wise One, as he led me to the shade of a huge tree which offered us protection from the heavy shower.

"This tree seems to be thousands of years old," I remarked, straining my eyes and neck to estimate its height and its span. Its thick, close-knit branches spread like an impenetrable roof overhead, allowing not a drop of rain to reach us. "Just see how huge the trunk is! I bet four people could stand around it, with their arms outstretched on either side, and still not encircle it fully! And look at the bark of the tree! It is as solid as armour…"

As I walked round the tree, looking at its trunk, my eyes fell on the words that had been painstakingly carved on it – perhaps years ago. The letters had been cut into the bark with a knife, and although they had become brown with age, they still stood out with their emphatic message:

Always Expect The Best – But Be Prepared For The Worst.

The 7th Secret of Happiness

Always Expect The Best – But Be Prepared For The Worst

"Here is the seventh secret!" I exclaimed. "But to be frank with you, people find it difficult to accept it, whenever I offer this precept to them. They say they find it contradictory. 'How can one expect the best and still be prepared for the worst?' they demand of me. And I remember the days of my boyhood when we used to laugh at contrary proverbs – *Fortune favours the brave*, and *Discretion is the better part of valour*. What is one supposed to do? Rush in where angels fear to tread, or sit back and wait indefinitely for the perfect moment that may never come?"

The Wise One smiled. "There is always the golden mean, isn't there?" he remarked. "That's what this secret is all about. Bad things may befall us – and we must be on our guard. But this does not mean that we cease to act, that we give up on an active enterprising life. We go ahead with whatever we have to do, and hope that the best will come to pass."

I grew thoughtful.

We live in a world of uncertainty. In fact, modern philosophy goes so far as to insist that death is the only certainty of life – as for the rest, we simply do not know where life will take us.

I have always felt that we should take this in a positive way. All that is born must die; this is a fact well known to us. But if we develop an obsession about death, we can achieve nothing in life. At any rate, God did not give us this precious human life to be spent just waiting for death.

But still, I had had reason to say to the Wise One as I did, that people found this concept difficult to accept. I have had several brothers and sisters coming to me with tear-filled eyes and broken hearts, telling me, "You taught us to trust the Lord. You told us to think positively. Our loved one was admitted to the hospital. But he passed away! How can God be so cruel to us?"

It is to such people that I repeat: "Always expect the best; because human life is intolerable without the spirit of optimism and hope. Therefore, hope for the best; believe that the best will happen. But also bear in mind that God's Plan for us might be different from the plan that we have proposed for ourselves. He knows what is best for us. And there is a meaning of His mercy in all the events, accidents, disasters and tragedies that occur in our life. Accept them in this spirit. Be prepared to accept the worst, for the unexpected may happen. The secret of facing the unexpected without losing your inner calm and balance lies in acceptance!"

Not *my* will, but *Thy* Will be done, O Lord! If this be the motto of your life, you will learn to expect the best – but be prepared to meet the worst eventuality.

"Think of Sri Rama and Sita..." said the Wise One... and the familiar story played itself out before my mind's eye, as he narrated the event from the sacred *Ramayana*.

It is the eve of Sri Rama's coronation as the *yuvaraj* of Ayodhya. The ceremony, which was slated to take place on a future auspicious date, is forthwith advanced to the very next day – because King Dasharatha is disturbed by bad, inauspicious dreams. He is worried that a great sorrow, perhaps even death may befall him. Something tells him that Sri Rama must be anointed at once. Therefore, he calls Rama and tells him to prepare for the ceremony by fasting that very night.

While the Rajaguru, Rishi Vashishta, initiates Rama with due *mantras* for the pre-coronation fast, Ayodhya begins to celebrate the impending coronation. The people are thrilled and excited; they decorate their houses with flags, festoons and flowers. It is as if their own son/brother is going to be *yuvaraj* – for such is their love for Sri Rama.

In the meanwhile, dawn approaches, and Sri Rama and Sita are readied for the ceremony with grand robes and royal jewels. They await the auspicious call to the royal court. The call comes – but it is not what they expected.

I do not have to tell you the story – for you are all familiar with the events of the *Ramayana*. When Sri Rama enters his father's apartment in the palace, it is to see the king lying on the bare floor in unspeakable anguish. It is Kaikeyi who informs him that Bharata is to be crowned *yuvaraj* in his place; while he himself should go into the forest as an exile, for fourteen years.

No one in Ayodhya, in their worst nightmares, could have thought of such a monstrous possibility. We know, that when Kaikeyi demands those two 'boons' Dasharatha almost grows mad with grief. He rants, he raves, he curses, he renounces Kaikeyi as wife; then he pleads, begs, coaxes, cajoles her, finally even falling at her feet – all to no avail. But when Sri Rama hears the dreadful doom, he is calm and untroubled. Kaikeyi cannot believe her eyes – for there is not the slightest sign of disappointment or anger on Sri Rama's face. Smiling, he tells her that his father's promise to her would be fulfilled – he would leave for the forest that very day.

Passion, sorrow, despair and anger overrun Ayodhya. Lakshmana is furious; Kaushalya is devastated; the people are bewildered by the turn of events – but Rama, who is the victim of this cruel injustice, is calm and unperturbed.

Sita begins to weep – *not* because her husband has lost the opportunity to become *yuvaraj*, but because he wants to go to the forest *without* her! All she asks is that she should go with him – where Rama is, *there* Ayodhya is, as far as she is concerned. Such is her supreme love, that he cannot deny her request. She is allowed to accompany him. Overjoyed, she calls the poor people and gives away all her belongings and prepares to go to the forest. Lakshmana insists on joining them, and the people of Ayodhya are faced with the unbelievable prospect of letting their beloved Rama and Sita go into exile.

Let us remind ourselves that it was Lord Vishnu who had assumed the form of Sri Rama. Even He, the Almighty Lord, accepted that He had to go through the sufferings, sorrows and experiences appropriate to his incarnation. Without a protest, indeed, with a smile, he accepted the worst.

"What a wonderful example the Lord and His divine consort offer to us in the *Ramayana!*" the Wise One remarked. And he had even more stories to narrate to me.

Amir, a prince of Khorasan, lived a life of luxury. Such was the splendour of his lifestyle, that three hundred camels would carry the pots, pans and utensils of his camp kitchen, when he set out to fight wars.

During one of his military campaigns, he was defeated by a powerful caliph. His army was surrounded by enemy soldiers on all sides, and it was expected that at any minute, he would be taken prisoner by the caliph.

Misfortune does not exempt a man from hunger! When Prince Amir saw his chief cook nearby, he requested the good man to prepare a meal for him.

The cook had a little rice, which he put on the fire. Then he went to see if he could find a few vegetables or at least some onions, so that he could add some flavour to the rice.

A stray dog was passing by, and he was attracted by the smell of the food. He put his nose into the pot, and feeling the heat of the fire, he tried to jerk his face free. But he was so clumsy that the pot stuck to his head and he began to run helter skelter in panic, spilling the rice all around him.

Prince Amir burst out laughing at the sight. His companions asked him how he could laugh, when the last morsel of food that he could eat as a free man had been snatched away by the cruel hand of fate.

Prince Amir pointed to the dog rushing around the camp and said, "Only this morning, it took three hundred camels to transport my camp kitchen; and now, one dog has managed to carry it all away!"

The prince was able to face the worst with cheerfulness. If he could smile in the midst of such privation, can we not also learn to accept the ups and downs of life with equanimity?

Rajaram was fabulously wealthy. Not only had he inherited a great deal of wealth from his father, who was a prosperous merchant; but he had amassed four times more wealth by his own hard work and wise business deals. But he was grieved by the fact that his own son was a wastrel, a profligate, who did not know the value of money. No matter how hard he tried to persuade his son to mend his ways, the boy refused to listen. Rajaram was saddened by the thought that all the wealth that he had acquired with such care, would be squandered away by his worthless son. But what made him even more anxious was the fear that his son would one day be reduced to a pauper, with no one to help him or support him or offer good counsel to him.

Finally, when Rajaram was on the point of death, he called his son to his bedside and said to him, "My dear son, all that I possess, I'm leaving to you. As long as I was up and about and alive, I looked after your every need, and still managed to keep your fortune intact. Now, the management of your wealth passes into your own hands.

"I only have one warning to give you. Wealth can vanish sooner than you expect, unless you manage it wisely and well. Therefore, please change your ways! Should you ever fall into trouble, should you ever be desperately in need of help, go to my *pooja* room where my copy of the *Valmiki Ramayana* is kept. Open the sacred text and read a stanza. Sri Rama, whom I have worshipped devoutly all my life, will surely come to your aid."

Rajaram died shortly thereafter. The worst that he feared came to pass. The son surrounded himself with philanderers like him, and squandered his wealth away. The wealth that had been amassed through generations was wasted in a matter of years.

With the money, the so-called 'friends' too disappeared. Filled with remorse, the son remembered his father's dying words and went to the huge volume of *Ramayana* in the *pooja* room and opened it. He was astounded! For, his father had carved out a large cavity in the middle of the book and it was filled with precious stones of great value. Using this, the last of his inheritance, with great care, the son prospered again.

Rajaram had proved that he was a wise man; he had hoped for the best, but he had been prepared for the worst – that his son would not mend until it was too late. To this end, he had preserved a little fortune to be kept aside for the son, when all else was lost!

We live in a frenzied age when unexpected things happen to us all the time. My friends tell me that accidents and fatalities fill the local news in the daily paper; in fact, they say they actually witness accidents happening before their very eyes, when they travel to work. Sometimes stocks and shares soar in value; suddenly they crash – and people lose their fortunes. Every day working people encounter irritation and ill will. The only way we can maintain our inner peace and balance is to do our duty well – and leave the rest to God.

Hope for the best – but be prepared for the worst.

"But why does the worst have to happen?" someone once asked me. "Why should God permit good people, innocent people to suffer?"

My answer to him was this: in truth, good people can never suffer. If an innocent person undergoes suffering or distress, the little evil that is within him is being transmuted into good. How does evil become good? The same way that gold is purified – by passing through fire! When a good man passes through the fire of suffering, the evil in him is burnt away.

Significant are the words of Sadhu Vaswani:

> Every great one of humanity has had to bear his cross. Krishna and Buddha and Jesus walked through the valley of the shadow of death. Then who are we to say that we must escape sorrow, anguish or pain? We too, must bear our cross – bear and bleed. And when we bleed, let us remember that the Will of God is working through us: and through suffering and pain, God's Will is purifying us, preparing us for the Vision of the One Lord of Life and Light and Love, in all that is around us and within us. Suffering is the benediction which God pours upon His beloved children to whom He would reveal the infinite meaning of His mercy – reveal Himself, His wisdom and His love!

"God has created a wonderful world for us," the Wise One said. "He wants each one of us to be successful, prosperous and happy, to enjoy all the good things with which his universe is filled. If I am not happy, prosperous and successful, it must be because I have broken some natural law in this or the previous births. Nature works in a simple way. If your thoughts, words and actions are in obedience to her laws, you may be sure of a happy, harmonious life.

"I firmly believe that at the heart of everything – everyone – is goodness. And this is true for every experience, howsoever unpleasant it may appear to be. Life is a mixture of the pleasant and the unpleasant. Sometimes, all our wishes seem to come true; we knock and the doors are open to us; we ask and we are given.

"But at other times, God deliberately seems to say 'No!' to our prayers. If He does so, it is surely because He knows that what we ask for, cannot bring real good to us. And so what we regard as the worst happens..."

I thought of the great English poet, William Blake, who says in one of his poems, "Joy and woe are woven fine, a clothing for the Soul Divine!" And the Psalmist too declares: "Weeping may endure for a night, but joy cometh in the morning!"

"Joy and sorrow follow each other, even as day follows night," continued the Wise One. "But when the worst happens, when we face disappointment and failure, the period of suffering appears to be interminably long. A year of joy is but a day: and a day of suffering appears longer than a year, doesn't it?

"True, the unexpected, the unwanted when it happens, brings suffering with it. But suffering is a part of life; suffering is a teacher. We would miss some of the best lessons in our life if suffering did not come to us. Alas, many of us do not recognise this truth, and do everything we can to avoid the painful, unpleasant experiences of life. When the worst happens, when trouble approaches, we try to run away from it: but trouble can never be dodged. The unpleasant experience may recede for a while – only to return in a more formidable form. By refusing to face the worst, we invite more trouble, perhaps greater trouble, at a later stage.

"There are some people who adopt a slightly different attitude when the worst happens. They simply resign themselves to the experiences which fall to their lot. They do not resist: they become resigned. They are the kind of people who say, 'What cannot be cured must be endured.'

"But there is a third way of meeting the worst that happens – the right way. The first way – the way of avoiding trouble – is folly. The second – the way of becoming resigned, passive submission – is *avidya*, ignorance. The third is the way of greeting the worst, the unwanted, the unexpected trouble, as a friend. Do not try to avoid it; do not try to run away from it – you will not succeed. Do not allow trouble to overwhelm you. But move forward to meet trouble, to greet it with the words, "Welcome, friend! What message do you bring to me from the Lord?" and you will find that every trouble is a soiled packet — soiled only on the outside, but containing a precious gift inside. Every unpleasant, unwanted experience brings with it a wealth of wisdom and strength. The person who knows this, is prepared to face the worst; he greets troubles with a smile. He is a true victor, and his way is a way of victory."

I nodded in silent agreement.

I often tell my friends the story of one such man; he had a flourishing business. Everything seemed to be going well for him. Suddenly one night, when he was out of town, his shop and house caught fire, and all that he possessed was reduced to ashes. Property worth crores was lost.

What did he do? Shed tears? No! Did he curse and fume in anger? No! Did he accuse God of deserting him? No! On his face was a smile, and lifting up his eyes, he asked, "Lord, what wouldst Thou have me do next?"

The Lord showed him the way. And over the shambles which was once his shop, he put up a sign board on which were the following words:

Shop burnt!
House burnt!
Goods burnt!

But Faith not burnt!
Starting business tomorrow!

He was a man who knew the right way to meet trouble. He knew how to take on the worst.

Yes, the worst that we fear comes to pass sometimes. But bad things happen to good people so that they may grow better, nobler, purer.

Wealth and pleasures and power and honour are not as good as they seem to be, though they seem to be the best things in life that we may hope for. In some cases, they may actually degrade a man and make him corrupt. In our ancient legends, there is a suggestive story told to us of Kunti, who was once permitted to ask a boon of Sri Krishna. What she asked for was that she might have a little suffering all the time. In suffering, she said, we remember the Lord; in pleasures and enjoyments, He is often forgotten.

When the best happens, we forget the Lord; when the worst comes to pass, we cling to His Lotus-feet!

Thomas Merton writes in *The Seven Story Mountain*:

> The truth that many people never understand until it is too late is that the more you try to avoid suffering, the more you suffer; because smaller, insignificant things begin to torture you, in proportion to your fear of being hurt. The one who does most to avoid suffering is, in the end, the one who suffers most.

I remember an old rhyme:

I walked a mile with Pleasure:
She chatted all the way,
And left me none the wiser
For all she had to say.
I walked a mile with sorrow:
And never a word said she!
But oh, the things I learned from her,
When sorrow walked with me!

Disappointments, suffering and failure come to us in many guises. There are physical sufferings associated with the body; intestinal disorders, exhaustion, muscular pain etc.; failing vision and hearing in old age with their attendant problems; serious afflictions like cancer, cardiac problems and ever new, ever unfamiliar diseases like SARS and leptospirosis etc.

Then there are the afflictions of the heart and mind – like disappointments in love and friendship, betrayal, loss of faith in near and dear ones, lack of appreciation and sympathy.

There are intellectual sufferings too – like an unrewarding, unsatisfactory job, frustration with our own limitations, boredom in the workplace and injustice in the recognition of merit.

Surrounded on all sides by disappointments and failures, we become like rudderless boats tossed on the high seas. Happiness seems to be lost, somewhere at the end of a rainbow that is *not* visible on our horizon.

Bishop Fulton Sheen enumerates ways of facing suffering and disappointments effectively: according to him the first way is that of *stoicism*, which tells us to grit our teeth and bear suffering patiently and with fortitude. The second is the way of Buddhism, which sees all suffering as self-inflicted, as a result of desire. As one conquers desire, one also overcomes suffering.

The third way that Fulton Sheen speaks of is the Christian way, which teaches that pain and suffering can be transcended through love.

The Hindu way of life, I must add, teaches us yet another way to overcome suffering – this is through loving surrender to the Lord. For does He not promise us in the Gita: "Renouncing all rituals and writ duties, come to Me for single refuge. Do not fear, for I will liberate thee from all bondage to sin and suffering."

Yes, when the worst happens, when suffering strikes, there is meaning to be found in it – but this meaning is available only to those of us who accept suffering with faith.

"It is hard to suffer," says Paul Claudel, "and not to know the *value* of suffering."

Don't let the worst sap your spiritual strength! Don't let failure and disappointment mar your progress. As Samuel Smiles writes:

> Failure is the best discipline of the true worker, by stimulating him to renewed efforts, evoking his best powers, and carrying him onward in self-culture, self-control, and growth in knowledge and wisdom.

What is the worst that can happen to you at this stage in your life? Close your eyes and force yourself to think of the worst: when you have faced up to it, you will find that there is nothing you have to fear or avoid any more!

Disappointment, pain and suffering have moulded all the great ones of history in East and West. Trials, tribulations and hardships came their way – in fact, they had more than their fair share of it all. But they were not daunted! They grew stronger, more positive, more determined than ever before. For many of them, defeat and disappointment marked the beginning of a new life – a real blessing in disguise.

I looked at the Wise One. He was watching me intently, and he smiled. "May I hear what you are thinking now?" he enquired softly. "I'm sure that I can learn something valuable from your reflections."

I recited to him the beautiful lines that I had read recently:

> For every pain that we must bear,
> For every burden, every care,
>   There's a reason.
>
> For every grief, that bows the head,
> For every tear drop that is shed
>   There's a reason.
>
> For every hurt, for every plight,
> For every lonely pain-racked night
>   There's a reason.

But if we trust God, as we should,
It all will work out for our good.
He knows the reason.

"That is just splendid! Beautiful!" exclaimed the Wise One. "That's a poem which says it all, doesn't it?"

"Oh look, look!" I exclaimed in delight. "The rain has stopped now, and there's a beautiful rainbow!"

"What a wonderful sight!" agreed the Wise One. "And the rainbow is a reminder to us that there is so much to be happy about in God's good world."

We left the shelter of the tree and walked out into the evening sunshine. Ahead of us stood a beautiful monument – an exquisitely sculpted structure, with intricate carvings and frescoes. Moving closer, I read the inscription carved over the entrance:

You Should Be Full Of The Spirit Of Wonder That Belongs To Children.

The 8th Secret of Happiness

You Should Be Full Of The Spirit Of Wonder That Belongs To Children

"A wonderful secret!" I said to the Wise One delightedly. "It reminds us that there is a lot we can learn from children."

We went up the beautifully carved steps into the monument. It was a small structure – but its beautiful artwork and frescoes made it unique and special. On the walls inside were intricate carvings and relief work, depicting scenes of celebration, joy and happiness. The fresco in a corner particularly attracted my attention. A mother held her small child in her arm and pointed to the full moon in the sky. The child gazed at the moon, utterly fascinated, and its eyes were wide with wonder...

Sadhu Vaswani often urged us, "Everyday you must spend sometime with children!"

He himself was very fond of little children. He often said he beheld child Krishna or the Christ-child in their tender, innocent eyes.

Once, he was playing with some children. Someone asked a child in the group, "Do you know with whom you are playing?"

"I don't know who he is," said the child in his wide-eyed innocence. "All I know is that he loves me!"

Sadhu Vaswani said that it would do a spiritual aspirant a world of good to spend time in the company of children – for children have so much to teach us.

"Be like a child!" said the Wise One, startling me out of my reverie, amazing me by the insight with which he seemed to echo my own thoughts. "Cultivate the trust and faith that the child has; take life as it comes, even as a child does; enjoy your life in carefree innocence, like a child!

"There are people, who, after a particular age, stop enjoying life as children do. They exclaim, 'We are not children and our life is not the same any more!'

"Have you heard of Lewis Carrol's wonderful novel, *Alice In Wonderland?* Carrol wrote it for his niece, it is said. But today, *Alice* is a classic that is loved by everyone who loves books. It has rightly been said that *Alice* is not just a children's novel, but a novel that appeals to the eternal child in all of us – whether we are eight or eighty. If you miss out on this child, you miss out the best part of your life.

"We are *always* children of God. Therefore, let us live like children who know that their mother or father is close to them, watching them, taking care of them."

Once again I thought of Sadhu Vaswani's words to us: "Hand yourself over, in child-like trust to the Lord. Have you ever seen a child living under a cloud of gloom or anxiety?"

So it was that Jesus said, "Of such as children is the Kingdom of God." Once, when children were told to keep away from Jesus, and not to disturb Him, He admonished His disciples by saying, "Suffer the little ones to come unto Me; for of such is the Kingdom of God." And the Kingdom of God is the Kingdom of happiness!

"Look at children!" said the Wise One. "They are so full of fun and laughter and happiness. Little things make them so happy…

"A little known incident from the life of Aesop reveals a totally new dimension to the great story-teller whose fables are world-renowned…"

One day, Aesop was playing with little children, happily shouting and laughing with them.

An Athenian passed by; he expressed surprise that a mature adult should waste his time thus.

In answer, Aesop picked up a bow, and unstringing it, laid it on the ground. To the Athenian, he said, "O, wise one! Tell me the meaning of this unstrung bow!"

The man was perplexed. He said, "I don't know! Can you tell me what it means?"

And Aesop said to him, "If you keep a bow always bent, it will lose its elasticity. But if you let it go slack, it will be fitter for use when you need it."

"Are we not, many of us, like the bent bow, always highly strung?" the Wise One turned to ask me. "We need to unstring ourselves, to relax from time to time, that we too, may be 'fitter for use' when we are called to action. And what better way to relax than in the company of the little ones?"

Children have so much to teach us. Two children went out for a walk with their father. One of them was a toddler, and the father held him by the hand.

The other said, "I'm a big boy now, Papa. Let *me* hold your hand!"

And so they walked along, hand in hand, when suddenly, they stumbled on a boulder, which they had failed to notice. The older boy lost his grip on his father's hand and fell down, bruising himself badly. The toddler was safe in the grip of the father, for the father's hold had tightened automatically, saving him from the fall.

The older boy represents self-help in spiritual matters; the toddler symbolises the spirit of self-surrender. Here too, the child teaches us — Trust in the Lord utterly, and you will be safe, secure and happy!

A science teacher was talking to her young class V students. "Modern science has wonders to make our lives better in every way," she said to them. "Think of all the benefits science has conferred upon us," she continued, "Just imagine what life will be without all those wonderful machines which our scientists have invented."

"Now I would like you to tell me some of these wonderful machines that make our lives easier," she said to her class.

The children came up with all the stock answers – the telephone, the cell phone, TV, airplane, motorcar and so on.

When the first rush of answers was over, a lull prevailed in the class. "Yes? Can you name a few more of those wonderful machines?" the teacher asked them again.

Little Jyoti put up her hand, slowly, thoughtfully.

"Yes Jyoti, what is it?" said the teacher encouragingly.

Jyoti got up. "The most wonderful machine that I have ever seen is a hen!" she announced.

"A hen?" said the teacher, thoroughly bewildered. "Do tell us how a hen can be a machine – and a wonderful machine at that!"

"Well," said Jyoti. "Can you think of any other machine which will take up all the droppings and leavings in the backyard and turn them into fresh eggs?"

Children look at the world with a sense of wonder and amazement. Their perspective is fresh and original. All of us need this sense of wonder to discover the beauty and happiness that are all around us in the universe. God made it all for us to wonder at and to enjoy.

The child is so given to a sense of wonder and amazement, that he is constantly asking questions: why... how... when...?

Little Pinky and her father were walking to school. As they passed an electrical transformer, Pinky wanted to know, "How does electricity pass through thin wires?"

"I don't know," said her Dad. "I will read up and then answer your question."

A little while later, Pinky asked, "Dad, what causes thunder and lightning?"

"To tell you the truth," her father confessed, "I'm not quite sure myself."

A few minutes passed. "Tell me Dad..." began Pinky again – and then subsided, "Well... never mind."

"Go ahead," said the father, "Ask questions. You must ask a lot of questions. How else will you learn?"

The father may not have been able to answer all Pinky's questions; but he certainly had a point encouraging her to ask more.

"Wonder," Aristotle said, "is the first cause of philosophy."

It is the child's instinct to ask questions, because the child is evolving, growing intellectually. Human civilisation was possible because man began to ask questions about himself and the world that surrounded him. In the ultimate analysis, the life spiritual too, begins with questions such as these: who am I? What is the purpose of my existence?

All of us wonder about the world, about our life. All of us ask questions. From the moment we learn to form thoughts into words, we begin to enquire about the world and things. Some of us acquire a great deal of knowledge in the process. As the poet Coleridge puts it:

> In wonder all philosophy began, in wonder it ends, and admiration fills up the interspace; but the first wonder is the offspring of ignorance, the last is the parent of adoration.

Wonder leads us to questions; questions lead us to knowledge and awareness; but for the sensitive, thirsting soul, questions do not cease with superficial knowledge; the more we know, the more we realise how very little we know. There are very many common, natural phenomena that we still cannot understand, though we have made tremendous 'progress' in science. Scientists enquiring into the origins of the universe, the formation of the earth, the nature of the planets and stars and the movement of the sun and the moon, still retain this sense of wonder. Intelligent, sensitive and quick to grasp things, they are still filled with amazement at what they see. They know that with all the progress they have made, they have still just managed to scratch the surface, in their attempt to understand the myriad wonders of this universe. And this sense of wonder always keeps them curious, always interested, always eager to know more – like little children.

Thus the realisation that our knowledge is limited has taught people to admire and adore what lies beyond: what they may perhaps never really come to *know* – except intuitively, spiritually.

Thus it was that Von Braun, the scientist who played an important role in the Apollo missions to the moon, confessed:

> Manned space flight is an amazing achievement, but it has opened to us thus far, only a tiny door for viewing the awesome reaches of space. Our outlook through this peephole at the vast mysteries of the universe only confirms our belief in the certainty of the Creator.

It is my belief that children respond to this sense of wonder and beauty and amazement much more than adults do. It is as if we grow jaded, dull, colourless and unappreciative as we get older, and begin to take things for granted.

Look at children! The sight of a dog, a cat, or a cow fills them with inexpressible delight. Their eyes grow wide and round, like little saucers. They look at you with urgent appeal, asking you to join their ecstasy at the sight before them. "Bow Wow! Bow Wow!" they exclaim. Or "Meow, meow!" or "Moo! Moo!" And, if an elephant should appear before them, their joy knows no bounds!

If our education is to be whole and well-rounded, it must be enriched by a sense of wonder, and the appreciation of all that is beautiful. An education that neglects the beautiful in nature and art, is like a barren wilderness without colours, without flowers and the music of the birds.

"What is the best education?" they asked Plato.

The great philosopher replied, "It is that which gives to the body and to the soul all the beauty and all the perfection of which they are capable."

"I am afraid we are living in an age when we uphold only material achievements, while beauty, charm, grace and the sense of childlike wonder are neglected," the Wise One remarked. "We would do well to heed the warning of Emerson: 'Never lose an opportunity of seeing what is beautiful; for beauty is God's handwriting – a wayside sacrament. Welcome it in every fair face, in every fair sky, in every fair flower, and thank God for it, as a cup of blessing!'

"Stroll about in a garden; climb a mountain; listen to the chirping birds; watch the glory of the sunset and sunrise; feel the cool breeze blowing against your face; listen to the music of the moving river; take in the majesty of tall trees and multi-hued flowers. Don't these things fill you with a sense of beauty and wonder? Don't they fill you with amazing happiness?

"Keep the child in you alive! Keep a sense of wonder – and you will discover beauty and happiness in everything, everybody around you. God made this world for you – to love, to enjoy, to experience as His child. His kingdom is yours – for you are His loving child. The beauty and joy of this universe is yours by birthright! Only keep your eyes open – your physical eyes and the eyes of the spirit – so that the beauty and the wonder are not lost on you.

"Take time to appreciate the beauty of the world: the glorious play of the colours at dusk; the twinkling of the silvery stars studded in the dark velvet sky at night; the lush green meadows; the soaring birds with their perfect flight formations – oh, the beauties of nature are indeed endless!

"When lightning and thunder flashed, Mira beheld the form of Krishna in the dark clouds and she was filled with ecstasy. *'Hari aawan ki awaaz aaj suni main'* she sang. I have heard the sound of Hari approaching!"

We sat on the steps of the monument as night fell gently and the silver disc of the moon arose in the evening sky. In my heart within, I could hear Krishna's flute and Mira's song... and the distant thunder...

"Time to move on..." the Wise One announced, leading the way forward.

Our path now skirted what appeared to be an orchard, and we gathered a few fruits for our simple repast. A little further, we came upon a spring – and I suddenly realised I was very thirsty.

"You have given me so much to imbibe, so much to think about," I said to the Wise One, as we quenched our thirst in the spring. "I have even forgotten that I could be hungry or thirsty or tired. If we had not found this spring or these fruits, I believe I could have just carried on, looking for more secrets of happiness!"

The Wise One smiled. "We may forget ourselves," he said, "but the Lord always provides for our every need."

"We should find a proper shelter for ourselves tonight," I said, glancing at the sky anxiously. "I do not want to get caught in another thundershower."

"As I said, the Lord will provide," the Wise One assured me.

Sure enough, he was right. A little distance away, we came across the remains of what appeared to be a farmhouse – for there were two huge granaries on either side of the building. The massive granite pillars of the front porch and the spacious *verandah* which the steps led upto were still intact. The shelter seemed to welcome us warmly at the end of what had been a long and eventful day.

We sat on the *verandah* and ate our fruits. Grown in their natural state – I should say, grown almost wild – they tasted simply delicious. If only people lived here, I thought to myself, how they would enjoy the land and all its unspoilt bounties…

When we had eaten, I got up to explore what was left of the house, out of curiosity. The doorframe leading inside the building was intact, but the door had disappeared. We stepped across the threshold into a large hall. In the silvery moonlight which came in through the open windows, I saw an inscription on the wall before me:

Keep Your Body Healthy And Strong.

The 9th Secret of Happiness

Keep Your Body Healthy And Strong

"Here is the ninth secret!" I exclaimed.

"Happiness and good health go together, don't they?" the Wise One said. "We need to pay attention to our mental, physical and spiritual well being, if we wish to be happy. We cannot take good health for granted…

"It has rightly been said: health is wealth; health is happiness. A sound mind in a sound body is a vital requisite for health. Wouldn't you agree?"

I nodded in complete agreement. Life, as I have said repeatedly, is God's greatest gift to man. It should be a wonderful, joyous pilgrimage – not an anxious, harried, disturbed existence, which it has become for millions of people today.

In Russia they say that the people's health is the nation's wealth. Our ancient scriptures take physical well-being, well beyond the idea of wealth – *Shariram Brahma Mandiram* is what we are urged to remember. The body is the temple of the Lord. It is foolish to dismiss the body and its physical well-being as unimportant and unnecessary in the spiritual scheme of life. I myself always urge my friends not to identify with the body – but that is only as a prelude to remind them that the body is the temple of the immortal soul that resides within! Will you live in a dilapidated, ruined, crumbling, unsafe building? Why then should you condemn your soul to dwell in a neglected, unhealthy, unfit body during its earth-sojourn?

"The value of the human birth lies in this," said the Wise One, "that dwelling here on the earth plane, we are given the opportunity to build up good *karma* and live a meaningful, healthy, happy, harmonious life. The body is the instrument which makes this possible – and therefore, we must do all we can to keep the body healthy and fit.

"People have described the body as a 'miracle machine' – a marvel of God's creation. But like all machines, it is subject to wear and tear. It must be taken good care of. The body needs good food, healthy exercise, fresh air, clean water and sufficient rest, in order to function at optimum efficiency. Good health is something that we cannot take for granted.

"Our great sages have taught us that man is a total being – not a mere physical organism. Within each one of us is a vast spiritual *shakti* which all of us use to a greater or a lesser extent, adapting ourselves to our worldly conditions and circumstances. It is our mental and physical well being that makes this channelisation possible. I, for one, firmly believe in the holistic concept of health and harmony – the well being of mind and body must go hand in hand with the power of our spiritual *shakti*. The possibilities that the world offers for our spiritual evolution are limitless; the spark of the Divine in us makes our spiritual *shakti* endless; given the two, how can there be a limit to our progress? All we need to do is tap our potential, and put it to the best possible use – and life here on earth, can be a veritable heaven of happiness!"

I thought of Sadhu Vaswani, who firmly believed that the birth of a new physical culture, the development of a new sense of physical discipline was vital for the renaissance of India – as indeed, for the rejuvenation of the individual's life. According to him, 'softness' was one of Hindu society's great sins – by 'softness' of course, he meant lack of discipline. He wanted young people to develop a new spirit of adventure – a new spirit of courage which would enable them to encounter every danger and difficulty with confidence and optimism. His message to young India was: Be simple, be manly, be hard! He believed that physical discipline should go hand in hand with mental and spiritual training – and this was the ideal practised in his *Shakti Ashram*.

"Our physical well being is closely allied with our mental, emotional and spiritual well being," the Wise One resumed. "Remember, we are born on this earth as physical beings – and it is foolish to ignore our bodies. Spiritual health cannot be achieved at the expense of physical health.

"Take care of what God has given you. Have you seen an unweeded, overgrown, neglected garden? Or, to use a more 'modern' metaphor, have you seen a car that is unwashed, covered in dust and filth, filled with junk and rubbish on its seats?

"A young man was once asked to drive such a car; he refused outright.

"Don't be taken in by the looks," they said to him. "It's ok, it will start."

"I don't think I would like to drive a car like this," he said firmly. "It makes me feel unkempt, shabby and dirty."

"I don't blame the young man – do you?"

I thought of some of my own friends. I know very many busy men, executives, professionals and business people who take a few minutes to clean and wash their own car, before they drive out to work everyday.

I know very many busy housewives and working women who will never go to bed before they have cleaned and wiped and washed their kitchen surfaces clean.

If people can be so particular about their cars and kitchens, how much more concerned ought we to be about our good health?

"I have said repeatedly that you are responsible, you are accountable for your own happiness," the

Wise One continued. "There is no use pointing your finger at others, and blaming them for your problems. So begin by assuming responsibility for your life – and your health. Don't make excuses; don't offer justifications and explanations. Take responsibility for the choices and decisions you make…"

And he gave me what was actually an invaluable manual for health and well being, which I enumerate hereunder for the benefit of us all:

Good health is your birthright:

Don't accept disease and illness as a matter of course. Your body reacts to your attitude. Get rid of negative emotions; change your attitude and improve your sense of well being. Induce cheerfulness in your life by being brisk and optimistic. Practise relaxation techniques.

Detoxify your system:

Say "No" to alcohol and "Never!" to drugs! Avoid excessive intake of coffee and tea. Avoid the use of too many cosmetics. Spend a few minutes everyday in silence.

I could go on and on! Our systems need to be cleansed and purified to eliminate toxic overload, and restore the body to its natural balance.

Think young!

Old age is in the mind. You are as old or as young as you think yourself to be. If your mind is always open to new ideas and new experiences, if you are always ready to undertake new experiments in the great laboratory of life, you will remain young in spirit – forever!

It is in the nature of all matter to change with time. Wood, rock, stone, soil – you name it, it disintegrates with time. So does the body. But what is ageing to the body, can be the maturing of the mind and the evolution of the soul! And we know age cannot affect the spirit within you.

Take Care of your Thoughts:

For thoughts have power over the body. *We become what we think*, wise men tell us. When our mind is affected by negative thinking, we fall an easy prey to illness and disease.

Thoughts are forces. Thoughts have power. Thoughts produce vibrations, which affect the tissues and the blood chemistry. For example, it is a medically proven fact that anxiety and stress lead to acidity, ulcers and other digestive disorders.

On the other hand, positive thoughts are healing, health-giving, vital forces. A happy mind is the greatest aid to a healthy body. By focussing on positive thoughts, we contribute to our own good health and well being.

Realise The Value of the Breath:

Many of us are unaware of the value of breath in building up a healthy body and a happy mind. Breath is life! Breath takes in that vital element called *prana* which is the subtle force, the essence of life. But the sad fact is that, we have lost the natural, proper way of breathing! We breathe through the mouth, we breathe in a shallow, superficial way – an incorrect, bad habit, making us prone to diseases. Shallow breathing also leads to depleted energy levels.

Don't forget Vitamin-W!

A doctor friend of mine calls Water and Walking the 'real vitamins' – the vital Vitamins-W.

Walking is the best form of physical activity – it is easy and simple, and it has been called the queen of exercises. When you take a brisk walk, you will see for yourself that you feel light and energetic. Walking gives exercise to all parts of the body, and ensures good circulation. This creates even more energy for work. Walking also relieves tension and anxiety.

As for water, we cannot overlook it's importance for the system. Even in the absence of other foods, man can subsist on water alone for several days. This is because over 70% of the human body is composed of water. Unfortunately, we fail to drink enough water everyday.

Water helps to flush out the toxic wastes in your body; it also controls the body temperature. Experts have calculated that there is a daily water-loss of about four and a half pints from our body through skin, lungs, alimentary canal and the kidneys. Needless to say, this loss must be replenished.

Spend A Few Minutes In Silence Everyday:

People often tell me that they are so stressed and tense that they long to run away from it all, and fly to a quiet and a beautiful place far away. The practice of silence can be like your personal jet which will enable you to reach those sublime spaces *within* you!

Practise brahmacharya:

Literally, *brahmacharya* means, "walking with God."

All the major religions of the world talk about the necessity of self-discipline, especially the control of the lower passions. However, our Hindu scriptures have attached a profound significance to the concept of *brahmacharya*. In its highest form, it implies the consciousness of the concept that we are *Brahman: Aham Brahmasmi*. In a more practical sense, it implies the practice of celibacy and restraint of sex indulgence. When sexual energy is brought under control, all other aspects of our life are automatically brought under control. Such a state of self-discipline is conducive to our health, happiness and spiritual progress.

Let me sum up for you the **right choices** you must make to achieve good health and happiness.

a. *Choose God's Love:* He wants you to live life to the fullest – not merely to exist. Accept His love, and you will find power and vitality and positive vibrations flowing into you.

Begin the day with God; take His presence with you wherever you go, whatever you do; end the day with God. When His name is not on your lips, let it dwell in your heart.

b. *Choose Good Health*: Don't take your well-being for granted. Tread the right path, choose all those aspects that will ensure your well-being.

c. *Choose The Right Food*: In practical terms, food can be of two categories: food of violence *(himsa)* – food that includes fish, flesh and fowl; and its alternative, the food of *ahimsa* or non-violence – in other words, a vegetarian diet.

During the last fifty years or more, medical experts and nutritionists have largely inclined to the opinion that a vegetarian diet is the best option for good health.

It was Mahatma Gandhi who said, "I hold flesh food to be unsuited to our species. We err in copying the lower animal world if we really believe that we are superior. Experience teaches us that animal food is unsuited to those who curb their passions."

There was a time when Westerners dismissed vegetarianism as "the cult of the crazy". Today, the tide has turned. An ever increasing number of people all over the world are turning to vegetarianism as a way of life which leads to health and strength of the body, mind and soul.

Eat less – not more! Lukmaan, the physician and healer of antiquity, tells us, *"Kam Khao, Gam Khao!* i.e. Eat less – and don't react hastily and rashly. If you do these two things – eat in moderation and control your anger, you will be healthy and happy!

d. *Choose A Healthy Environment*: Create a healthy mental and physical environment to live and work.

Let fresh air and light stream into your homes. Do not shut yourself in centrally heated or air-conditioned cages. If you are forced to work in such an environment, take in as much fresh air as you can, through daily walks in the open.

Choose a healthy mental environment by dismissing worry, anxiety and negative thoughts out of your life. Choose optimism, positive thoughts, peace and joy.

We can and we must make the right choices to keep ourselves fit and healthy. God has given us the power and wisdom to do so. And, should you fall ill, do not forget to 'consult' my favourite doctors: Dr. Quiet, Dr. Diet, Dr. Sunshine and Dr. Laughter!

The Wise One smiled at me, as he came to the end of his fascinating discourse on good health. "I'm sure you're aware of all this," he said. "But you must continue to emphasise these precepts for the benefit of those who turn to you for help and healing."

"I will," I assured him. "You have indeed, given me a treasure of wisdom, and I have inscribed your words on the pages of my mind."

"Time to rest now," the Wise One said.

We found our own comfortable corners on the spacious *verandah*, and I slipped into a peaceful sleep…

We awoke with the dawn, and went to the spring for a freshening wash and clean-up. Then we set out to explore the surroundings.

A little distance away, we saw what appeared to be huge stables. There were at least fifty stalls around a huge open courtyard, with posts and pegs to tether horses, and huge water troughs out of which ten horses could drink at a time.

Just above the main entrance to the stalls, I saw an inscription:

You Don't Have To Win All The Time!

The 10th Secret of Happiness

You Don't Have To Win All The Time!

"How true!" I exclaimed. "Here is the next secret – and so few of us realise the truth of this statement!"

"People whose goal is to win, win *and win* all the time, end up enjoying their lives less and less," said the Wise One.

I nodded my silent agreement.

I wonder how many of you remember Richard Nixon, the American President who ran for re-election in the year 1972. During his campaign, he called his workers and said to them, "We must win at all costs.'

We must win at all costs. This gave his people the message that they could do anything they wanted – right or wrong – to bring votes to Nixon and the Republican Party.

What followed was one of the most notorious political scandals of the twentieth century: Nixon's aides staged a break-in at Democratic Party Head Quarters in the Watergate Building, and planted bugging devices. Their aim was to 'tap' the phone conversations of the Democrats, find out their election strategies and secrets and counter them. They engaged in an endless series of what Nixon himself called "dirty tricks". I read somewhere that one of them even called up a Pizza delivery outlet and ordered for one hundred pizzas to be delivered to the office of an opposition candidate – just to cause him embarrassment and discomfiture.

This was not all. They handed out phony notices informing the public that Democratic Party rallies and meetings had been postponed. They called up conference venues and auditoriums booked by opposition candidates and cancelled their reservations. They resorted to every unethical measure, every dirty trick in the book to make sure that their candidate, Richard Nixon, won the election *at all costs*.

The sad truth of the matter was that Nixon was winning the polls anyway – and would probably have done so *without* the need to indulge in such tricks. However, he was not prepared to take any chances; he wanted to "make assurance double sure," as the saying goes. And, under his personal instructions, "all the President's men" stooped as low as they could, stopping at nothing to ensure his victory.

Nixon did win the 1972 elections. But his celebrations were short lived. When journalists investigating the 'Watergate Scandal' uncovered all the sordid details and 'broke' the story in the print and electronic media, it made world news headlines. The conscience of the American nation was stirred – and impeachment proceedings were started against President Nixon. Finally, in the eleventh hour, Nixon had the good sense to tender his own resignation, rather than face the utter ignominy of impeachment – forced resignation from the highest office in the land under judicial and legislative orders.

The man who wanted to win at all costs not only disgraced himself completely and utterly – he also paved the way for a Democratic victory in the elections that followed. The public were disgusted with the dirty tactics adopted by him – and the disgust rebounded on the Republican Party even after he quit.

Friends tell me that there is yet another phone-tapping scandal being uncovered in Indian politics. I am not generally concerned with the political developments and news; but when I hear of such incidents, I am pained by this fanatical desire to bring down one's political adversaries and ensure one's own interests at any cost!

"Why are people so obsessed with winning?" I asked the Wise one.

"History is replete with examples of desperate leaders and generals who were convinced that they had to win all the time," he replied. "Edward II and Richard II of England were actually put to death by their own noblemen – subjects who owed loyalty to them. These kings had misused their 'Divine Right' as kings to indulge their own whims and desires; no sane counsel or political advice would convince them to alter their dictatorial tendencies. Their reigns were marked by strife, violence and bloodshed which almost threatened the British monarchy. But in the end, they vanished without a trace from the body politic – unwept, unlamented, confined to the dark and dismal pages of history, which deal with the fall of tyrants.

"Do not imagine that this 'Win-at-all-costs' attitude is the sole prerogative of kings, generals and leaders. It can also afflict 'commoners' like you and me. Take businessmen who adopt illegal measures to make a profit; take individuals who bribe their way into 'deals' and 'contracts'; think of all the people who have made corruption an ugly and inescapable reality in our country – how and why does it happen? Only because some men are determined to win at all costs…"

I was reminded of yet another recent scandal – an academic shame that had shocked the nation. Question papers of the Common Entrance Test to the nation's premier management institutes were 'leaked' to young men who were prepared to 'pay a price' for them. This really saddened everyone who was associated with education and academics. The boys had decided that they had to be on the top – they had to secure admission to the institute of their choice – and were prepared to adopt any kind of unfair means at their disposal.

My Master, Sadhu Vaswani, was a brilliant student right from the days of his childhood. He stood first in almost every test and examination conducted in his class.

In one of the tests, when the result was declared, the teacher announced that it was Thanwar (Sadhu Vaswani's first name) who had topped the class with 73% of marks. The student who obtained the second rank had scored 65%.

The answer books were given back to the students. Like all top-ranking students, Sadhu Vaswani checked his total – and found that he had secured not 73% but 63% marks.

Immediately, he went up to his teacher and said, "Sir, there has been a mistake. I should have received not 73% but 63%. It follows that I must get the *second* rank, not the first."

The teacher was moved by the young boy's spirit of truthfulness.

How I wish some of our youngsters – and their parents – could emulate Sadhu Vaswani's example!

I know a sister who works in one of Pune's prestigious schools. She tells us that every month, after the Unit Test results are declared, she is confronted by angry and aggressive parents demanding ½ a mark and one mark more for their children – for after all, the tests are often just out of ten marks. But such is the spirit of competition, such is the intensity of the race to win, that parents who ought to know better, grow angry and agitated over half a mark, setting a poor example for their children.

In the sixties and seventies, the 'Stars' of Indian Tennis were two 'gentlemen' players – Ramanathan Krishnan and Vijay Amritraj. They did *not* win any major tournament – perhaps they got to the second round or the quarter-finals of Wimbledon. But sports enthusiasts all over the world, and even their opponents loved and admired them for their genuine spirit of sportsmanship. They never shouted or swore at their opponents; they did not create scenes on the tennis court by yelling abuse at the linesmen and the referees; if they won a match, it was with a smile and a handshake for their opponent; if they lost, it was still with a smile and handshake – they never allowed victory or defeat to counter their courtesy and good manners. I am told that when the world champion Bjorn Borg defeated Vijay Amritraj at the Centre Court of Wimbledon, he raised his racquet in honour of his losing opponent and applauded his game – and Wimbledon witnessed the unprecedented spectacle of the entire audience rising to give a standing ovation to the loser in a tennis match!

Today, the winning-at-all-costs attitude has vitiated several sports including athletics and cricket. I am deeply pained to read about athletes testing positive for banned drugs, and even being stripped of their gold and silver medals. And the details of illicit betting carried out between professional cricketers and unscrupulous bookies, tarnished the very name of cricket – all because a few men had to win all the time!

The obsession to win, to achieve spectacular success, has had an adverse effect on us – we simply do not know when to stop, when to say enough is enough. This has led to excess – in some cases to burn-out, exhaustion and needless over reaching. We do not know when we have made adequate profits, when we have done enough, said enough, eaten enough or even lost enough weight. We do not realise too, that we have accumulated enough recognition. We feel, on the contrary, that we can never achieve enough!

I have always said that failures are not stopping stones – but *stepping* stones to success. And the mark of the truly happy man is that he accepts that he can sometimes win, and sometimes lose.

Inventor Charles Kettering talks about "failing intelligently" or "failing successfully". What does this mean? He tells us that when we have failed, we must try to analyse the situation and find out *why*. He also offers us these suggestions for turning failure into success:

1) Face defeat honestly – do not fake success.
2) Don't waste failure – exploit it to eliminate your weaknesses and get to know your strengths better.

3) Never use failure as an excuse for not trying again.

So far from successive wins, winning after initial failing can give us more satisfaction and a greater sense of achievement – besides preventing pride, arrogance and egoism from raising their ugly heads in our lives.

I wonder if you have heard of Akhwari, the athlete from Tanzania. Marathon runners talk about him with great admiration. His achievement? He finished *last* in the Marathon race at the 1968 Olympics. No last-placed athlete had ever finished so late as he did. A record failure, would you say?

You would be mistaken!

As he was running the race, he was badly injured. But he continued, hobbling into the stadium with his leg bleeding and bandaged, hours after the winners had romped across the finishing line, and long after the rest of the runners had completed the race. There were hardly any spectators left in the stadium when Akhwari painfully crossed the finishing line.

"Why did you continue to run the race when you were in so much pain?" someone asked him.

Akhwari's reply was simple. "My country did not send me all the way to Mexico to start the race. They sent me there to finish."

We can all learn a valuable lesson from the attitude of this brave athlete. We must not 'run' the race of life for awards and honours. We must run with endurance, so that we will have finished what God wanted us to do.

"I know winning can give a great deal of personal satisfaction," I observed, coming out of my prolonged reflection. "But I can't understand why people stoop so low as to win by fair or foul means."

"There is a win-win attitude that can help all of us," said the Wise One. "It is to accept success and failure with equanimity and to continue to put in one's best efforts, unmoved by praise or blame. This is exactly what The Lord advises us in the Bhagavad Gita : Do your duty: fruit is not your concern. How I wish more and more of us would follow His advice!"

We walked down the path that led out from the stables. Some distance away, we saw the stream flowing. On the bank ahead of us, I saw a curious device. Two poles leaned out at an angle towards the stream. On either side of the poles were strong metal handles. Attached to the poles were two huge leather containers.

"What on earth is this?" I exclaimed, examining the device closely.

"It is an old irrigation device that was in use by our farmers till the middle of the 20th century," smiled the Wise One. "Come, let me show you how it works…"

He took hold of the handle on one side and bade me do the same on the other side. Together, we rotated the handles round and round – and to my amazement, the leather containers dipped into the stream and came up with water to the brim; and, as we continued rotating the handles, they emptied the water into the deep and narrow channels that had been cut into the river bank, leading to the fields nearby.

"Two sturdy farmers – rather more healthy than you and me – operating this device, could irrigate a large field in a few hours!" the Wise One explained. "No electricity, no generators, no motors, no pumps – sheer manpower!"

"Amazing!" I exclaimed, holding on to the poles and studying the device carefully. I caught sight of the message straightaway, for I had been looking for it this time. There it was, in duplicate, inscribed verbatim on both the poles:

Friends Are More Important Than Money.

The 11th Secret of Happiness

Friends Are More Important Than Money

"Here is yet another secret that reminds us that true happiness can never be selfish," I observed. "We cannot buy happiness with money; we cannot attain happiness through power or position; and what is happiness, if we have no friends to share it with?"

"A true friend is indeed the greatest of treasures," the Wise One agreed. "Our poets tell us we can find rubies and emeralds and precious gems easily – but a true friend is rarer than all of these!"

I nodded solemnly.

A man once said to me, "I don't mind losing money – but I can't afford to lose a true friend. To me, a friend is far more precious than money."

"Who is a true friend?" the Wise One mused. "A true friend is even one who knows my failings, imperfections, weaknesses, limitations and lapses – but still loves me for what I am. He does not flatter me; he does not deceive me with insincere praise. He accepts me with all my failings, encourages me to improve myself and supports me with his love and affection."

I recalled the words of Herbert Hoover who said, "We need the whole world as a friend." Even loftier was the vision of Sadhu Vaswani, who urged us to be friend of man, bird and beast, to recognise the fellowship of all creation, and to protect the dumb and defenceless creatures like our own younger brothers and sisters in the One family of creation.

> I would be friend of man and bird and beast
> I would the One *Atman* greet in west and east…

Such a man is indeed a friend of all the world – a friend to the good and the bad, to the rich and the poor, the saint and the sinner, the needy and the underprivileged. He is also a friend of all the creatures that breathe the breath of life, a friend of Mother Earth, Father Sky, Brother Sun and Sister Moon – and a friend of the friendless.

Such a man is not only happy himself – he makes everyone around him happy!

When Abraham Lincoln was the President of America, he used to receive appeals from soldiers for pardon and release from prison. Invariably, these appeals would be strengthened by earnest recommendations from one or more friends.

One day, he received an appeal which stated that the prisoner had to plead his own cause, because he had no friends to turn to, no one to take up his case.

Lincoln was so moved that he observed, "If indeed this man has no friend, I shall be his friend!" Needless to say, the soldier was pardoned.

"Friends there may be many, but true friends are few," observed the Wise One. "And a true friend is the greatest blessing in your life – far more valuable than your wealth and possessions; for a true friend, as I said, is rarer than diamonds and precious stones.

"All of us like to have such friends. But if you want to have a true friend, you must *be* a friend. Let me quote these famous lines which I have always cherished:

> I went out to find a friend,
> I could not find one there;
> I went out *to be* a friend
> And friends were everywhere!

"There are three marks of a true friend," he continued:

1. If he finds you moving on the path of evil, he will do all he can to set your feet on the path of righteousness.
2. He will tell you the truth about yourself and the world, even at the cost of incurring your displeasure.
3. When you are in trouble or in need, he will be the first to rush to your help.

"Someone once asked me about give-and-take between friends. I replied, 'You give to your friend the true love of your heart and good, sound advice.

You take from a friend – nothing! For, if you wish to *take* something, you cannot be a true friend. I believe firmly that a friend is always a giver.'"

I nodded my assent.

Friendship has rightly been described as the highroad to happiness. A popular song calls friendship "the only ship that never sinks."

"No man is without hope," said R.L. Stevenson, "while he has a friend."

An inspired writer has this to say about friendship:

> If life is to be rich and fertile, it must be reinforced with friendship. It is the sap that preserves life from blight and withering; it is the sunshine that beckons on the flowering and fruitage; it is the fresh dew that perfumes life with sweetness and sprinkles it with splendour; it is the music tide that sweeps the soul, scattering treasures...

"True friendship is never influenced by money, wealth, status or position," continued the Wise One. "It is truly disinterested, and often based on mutual sacrifice and selflessness. True friends do not expect returns or rewards for their services to us. For, as I have said earlier, friendship must be valued for itself, not for what can be got out of it.

"If two people appreciate each other because they derive mutual benefit and advantage from the other's presence, they are merely acquaintances with a business understanding – not friends in the true sense of the term. Shall I tell you another of my stories ...?"

There were two friends, Daulat Ram and Dhani Ram. They worked together as partners in a financial company. They had put all their money into the business, and for a while, they did very well. Then one day, the markets crashed and they were ruined. They blamed each other for their loss, and became estranged. Each went his own way.

After about a year, they both met outside a bank. They found themselves profoundly moved. They admitted to each other that the loss of money was nothing compared to the loss of friendship. "Money is like a glove," said Daulat Ram, "but friendship is like your hand. Money is useful, but friendship is essential."

"To seek friendship for its 'utility' is as futile as looking for a pot of gold at the end of the rainbow," the Wise One said.

A senior bureaucrat visited a primary school, and was surprised to see the children in Class III using sign language.

"I did not know you had children with hearing and speech impairment," he remarked to the class teacher.

"As a matter of fact, Sir," the teacher explained, "we have just one boy, Vikram, who is a deaf-mute. Because we do not want him to feel lonely and left out, all his friends and teachers have learnt sign language."

Man is a social animal – he cannot exist without a meaningful and worthwhile social contact. And a friend can offer us a lot. A generous friend will always support us; a prudent and reliable friend can be trusted to give us the right advice; a cheerful friend can be counted upon to enliven our life.

It was Seneca who said, "Of all felicities, the most charming is that of a firm and gentle friendship. It sweetens all our cares, dispels our sorrows, and counsels us in all extremities."

I'm sure all of you have heard of the famous book, *How To Win Friends And Influence People*, by Dale Carnegie. He gives us a formula for making friends in two statements:

1) Be interested in others.
2) Do things for other people.

This breaks up into the following suggestions:
- Speak cheerfully to people.
- Smile at people: it costs nothing, and affords so much pleasure.
- Call people by name. It makes people very happy to hear their name uttered.
- Be helpful.
- Be cordial and genuine.
- Take real interest in people and what they do.
- Be generous with your praise and appreciation. Be sparing in your criticism.
- Respect others' feelings. Be considerate and sensitive to their concerns.

- Respect others' opinions. Remember there are three sides to any controversy: yours, the other person's and the right one.
- Be of service to others. What counts most in life is what we do for others.

As there are do's, so too, there are don'ts:
- Do not indulge in gossip and back biting. It is not your business to report what others said, or what unkind things were spoken about another person.
- Do not jeer at others' weaknesses or infirmities.
- Do not laugh *at* others – by all means laugh *with* them.
- Do not ridicule someone about his status, race or religion.
- Do not harp on his mistakes.
- Do not play silly practical jokes.

"The art of pleasing requires only the desire," writes Lord Chesterfield. Indeed, the desire to be liked, to enjoy the affection of friends, to get along well with everyone around us is instinctive in most human beings. "A person completely wrapped up in himself makes a small package," says Harry Fosdick.

George, Sam and Rameck were 'coloured' boys who grew up in the harsh inner city area of Newark, New Jersey. Wishing to keep their sons off the streets, their mothers forced them to focus on educating themselves. In the ninth grade, the boys made a pact to become doctors – *together*. After years of constantly helping, encouraging, pushing and challenging each other, they made it – they graduated from Medical School in 1999. Well-settled and well-off, the friends practised medicine in their old neighbourhood!

As a teenager, Shelly Brady met Bill Porter, a door-to-door salesman afflicted with cerebral palsy. Bill became Shelly's lifelong friend and mentor, also her hero, because of his courage, perseverance and positive attitude to life.

Much later, when Shelly had grown up and Bill was too old to make ends meet, Shelly bought his house to make sure that her friend would have a place to live in for the rest of his life. "There comes a time when your heart opens up and you are absolutely there for anything, for the sake of your friend," Shelly says. She has written a book about her experiences with Bill called *Ten Things I Learned From Bill Porter*, which is a heart-warming story of their unique friendship.

When you share your joy with a friend, your joy doubles; and when a friend is there to grieve with you, you grieve less. And so it is that Bacon says, "Without friends the world is like a wilderness."

"How can one be a good friend?" I asked the Wise One.

I would like to offer to you his answer to my question, in the form of ten tips, ten practical suggestions which I would like to call the *Ten Fingers Of Friendship*. When friends clasp their two hands, five plus five, ten fingers come close to each other. These ten fingers tell us the following:

1. ***To be a friend, you must be a good listener:*** It was Benjamin Disraeli who said that nature has given us two ears – but only one mouth. Also remember, the ears cannot be closed, whereas the mouth can be closed. The mouth has two fences which act as a barrier to unnecessary speech – the teeth and the lips. Once a word leaves your mouth, you cannot take it back. Think twice before you speak anything. Of the unspoken word, you are the master; of the word you have spoken, you become the slave. Let not a word spoken in anger or harshness or out of turn, affect your friendship. Listen to your friends with attention, affection and understanding. Listen not only with your ears, but with your heart.

2. ***Learn to appreciate your friends:*** Do not take your friends for granted. Appreciate all that they do for you. Follow Leonardo Da Vinci's advice: *Reprove in private and praise in public.*

3. ***If you would be a true friend, you must grow in the spirit of forgiveness:*** Give generously to your friends – also forgive them. God's forgiveness to us is unlimited – let us therefore, forgive our friends.

4. ***Never forget a friend's name:*** That is a lapse on your part which can really hurt your friends.

5. ***Make promises sparingly:*** But if you make one, make sure you fulfil it with the least delay.
6. ***Do not preach what you cannot practise yourself:*** It is necessary for you to bear witness to whatever you say in your own life and actions.
7. ***Be cheerful:*** Smile as much as you can. Learn to laugh with your friends.
8. ***Discuss, but do not argue:*** You may win the argument – but lose your friend.
9. ***Accept criticism in the right spirit:*** If you happen to be in the wrong, admit it.
10. ***Always be on the lookout for opportunities to serve your friends:*** The opposite of love is not hate, but apathy. Henry Davidson says, "Radiate friendship – and it will be returned tenfold."

And last, but not the least, let me remind you – there is one friend who is a Friend of all friends. When all other friends fade away, this Friend remains firm with you. He is none other than God. Cultivate friendship with God; make contact with God. What a privilege it is to have a friend for all 24 hours of the day! He is a Friend, so understanding, so forgiving, you can share the innermost secrets of your heart with Him. Take God with you wherever you go – to your office, to the shop, to your place of work. Make God your personal friend!

"You have captured the very essence of true friendship," I said to the Wise One. "I shall treasure your words, and pass them on to as many people as I can."

We had now reached the edge of a small wooded area. As the day was getting warm, we decided to trek through the woods, for it looked cool and sheltered.

A footpath led into the wood and we decided to follow it. The path was barred by a small gate, and as I fumbled with the catch to get it open, my eyes fell on the message on one of the gate posts:

Accept Yourself As You Are – Unconditionally.

The 12th Secret of Happiness

Accept Yourself As You Are – Unconditionally

"Here is the next secret!" I said to the Wise One eagerly. "Each one seems more valuable than the other! I have found these secrets in the most unusual places – but I feel they ought to be carved in letters of gold, in a beautiful Temple of Happiness."

The Wise One smiled. "Carve them in your heart," he said. "That is where they belong."

"Tell me something about accepting oneself unconditionally," I requested him.

"Let me begin by asking you a simple question," said the Wise One. "Who are you?"

I waited to hear his answer.

"English grammar tells us that the right answer to that question is your name: *I am Malati Gupta;* or *I am Peter James;* or *I am Abdul Rehman.*

"On to the next question: What are you?

"According to the rules of grammar, the answer should refer to your profession or vocation: *I am a doctor;* or *I am a teacher;* or *I am a lawyer.*

"So who are you? Are you just a name or a profession?"

I grew thoughtful.

A recent survey found that when respondents were asked the second question, many women answered it rather diffidently. "I'm just a housewife," some of them said; or "I don't go to work," or "I just stay home and look after the family."

In my opinion mothers and wives who run their homes well amidst the challenges and problems we face today, are some of the bravest, most prudent and hard working people. And if they do not belong to the affluent class, their courage and perseverance are even more laudable.

Yet, I wonder, why did some of them deprecate themselves by talking so diffidently of themselves? Would a doctor have said, "I'm only a doctor"? Would a politician ever have said, "I'm only a politician?"

What is it that causes some of us to have a very low self-image? What is it that causes some of us to have very little self-esteem?

At a question-answer-session with young people, someone sent a chit to me asking the following question: "Can you please explain why I feel inferior and insecure when I am with people who are tall, fair and intelligent?"

Sri Krishna was not fair! Mahatma Gandhi was not tall! That did not stop them from having a great self-image and an excellent sense of humour.

I cannot understand why young people today aspire to look like film stars, models and sportspersons. How boring the world would be if we all looked like clones of each other – all of us 5'8", all of us fair, and all of us with identical sharp features!

You will not believe how unhappy people become, just because they don't like the way they look. Dark complexioned people wish to be fair; fair-skinned women wish they had less oily skin; men wish to be taller and more muscular; girls wish to be slimmer; boys wish to be smarter…

Why can't you like yourself as you are? Why do you make yourself unhappy over how you look, how you talk, how you walk and how you carry yourself? Who sets the standards by which you judge yourself?

Sociologists tell us that the plethora of advertisements and commercials that we see around us everywhere, set up impossible-to-emulate role models before a gullible public: men who are smart and rich and drive huge cars; girls who are picture perfect and made up from head to toe; impeccably dressed mothers who cook and clean and wash and serve meals without so much as a hair out of place…

We look at these images and we aspire after their unreality. We compare ourselves unfavourably with these 'celebrities' or with people whom we regard as being 'better off' than us; we begin to wish we were different. "If only I had her complexion…" "If only I could drive a car like that…" or "If I could speak like him…"

"You are unique!" said the Wise One, reflecting my thoughts. "God made you the way you are! God gave you a certain personality, certain features and a particular kind of temperament; He also gave you certain special skills and attributes which others lack. If God wanted you to be taller or slimmer or fairer, surely He would have made you so. And as I say to my friends repeatedly, God is all love; God is all wisdom; He is not likely to have made a mistake. I know some of you will not be satisfied with that explanation. You will probably turn round and ask me, Why has God been so unfair to me? Why has He not made me taller/ fairer/ richer/ more powerful/ more intelligent/ more attractive?

"Let me answer your questions with a story..."

Deepak and his father worked as farm-labourers at a huge estate belonging to a wealthy land owner. They and the other labourers lived in cottages allotted to them on the estate. Every morning they would be up by six, and set out to do the work assigned to them on that particular day. Some would work in the orchards; some would work in the cattle sheds; some would go to graze the cows and sheep. From six in the morning till six at night they attended to their work, and returned home for the evening meal.

Deepak grew bored with this unchanging daily routine. He longed to be somewhere else; he longed to do something different.

Sometimes, he happened to gaze across the perimeter fence, on the neighbouring farm. This was also a huge estate, and the farmhouse and the workers' cottages lay at a great distance from the fence. The house and the cottages seemed to shine in the noonday sun. It seemed to Deepak that they were made of gold. He imagined that the people who lived on that estate must be truly lucky.

The more he thought about them, the more his imagination soared. They must be eating good food, he imagined; they were cheerful and happy; they hardly did any work, but they were paid well, and their master must be a generous, kind man…

One day, the landlord gave Deepak a day off from work. Deepak decided to go across to the neighbouring estate and explore the farm and the people who lived there.

He let himself in through a gap in the fence and began to walk up to the farmhouse. As he approached the house, he saw a young boy of about his own age, walking towards him.

"Good day to you!" called Deepak excitedly. "Do you live here? Do you work here? You are so lucky! You must be very happy here!"

"I live here and work here – but who says I'm lucky? And where do you come from?"

"I work in the farm next door," Deepak replied. "I see your farm from our pastures, and it seems to shine like a golden dwelling! As I sweat and toil at my work,

I think how fortunate you people must be to live and work here!"

"I don't believe this!" exclaimed the boy. "That is exactly what *I* think when I look at *your* estate! Your houses seem so beautiful and picturesque from here! Your farm house looks like my idea of heaven. I often think that you people living and working on the other side of the fence must be the luckiest, happiest souls! Why, just turn around and look!"

Deepak turned round to look at his farm. It did seem to glitter like gold in the brilliant morning sunshine. The realisation dawned on him – that it was distance that lent enchantment to the view. Each of them thought that the other was better off. It was only when he got closer, that he could perceive the truth.

Psychologists tell us that the basic reason for several 'complexes' and negative feelings is the fact that people are not happy with who they are and what they are. They are not ready to accept themselves as they are. They don't like themselves. This leads to low self-esteem, insecurity and negative self-image.

Forensic experts tell us that no two human beings will have similar or identical fingerprints; each one is unique. Now, genetic scientists are telling us that our DNA is equally unique. God has chosen to make each one of us uniquely different. Why then should we wish to become copycats? Why should we wish to imitate others and make ourselves unhappy in the process?

"Let me tell you another of my stories ..." the Wise One began.

A wise old Indian Guru was approached by his disciple who had the following question to put before him: if it was true that God made all of us in His image, how come the Caucasian races are white, Africans are black and Asians are brown? Was not God being unfair and unkind?

The Guru had a lovely sense of humour. He said to his disciple, "God created the human race, and He decided to bake bread for all His children. The first batch of loaves was all undercooked. They looked white and pale, and the Caucasians got that lot. The second batch was overcooked and burnt black – the Africans got it. The third time round, God was extremely careful and that batch was baked just right – not too white, not burnt black.

"You, my dear student, are lucky to be born in Asia with your gorgeous brown skin!"

Let me assure my friends, that this was the Indian Guru's answer to his unhappy student. If he had been an African teacher, I'm sure he would have said, "Black is beautiful!"

"*Vive la différence!*" exclaim the French people. We too, must learn to appreciate our differences. We must learn to appreciate ourselves as we are. This does not mean that we must not learn from others, or indeed try to emulate others' good qualities. But, at the same time, we do not have to think badly of ourselves, nor feel insecure or negative about who we are and what we are.

Recently, I met a young mother who complained to me that she was exhausted, just taking care of her two children.

"Early in the morning I have to take Ramesh for tennis practise; then I return home and take Gita to the ballet class. At eight a.m. I have to pack them off to school.

"When they return in the evening, Ramesh goes to the computer class and Gita has music lessons. Then they both go to their maths classes and then Ramesh has his guitar lessons and Gita goes for yoga..."

"Isn't it a bit taxing for the children?" I asked her gently.

"But Dada, what I'm doing is really not enough!" exclaimed the young mother. "Why, my neighbour's children learn Karate and French and roller skating – and they are both athletic champions!"

In this case, it was the mother who was imposing standards on the children, demanding too much from them and wearing herself out in the process!

Many parents feel that their children are unique, special, gifted, sensitive. Family counsellor John Rosemont asks, "Is your child special... is he the most exceptional person in the world?" He himself gives the answer, "Of course – to *you!*"

You can and you must let your child know that he is very special to you – but it is not healthy to let him imagine that he is more gifted or more special than others. If you do, the child will grow up thinking that he is very superior, and deserves special attention and special privileges. This may make him selfish and envious and lead to a lot of unhappiness in later life.

The best thing that parents can do is to teach their children that they are unique in their gifts – as also are the other children – and that each one of them has a unique contribution to make in life.

You don't have to be the tallest, smartest or the most intelligent person! You must be at *your* best; you must do *your* best and that's what counts.

Whom are we trying to please by bending over backwards trying to be what we are not? If you set great store by what others think of you, you will reduce yourself to being a dull and pale imitation of others!

Parents, especially, must be careful in that they should not force their children to act out and fulfil their – i.e. the parents' – aspirations.

Neeraj was artistic and creative since childhood. He loved to paint, draw and sketch. Sitting at the back of the class, he would draw sketches of the teachers and his classmates, instead of doing his sums. The teachers would, of course, pull him up, but when they saw his sketches, they recognised his great talent, and let him off with the mild warning that he must pay more attention to his lessons.

Neeraj was intelligent, and he managed to pass his school exams reasonably well. That is when the real problem began.

His parents wanted him to become a doctor. His father was an eminent specialist and he had invested a fortune in setting up a state-of-the art Nursing Home. It was his wish that the hospital should be taken over, one day, by his own son. This seemed an entirely reasonable thing to both his parents.

As for Neeraj, his heart was in painting and drawing. He had already visited the local Fine Arts College, and talked to the teachers there. They too, had been highly appreciative of his talent and had assured him that he had a very bright future both in commercial art, as well as in freelance art. His ambition was to become a famous painter.

His parents would not hear of such a thing. How could he hope to earn his living by painting? Who would respect him in society if he did not have a worthwhile career? Who would marry him?

Neeraj's protests were silenced, and he was forced to take up medicine. As he did not score very high marks in the Entrance Test, his parents paid a fortune to get him a seat in a private Medical College.

Neeraj spent three of the most unhappy years of his life in the Medical College hostel. Though he struggled, he could not cope with his studies. He failed in his exams repeatedly. His classmates made fun of him and jeered at him. His professors had no patience with him.

In the fourth year, Neeraj was still stuck with backlogs from the first and second year – and could not be promoted. When his classmates passed out, he was still left with his second year papers.

That year, Neeraj attempted to commit suicide…

To cut a long story short, he was saved – but he was reduced to a nervous wreck. Above all, he began to resent his parents, as he held them wholly responsible for his plight. It took the intervention of a very understanding grandmother to nurse him back to good health and self-esteem. Eventually, the old lady used all her influence and authority in the family to persuade his parents to give up their ambitious plans for him and allow him to do what he wanted. When he was 25 years old, Neeraj went back to the Fine Arts College, and pursued his dream. And, no – he did not turn out to be a famous or brilliant painter, but he had the satisfaction of doing what he wanted in life – eventually.

Parents – accept your children as they are! Do not impose your dreams or aspirations on them. Do not expect them to fulfil your unrealised hopes and plans! They are not Xerox copies of you – they are precious individuals with their own unique set of talents and God-given gifts. You have, of course, given birth to them, brought them into this world and helped them grow up – but that does not give you the right to determine their future or dictate their choice of career. You must allow them to be themselves!

"You must be what you are!" the Wise One repeated. "You cannot become what others want you to be. You cannot live to please others, expecting to fulfil their dreams and following *their* stars instead of yours.

"God has made each of us for a distinctive purpose. He has meant some of us to become great artists; some of us were born to become great dreamers and visionaries; some of us were meant for professions like medicine, engineering, architecture or law.

"But there are a vast majority of us who are none of these things. May be God meant us to be good human beings; may be He wanted us to be the helpers and servers of humanity; may be He meant us to be kind, loving sons/daughters/spouses/parents. Why should we try to alter His Divine Plan? Let me tell you a story..."

A glistening new Ford car was speeding down the highway from Pune to Bangalore. The car had a single occupant – an affluent, well-dressed businessman, Mr. Ramesh Joshi, who had decided to drive his new car to Bangalore, for the sheer pleasure of the ride. Normally, he would take the flight on his business trips, and wherever he went, he was driven by his chauffeur. This long drive was actually a 'treat' that he had planned for himself.

Just past a difficult *ghat* section, the car began to stall. Mr. Joshi tried whatever techniques he knew, but it was not good enough. He could sense that the engine was slowing, and sure enough, the car came to a standstill.

Mr. Joshi got down and peered into the bonnet anxiously. Like so many other affluent businessmen, he had enjoyed buying and occasionally driving new cars – but he really did not know *how* they ran, or *what* made them run.

Now, as he peered anxiously at the 'inside' of his brand new car, he had no clue about why it had stalled.

He must have looked rather incongruous standing there in his expensive clothes, his gold plated wristwatch and high-styled dark glasses, for a few peasants and urchins had gathered around him curiously.

One little boy, wearing torn shorts, touched the shining new car and remarked knowingly to his companion, "This costs several lakh rupees."

"Then why has it stopped?" his friend asked pertinently.

Mr. Joshi cleared his throat and addressed a young man standing next to him. "Can you tell me where is the nearest garage? I need a mechanic to attend to this problem."

The good natured villagers held a hasty discussion among themselves and then a young man said that the nearest mechanic was his friend Shiva, whose 'shop' was two miles down the road, in the next village.

"Two miles..." said Mr. Joshi. "May be I should take a lift from someone..."

The group around him galvanised into animation. "*Saab*, you stay here with your car," announced the leader. "Chotu here will go to the village and fetch Shiva. And when Shiva comes *Saab*, you will have nothing to worry. He will get it started in no time."

A lorry that was rumbling down the road was waved to a stop. The driver was told about the problem with the car and he gladly agreed to take Chotu along to the village.

In the meanwhile, one of the boys had run out into the grove on the roadside and returned with a few guavas and custard apples, which were ceremoniously offered to the *Saab*. Ramesh Joshi realised that he was actually very hungry and gratefully accepted the fruits.

In no time at all, Chotu arrived with Shiva – this time, in a tractor which was travelling in the opposite direction. Mr. Joshi was taken aback at the sight of Shiva – barely out of his teens, wearing a khaki outfit covered in grease, hands and face blackened with grease, unkempt hair and a generally unwashed appearance. For a moment – just for a moment – he wanted to protest, "Are *you* going to fiddle with my new car? No way will I let you do it!" But he controlled himself.

"*Namaste Saab*," Shiva greeted him cheerfully. "What is the problem? Is there petrol in the *gaadi*? *Arre*, it seems brand new! If you would just move sir, let me take a look…"

He cast an expert eye into the bonnet, running his hands here and there, checking on a few nuts and bolts, and then he exclaimed triumphantly, "I knew it! It is a fuse that has become loose."

The small crowd clapped and cheered enthusiastically as Shiva adjusted the fuse and asked Mr. Joshi to start the car. Sure enough, the engine roared into life.

Mr. Joshi was thrilled. He wanted to show his gratitude and appreciation to the young people who had so spontaneously gathered around him, given him their company and support. He drew out his wallet and took out some money and offered it to the group leader.

"No *Saab!* Give your money to Shiva," the young man protested. "We only came to help you – not to take money from you."

Mr. Joshi remembered that he was carrying a bag of biscuits, chocolates and snacks with him for the journey. He took the bag from the back seat and offered it to the group. "Right," he smiled. "You won't take money, but you cannot say no to a few biscuits…"

'Alright *Saab*, if you insist," said the young man. Packets were opened and the snacks and biscuits distributed among the group. Mr. Joshi also received his own 'share'. The boys munched happily and pronounced the snacks, "First Class". Then a Mineral Water bottle was produced from the car, and was passed round.

When the 'meal' was over, the group leader said to Mr. Joshi, "Now *Saab*, please drop Shiva at his garage on your way, because he will be losing out on his business if he stays away."

Mr. Joshi gladly agreed, and the greasy young mechanic insisted that Mr. Joshi spread a newspaper across the seat, so that his dirty clothes would not 'spoil' the car. And the Ford car set off, to the cheerful waving of the small crowd.

For Mr. Joshi, the experience was an eye-opener. With all his wealth, status and education, he had been dependent on the kindness and co-operation of a bunch of poor villagers. And how splendidly they had responded! There are situations in life, he reflected, when your money and social position are of very little use. You have to accept your own limitations, and look to your fellow human beings for help and support.

We gain from others when we realise that as human beings, we are all inter-dependent. We learn from others when we realise that we need their help, and seek the same with humility. At such times, we come to realise how little we know, and how we cannot get on without others. However, we would miss these valuable insights, if our pride and ego stand in our way.

"There is so much wisdom to be learned from the people around us" the Wise One said. "Life offers so many opportunities for us to evolve emotionally and intellectually. And the most valuable lessons in life are learned when we accept ourselves unconditionally – realising our own limitations.

"Some of us are blessed with material wealth and riches; some of us are blessed with business acumen; some are gifted with artistic bent and creativity; yet others stand apart with their caring and compassionate attitude; a few of us are efficient and capable administrators; sincerity and devotion mark the efforts of some people; the world needs us all. We can each contribute our own special and unique efforts to make life more meaningful and beautiful. What matters is that we recognise the others' contributions and appreciate it.

"All of us, with our individual gifts and skills are like so many strings on God's lute. We will make divine music, when we function together.

"Many of us feel lost in the immensity of life. Many of us feel unwanted or insignificant in the workplace. Things seem to happen with or without our contribution. Major events and functions happen where we do not have a role to play. At best we are reduced to the level of bystanders or spectators; at worst, we feel unwanted, useless, redundant. This naturally causes a great deal of unhappiness in our hearts.

"We would do well to remember the words of Martin Luther King: 'Everybody can be great, because everybody can serve. You don't have to have a college degree to serve. You don't have to make your subject and verb agree to serve. You don't have to know about Plato and Aristotle to serve... you only need a heart full of grace, a soul generated by love.'

"We must accept that we cannot all be heroes and heroines in history; after all, history also needs its subjects, soldiers and servants. But that word 'servant' does not appeal to us. 'I don't want to be a *servant!*' we exclaim. 'I want to be someone more important.

"When Jesus's disciples got into an argument over who was holy and who would get places in heaven, Jesus said to them: 'Whosoever desires to become great among you shall be your servant. And whosoever of you desires to be first, shall be the slave of all. For even the Son of Man did not come to be served, but to serve, and to give His life as a ransom for many.'

"How many of us will be prepared to accept such a role? How many of us will do our best, in our allotted sphere of life, without worrying about 'greatness', 'fame', and 'popularity'? Can we live and work and do whatever we can to please God rather than gain the applause and appreciation of people? Can we do our best, knowing that our work may go unnoticed? Then, we can be truly happy . . ."

I was profoundly moved by the Wise One's words. It seemed such a simple thing: accept yourself. And yet most of us could not do it!

A group of executives and administrators were having dinner at a restaurant. They talked about the various problems that beset religion, and the talk turned to Christianity.

"If you ask me, Jesus should have considered his choice of followers a little more critically," one of them said. "He should have looked among rulers and leaders, or at skilled statesmen and gifted orators. Instead, what did he do? He went to the shores of Lake Galilee and called out four common fishermen – Peter, Andrew, James and John."

"I can't help thinking he might have chosen better," the man continued. "He might have chosen more educated, more cultured, more appropriate people, don't you?"

"I don't agree with you," said a diner who sat at the next table. "Excuse me, but I could not help overhearing your conversation. And I would like to say this on behalf of fishermen – they too have very many positive, strong points. They are resourceful, patient and persevering. They have the courage to weather many storms. They know how to take care of their boats, tackle and equipment. They know what it is to brave the elements and struggle against harsh conditions. They know how to work as a team and care for each other."

God chooses His own people for each task. To us, they might seem unlikely choices – but He knows they are right for His Plan. 'They' might be you and me – for we too, have our own role to play in God's scheme of things.

Management consultants tell us that young people very often take to 'padding' their bio-data or *curriculum vitae* (CVs) as they are called. What is 'padding'? We 'embellish' details about ourselves. We actually resort to untruths in order to impress our potential employers.

Often, young applicants claim that their hobbies are playing chess, bridge or some such game which they perceive to be 'intellectual'. They feel that such hobbies 'elevate' the impression they make on their potential employer. If they were asked a slightly difficult question about chess or bridge, they would be shown up as hypocrites or liars. Why can't we say instead, that our hobbies include reading, walking, cooking, listening to music or playing scrabble or monopoly? After all, this is what most of us do. If I were an employer, I would appreciate the honesty of someone who claims that she enjoys cooking in her leisure hours, rather than be impressed by someone who claims falsely that she plays chess.

A businessman writes that he had an application from a girl who claimed that she had experience in "foods and beverages." As this man was about to start a catering unit, he called the girl for an interview. He made it clear that he was not much impressed by her paper qualifications as by her experience in the foods-and-beverages area. Upon questioning, the girl had to confess the truth: what she had loftily described as "experience in food and beverages" was, in truth, nothing but the fact that as the junior most clerk, she had made the office tea twice a day, and taken the tea round to her superiors with accompanying biscuits!

When we decide to 'embellish' the truth about ourselves, or even exaggerate or lie in order to impress others, we are letting ourselves in for continuous falsehood. For we may be forced to utter more lies to 'prove' our earlier lies. Exposure would demean and degrade us. Instead, why not accept what we are, unconditionally?

The Australian psychiatrist, Victor Frankl, was arrested by the Nazis and thrown into a concentration camp to die. However, Frankl survived the horrors of the Holocaust to write *Man's Search For Meaning*, which became a bestseller. In this book, Frankl shares with us the great truth that his suffering taught him: "There is nothing in the world, I venture to say, that would so effectively help survive even the worst conditions as the knowledge that there is a meaning in one's life."

Each one of us has been created by God with a definite purpose, and a definite task assigned to us that we alone can do. We may not suffer, we may not be called upon to act heroically – but we are part of God's Divine Plan. If we accept the role that is assigned to us, there is no question of our being unhappy.

A brother complained to me wearily, "My life has fallen into a rut, a deadly routine. Everyday I awake, I rush about to get ready, I leave for work, I come home exhausted, eat and fall asleep. Where am I going? What am I achieving? Why has God condemned me to lead such a dull and repetitive life?"

Shakespeare viewed this 'routine' slightly differently. He compared the world to a stage, and all of us to actors; we have to play our parts on this stage, and our 'exits' and 'entrances' are all carefully timed.

Indeed, the world is like a theatre in which the cosmic drama of human life is unfolding. Since there are millions and trillions of us acting out our 'bit parts' here, we are only playing minor roles. Therefore, we are often forced to repeat our lines, appear in crowd scenes and not really given anything spectacular to do or say. We can 'act' our roles in a dull, bored way as disinterested actors do – or we can look at our 'role' as a wonderful opportunity to prove to the great Producer how good we are at whatever we do!

My friends who 'surf the Net', tell me that there is an online publication called *Journal of Mundane Behaviour*. Edited by a sociologist, this journal tells us that nearly 60 % of our time is taken up with 'routine' activities like cleaning, washing, shopping for groceries and commuting to work. How, can we make this 'ordinary' routine more meaningful?

When there is no enthusiasm and joy in the work we do, our days become dull and colourless. "The only way to keep life uncrushed," says a wise counsellor, "is to dedicate our life and actions to the Lord."

Let's make every day an important, ordinary day! Let's make our 'ordinary' life more meaningful by dedicating all our efforts to God. He does not expect great deeds and achievements from all of us. Does He not say to us in the Gita, "Whatever you do, whatever you say, whatever you eat, do it as an offering unto Me"?

The wise one and I had been walking through the woods all this time, our feet keeping pace with our thoughts, words and reflections. We now reached a clearing, where the thick undergrowth gave way to a grassy knoll, with scattered trees covered in green creepers. We sat down on the grass for a brief rest.

"May I say something?" I said to the Wise One. "I feel in a very paradoxical way that it is man's ego which prevents him from accepting himself as he is… it is paradoxical because ego makes him think he is the best there is, yet he cannot accept that he has weaknesses… isn't it strange?"

"It's not really paradoxical," the Wise One remarked. "Where ego dominates, reason takes a back seat, as does wisdom. How can a man attain self-acceptance without wisdom?

"The sad thing is, lack of self acceptance can only lead to eventual disillusion – and unhappiness. How many of us can actually say, 'I *like* myself as I am'? There are that many happy people in the world."

I was startled to find the next secret staring at me in the face. It was on an antique carved wooden piece that lay on the grass, just to my side. Eagerly, I lifted the carving, and read the next secret:

Believe In Yourself –Believe And Achieve!

The 13th Secret of Happiness

Believe In Yourself – Believe And Achieve!

"It appears to me that we are now involved with what Socrates held up as the ultimate aim of all learning and education," I observed to the Wise One. "We are now focussing on self-knowledge, aren't we? Accepting oneself unconditionally, knowing one's limitations, and believing in oneself..."

"Can there be happiness without self-knowledge?" the Wise One shot back.

"Know Thyself!" I repeated the famous dictum of Socrates. "But it's not easy, is it? We have just been saying that we must not over-estimate our own abilities; and now we are saying – don't let us under-estimate ourselves!"

"It's not as difficult as it is made out to be," the Wise One replied. "In management, they talk of SWOT analysis, don't they? It's nothing but a realistic assessment of our strengths, weaknesses, the opportunities before us and the threats and challenges that we are likely to face. This is essential not only for business success, but also for happiness in life."

We began to walk through the woods, as our interesting discussion continued.

"Let us say that I make a realistic assessment of myself," I argued, warming up now, "and I find that I really don't amount to much, what would you have me do next? Give up my ambitions? Or begin to think small, aim low...?"

"Please bear with me," I added as an afterthought. "You know I'm only trying to clear up the issues, not really trying to counter your wisdom."

"On the contrary, I enjoy this stimulating discussion as much as you do," smiled the Wise One. "We have to play devil's advocate with each other so that our thoughts may be clarified and our arguments strengthened and made more logical. I appreciate what you are trying to do, and I shall marshal my arguments to your satisfaction...

"Thus far I have stressed the need to accept yourself unconditionally, so that you are not led to unhappiness because of your own unrealistic assessment of yourself. Now it is time to tell you that this is *not* a formula for passive frustration and inferiority; nor is it a 'license' which permits you to stagnate with your weaknesses and limitations.

"Accept yourself as you are – but this does not mean that you cannot try to improve! Accept yourself unconditionally – but work on building your strengths and eliminating your weaknesses..."

I thought of the many people who often came to me with this problem. Try as they might, they swore they could not overcome their bad habits, weaknesses and temptations – it might be smoking, it might be overeating or trying to give up the food of violence: "We tried so hard, but we simply can't succeed!" was their constant chorus.

My friends tell me that around the end of December and beginning of January, enrolment in gyms and fitness centres in Pune is at an all-time high. People make new year resolutions to lose weight, keep fit and adopt a healthier lifestyle for the future – and the gyms seem to overflow with good resolutions. But by the time April arrives, the good resolutions have all worn out, and the drop-out rate is at its highest!

Overweight and obesity are weaknesses that people refuse to overcome. I know many men and women who succumb to defeatism and negativism when it comes to knocking off a few inches. "It's a hereditary problem," they rationalise. Or they say, "My metabolism is different," or even, "It runs in the family."

"Let me make it clear," the Wise One resumed. "It is not my intention to encourage a negative, defeatist attitude when I urge you to accept yourself as you are. This acceptance is *not* defeatism or refusal to improve. It is just a realistic assessment of your capabilities and strengths which will enable you to set targets and goals which you can achieve, and thus enhance your self-esteem and add to your happiness."

I remembered the occasion, several years ago, when a Local Inquiry Committee (LIC) from Pune University was visiting St. Mira's College for Girls, for the purpose of accreditation and affiliation. The college was still in its early days, and I happened to be the Principal. The committee visited the various departments and facilities in the College, assessing each criterion in the standardised form which had to be filled in by them and submitted to the University.

"Which is the largest room in the College?" one of the members asked me.

"The room for improvement!" I answered without hesitation, and this candid reply brought a smile to everyone's lips.

Yes – the room for improvement is the largest room in all our lives. The realistic appraisal and acceptance of ourselves does *not* exclude our obligation to improve ourselves in every way possible.

Recently, I read an article about *The Louvre* in Paris – probably the most famous art museum in the world. In this museum are displayed the original works of some of the world's greatest masters – including the *Mona Lisa*, by Leonardo Da Vinci.

The article said that aspiring artists have always been encouraged to come to the Louvre and "copy the masters." By imitating the work of great artists, they themselves have become better painters.

The article spoke of Amal Dagner, a 63-year old man, who has been duplicating art at the Louvre for 30 years. He is in awe of the great masters and says he still continues to learn from them. Asked how he could still carry on 'learning' for over 30 years, his reply was, "If you're too satisfied with yourself, you can't improve."

Accept your limitations – but do not give up the effort to make yourself better. Do not rest content with mediocrity – aspire to improve! Never, never, never, give up!

"Have you heard of A.J. Cronin?" asked the Wise One. "Let me tell you about this remarkable man…"

A.J. Cronin was a Scottish physician, who had aspired to become a writer. Forced to go on a medical leave due to an illness, he decided to try his hand out at writing a novel, during his days of enforced leisure. But when he was halfway through the novel, he became disheartened with his effort and relegated his work to the dustbin. He thought his writing was mediocre; not worth pursuing.

In this pessimistic mood, he was walking in the Scottish Highlands when he saw a man digging a bog. Bogs are marshy lands that are common in the Highlands. It takes tremendous efforts to drain them, only after which they can be put to any use, as pasturelands.

Cronin began to speak to the solitary highlander who was determinedly pursuing his tough task.

"Aren't you wasting your time?" he said gently. "Do you really think you will succeed in this task?" he asked the man.

Wiping his brow, the man replied. "My grandfather dug at this bog, but he could not make a pasture out of it. My father dug at it and he didn't succeed either. But my father told me that it is only by digging that we could make a pasture out of this useless piece of land. So I continue to dig."

Cronin was charged and motivated by the man's determination. He went back to his home, retrieved his manuscript from the dustbin and worked on it with perseverance, until he finished it. That was his first novel, *Hatter's Castle* – it sold 3 million copies, and made Cronin a world famous writer.

"Does life seem a harsh, useless, inhospitable 'bog' to you?" the Wise One queried. "You don't have to live with your frustration. You can convert it into a green pasture if you work with courage and conviction. Believe and achieve!"

At a critical juncture in Martin Luther's career, he had to cope with discouragement and setbacks. During those days, he would look up at the night sky to draw courage and inspiration.

"What do you see up in the sky?" a friend asked him.

"The sky is studded with a thousand stars, and there are no pillars to prop them and hold them up," said the great religious reformer. He drew encouragement from the idea that just as God's invisible support sustained the universe, it would support him too.

Mr. Brown had loved his parents' small back garden, which he had seen his father tend with loving care, as he grew up. As he went to work in a city, he himself did not have the chance to work in a garden of his own. However, his passion for gardening stayed alive in his heart. When he retired, Mr. Brown bought his dream cottage in the countryside; but its backyard was an overgrown plot of land covered with weeds and thorny bushes. Mr. Brown worked hard to clear the plot and in just two years, he had transformed it into a beautiful garden that became a showpiece for the whole neighbourhood.

One day, the pastor from the local church visited Mr. Brown's garden. "This is what I did..." "This is how I planned..." "This is what I thought..." Mr. Brown explained, as he talked about his garden. Pointing to a beautiful bed of flowers, he said, "Look at what I've done here..."

The pastor, at this point, felt constrained to correct him. "You must say, 'Look at what God and I did together here'..." he said gently.

Mr. Brown stopped and stared at him for a moment. Then he said with a grin, "Yeah, I guess you are right. But if only you could have seen the state this place was in when the Lord was in charge on His own..."

We laugh at this joke, but it expresses a great truth that when we believe in ourselves and work hard – God blesses our efforts. We become co-workers with God, to create our own achievements and build our own happiness.

I read of a woman lawyer in Orissa, over 40 years of age, who actually attempted to climb Mount Everest. Due to a technical problem, she had to give up the attempt, when she was within a few hours of actually reaching the peak. Not discouraged by the setback, she is planning another expedition to climb the world's highest mountain – and she is described as the first civilian, that is, a non-professional trekker to make the attempt on her own.

How does she practise for the feat in her native Orissa?

Her answer would surprise you. Next to her home is a small hillock, which is about one thousand four hundred and fifty feet high. She climbs that hill, carrying a thirty-kg. backpack with her – *ten to twelve times a day!*

As I write this, she is planning her next attempt at Everest, and this time she is determined to create a record by staying on the peak for the longest duration possible!

This woman certainly believes in herself!

At a question-answer session, a brother once said to me: "If we are imperfect, weak, incapable in certain respects, it is because God has willed that it should be so. Why then should we try to overreach ourselves? Why should we set ourselves impossible targets and try to become better than God made us?"

Rarely have I come across a more specious or more futile argument!

I said to this brother, "What is your reaction when a perfectly healthy, able bodied man comes to you, begging for alms?"

He did not hesitate even for a moment, before he replied. "Really, Dada, I have very strong views on the subject. I feel we must discourage begging at all costs. I would tell this man, 'Don't be lazy! You are able bodied. Go and work for your living!' I have no patience with these sponges who live off others' charity and alms. I think they are a disgrace to society."

"Well, that was your point of view and you have every right to express it," I said. "But suppose this man were to turn round and tell you, 'It's my nature to be lazy and poor. Why are you asking me to change my nature?' What would your response be?"

The brother grew silent and thoughtful. Obviously he would not have been satisfied with the beggar's response!

We are all here to put forth our best efforts. The ideal before each one of us is the ideal of perfection. It was Jesus Christ who urged us, "Be ye perfect, even as your Father in Heaven is Perfect." This is the way that we can believe and achieve. The alternative is to live a lazy life like the beggar – and refuse to improve our condition.

"We have said this again and again," said the Wise One. "Happiness cannot be measured in terms of money, power, position, wealth or social status. For a man may have all of these and still be miserable. The world thinks that a millionaire is a 'successful' man. Success must be measured by the yardstick of inner happiness – your ability to be happy and make others happy; the ability to love and be loved by others; the ability to live in harmony with those around you, with your own self and God's cosmic laws…

"True success, true happiness lies in freedom and fulfillment. How can you feel a sense of fulfillment if you don't put forth your best efforts?"

"How may we believe and achieve?" I asked him.

His valuable advice, I present to you in the form of nine practical suggestions, which I would describe as the software for success:

1. Do only that which you feel is right and true. Nothing in life brings about unhappiness and failure more surely than lack of integrity.
2. Do your best each day. Let this be the motto of your life: only the best is good enough for me! When you give to the world the best you have, the best will come back to you.
3. Fully trust in the Divine wisdom that designs and orders the scheme of things. There is a meaning of mercy in all that happens.

4. Plan carefully for each day. Budget your time. Take care of every minute of your time.
5. Begin the day right. Wake up each morning, full of hope and expectation.
6. Never give up! Persistence pays!
7. Tact is as important as talent. Therefore, speak politely; act courteously; respect everyone you meet.
8. Stay young at heart. Age is a state of mind.
9. Reach out to others. You succeed in the measure in which you help others to succeed.

"Why are some of us better, more successful than others?" the Wise One mused. "That is like asking the Principal of a school, 'Why are there so many different classes in your school? Why is it that some children are in the fifth class, while some are in the eleventh class? Don't you want all your students to pass the High School examination?...'

"Yes, the Principal would like all his students to pass the highest examination, eventually. But in order to do that, they have to go through different stages of education. Likewise, we have to keep striving constantly, seeking 'promotion' to the next higher level, seeking maturity and wisdom, striving to become better and better in every way..."

"How can I become a better person?" a youngster once asked me.

I replied simply, "By being a better person, surely!"

That was in fact, the gist of what the Wise One had been telling me all along. Everyone of us has some weaknesses, some imperfections, some undesirable qualities. We must try to assess our own weaknesses and work hard to eliminate them.

If that seems daunting to you, select just one of your weak points to work on! If you try to tackle your flaws all at once, you may be disheartened by your lack of progress. Select just one weakness and focus your efforts on it: don't dwell on the weakness itself – that will only strengthen your weakness. Rather, focus on your resolution to conquer it.

For instance, if you are easily given to anger, you must not think of your short temper, but of its opposite quality – serenity, peace and tranquillity. The more you focus on these positive qualities, the sooner you will find that these qualities enter your being.

"Remember," the Wise One said softly, "You become what you think! Think better thoughts, higher thoughts, and you will surely become a better person. You will really believe and achieve!"

"This has been one of the most inspiring sessions we have had," I said enthusiastically. "I wish you could just go on and on…"

I caught sight of a kite that was lodged in the thick foliage of a tree near us. "Hello!" I exclaimed. "I wonder how long ago that kite was flown by one of the residents of the realm of happiness…"

Carefully, I disentangled the kite from the tree. It was a beautiful, handmade kite, embellished with artistic, handpainted designs. Across the width of the kite, I discovered the next secret imprinted in exquisite calligraphy:

If You Would Be Happy, Always See The Good In Others.

The 14th Secret of Happiness

If You Would Be Happy, Always See The Good In Others

"This links directly with the last secret, doesn't it?" I said to the Wise One. "I must realise my limitations and weaknesses – but I *must not* focus on the faults and weaknesses of others. I must look at their good points instead. Isn't that so?"

The Wise One smiled.

"If you would be happy, I urge you not to look at others' faults," he said. "By focussing attention on people's faults, you only draw negative forces to yourself."

"Some of us insist on pointing a finger at others' shortcomings. 'Someone's got to change all that is wrong with this world,' we proclaim. Let me tell you, fault-finding and magnifying others' mistakes are poor ways of changing the world!

"When I find fault with others, I regard myself as superior – better than another. This is pride, this is egoism. This must be overcome if we are to be truly happy.

"Let me tell you a beautiful incident narrated to us by the great Sufi poet Sadi..."

When Sadi was a young boy of six, his father, a *dervish*, took him to the mosque where a night-long vigil was being observed. As the night grew, Sadi found that one after another, the people who had assembled at the mosque began to fall asleep. Even the *mullah* had nodded off. Only Sadi and his father had remained awake.

The little boy whispered into the ears of his father, "Father, only you and I are keeping the vigil. All the others have fallen asleep."

Sadi's father admonished him, "It is better to go off to sleep and not observe the vigil, rather than find fault with others and think ourselves superior."

"If you wish to be happy," the Wise One said, "you can begin by thinking, 'Everybody has something good in him; there is something that I can learn from every human being.'"

I recalled that the great Prophet of the Baha'i faith, Baha'u'llah, said to his disciples again and again, "If you find that there are nine vices and only one virtue in a man, forget the nine vices, and think of his one virtue."

"See only the good in others," repeated the Wise One. "When you do this, you will find yourself growing better and better. If you see only people's faults and failings, you will only heap those on yourself, and consequently become more and more unhappy. Shall I tell you another story...?"

Tina was a 'special' child – severely challenged physically and intellectually. Her parents brought her to experts who would observe her carefully, assess her capabilities and suggest a child-centred approach which her parents could adopt to teach her at home. The experts would not impose any set programmes on Tina; rather they would learn *her* preferences and inclinations first, and allow the child to guide them in helping her. During successive sessions, trained volunteers and special teachers would observe the child, and share their observations with each other and the parents.

At the end of the third day's session, Neela, one of the volunteers, said enthusiastically, "Yesterday, Tina was not ready to move out of her place; but this morning, when I held out a toy to her, she actually took a few steps in my direction."

Shanti, another volunteer, added, "This afternoon, when I showed her a teddy bear, she laughed happily and came near me to touch the teddy."

Tina's mother, who was listening open-mouthed, interjected at this point, "But...but she *cannot* walk!"

"Oh?" said the volunteers politely, "We really didn't know that!"

"I narrated this real-life story to tell you how the teachers and trainers of 'special' children do not pre-judge the capabilities of their young wards," the Wise

One added. "This is an attitude we will all do well to adopt."

I nodded my assent.

We have ingrained notions of what is right and wrong, what is proper and improper, what is acceptable and unacceptable. When we impose our narrow and harsh judgements on others, we condemn ourselves to a critical attitude and lose out on a lot of good cheer and joy that comes from being open-minded.

Two women met at a party. The talk veered round to the dresses they were wearing. "My husband brought this material for me last year," said the first woman proudly. "In fact, he chooses all my clothes. I wouldn't dream of ever buying anything on my own, because he has such excellent taste!"

"As for me, I wouldn't ever take my husband shopping with me," exclaimed the second woman. "It is quite enough if he gives me the money. I will never, ever let anyone choose the clothes that I wear. I'm too independent for that,"

The first woman immediately judged her friend to be an arrogant, egotistical lady who treated her husband like a money-making robot. The second woman put the first down as a 'door mat' who had no opinion of her own. A rigid opinion was formed on both sides; feelings hardened, and a budding friendship was nipped in the bud.

Each one to his or her taste! Why do we have to express our opinions on everyone's behaviour and pass negative judgements on everyone who does not think and act like us?

Today, there are several married couples who are so intolerant of each other, that they file for divorce, "on grounds of incompatibility". I often remark that "emotional incompatibility" is a myth invented by divorce lawyers to make money out of others' misfortune and unhappiness. To my mind, there is no such thing as incompatibility. There are only misunderstandings and mistakes which can easily be set right, when people have the will to do so.

The greatest famine in the world today is the famine of understanding. No two people are prepared to understand the other person and look at life and its problems from the other's point of view.

"None of us is perfect," the Wise One observed. No man or woman can ever be perfect. It was Jesus who said, 'Call me not perfect. Alone the Father in heaven is perfect!' Marriage, friendship, any relationship or business partnership involves two imperfect human beings trying to live together, work together or establish a link. Unless we learn to accept people as they are, we will lose all possibility of finding happiness in our relationships."

As always, the Wise One had got it right. Resentment and negative judgements actually hurt us as much as they hurt others. As Benjamin Franklin says, "Whatever is begun in anger, ends in shame."

A stranger arrived at the gates of a city, which he was visiting for the first time. An old woman sitting on the roadside greeted him, "Welcome to our city!"

"What kind of people live here?" the stranger asked her.

"What kind of people live in your home town?" the old woman asked him with a smile.

"Oh, they were terrible," swore the stranger. "They were mean, nasty, malicious and selfish. They were impossible to live with."

"You will find people here are pretty much the same," the old woman said to him.

A little later, another stranger arrived at the city gates, and was welcomed by the old woman.

"What kind of people live in this city?" the second traveller asked.

"How did you find them in your home town?" the woman asked him.

"They were a wonderful lot – hard working, friendly, and easy to get along with."

"You will find the people here likewise," the old woman assured him.

Approach people with love and understanding – and you will find the same reflected in their approach to you.

It was Thomas Merton who said, "Saints are what they are, not because their sanctity makes them admirable to others, but because the gift of sainthood makes it possible for them to admire everyone else.'

Dr. Richard Seltzer, the well-known surgeon, carried out a surgery to remove a malignant tumour from the cheek of a young woman. Though he had carried out the surgery with great care, he had to make a crucial decision to cut a little nerve in order to remove the tumour completely.

Now, the young woman would have a crooked, twisted mouth all her life – for the tiny nerve which had been cut was the one which moved the muscles of her mouth.

When her husband visited the woman after her operation, her eyes filled with tears. "Will my mouth always be like this?" she asked Dr. Seltzer.

"Yes," said the doctor gently. "You see, we had to cut a little nerve in order to remove the tumour completely."

The woman nodded, silent in her misery.

Her husband bent down to kiss her forehead. "I like it," he said to her. "You look really cute."

Dr. Seltzer was amazed at the power of the man's loving kindness which could look beyond the scars and the disfigurement, and offer such comfort and support to the wife in her pain and suffering.

See the good in everyone! A friend who teaches at a National Open University once told me that she gets very different students from very different backgrounds. There are housewives from the age of twenty-five to fifty-five, who were married early and were unable to pursue higher education; there are men who were compelled to take on the burden of supporting their families at a very young age, and had to stop their schooling; there are others, better qualified, who wish to acquire more degrees and diplomas and improve their prospects now; and there are the retired folk, sixty plus, who are eager to catch up on the education they missed out long ago…

"All in all, it's a very mixed bunch of people we get," the friend said to me. "But there's one thing they all have in common – they are determined to educate themselves, determined to get that precious college degree which they missed out on."

Not being young, not being used to the rigorous routine of the education system, they have very different learning problems from ordinary students. They are always attentive; but they do not have all the basics. They never ever miss their Sunday classes (they meet only on Sundays – the rest of the inputs are through audio, video and self-teaching manuals); but they still lack a lot of background information.

The Open University concept was envisioned just in order to give such people a second chance, and so the instructors are given training to treat their 'mature' students with kindness and courtesy, and, above all, to motivate them by encouragement and appreciation.

My friend told me that when they were correcting assignments and tests, these instructors were requested *not* to use red pens – for red ink, as you know, is traditionally associated with mistakes, errors or 'wrongs' and negative comments. So even if an assignment had several mistakes, the student would not get back his paper covered with angry red marks. Instead, the teacher's 'suggestions' for rewriting would be found alongside the original mistakes. The teachers were also asked to identify ideas and expressions that were good, and show their appreciation by a double tick (✓✓). And, they had been told to write a positive, encouraging comment at the end of each assignment, bringing out the student's good points and urging him to do even better next time.

Don't you think even 'regular' students in our schools and colleges would do far better if we adopted such a positive approach to them?

Sadhu Vaswani had just such a vision of an ideal school where a teacher would be the *friend* of the children, rather than a disciplinarian or an authority. When he was very young, he once happened to smile in class, as a thought passed through his mind. The teacher asked him why he was smiling; and as the little boy did not answer immediately, the teacher grew angry and slapped him!

In the heart within, Sadhu Vaswani resolved that when he grew up, he would start schools of a very different type where teachers would be friends of their pupils – where they would neither spank nor scold the children, but touch them with reverence and treat them with love. This resolve came true when he founded the Mira movement in Education.

Today, you will be happy to know that the MIRA institutions encourage their students to do their best in every sphere of activity. Of course, academic excellence is encouraged and gold medals and cash prizes are given away to the toppers in each class and each subject. But others are not kept out on the Annual Prize Distribution day! There are Prizes and trophies for Service, Simplicity, Prayer, Cheerfulness and Compassion! There are prizes for performing arts, elocution, debates, general knowledge and music. At St. Mira's College, they have done away with 'consolation' prizes which sound derogatory – instead, they have 'Appreciation' prizes!

Two passengers were travelling in a First class compartment on a rather lonely and bandit-infested stretch of the Central Railway. One of them was a God-fearing, pious shopkeeper, who happened to be carrying a considerable amount of cash with him. The other man was in fact a habitual criminal, whose sole occupation was to travel in buses and trains all over the area and loot unsuspecting passengers. He had got wind of the fact that the shopkeeper was carrying a lot of money, and planned to rob him as soon as night fell.

The shopkeeper, poor soul, had no inkling as to the other man's true nature. In all innocence he asked the man, "Where do you think I should put my money away, safely for the night? I don't want to lose it to a dacoit, you see. May be you will help me with your valuable suggestion?"

The criminal was so shocked that his mouth fell open. What a fool this chap is, he thought to himself. However, he composed himself and said to the man, "Sir, I would advise you to put the money at the place which you consider to be really safe – say, under your pillow, or close to your hand or even locked up in you suitcase".

"Thank you, my friend," said the shopkeeper solemnly. "I shall do exactly as you say!"

When darkness fell, the shopkeeper actually shared his food with the criminal, chatting amicably all the time. As for the thief, he was laughing inwardly at his gullible companion. He would loot the man's money and get off the train at midnight – and none would be able to trace him. For, as always, he was travelling under a false name with a non-existent address.

The two men made their beds and the criminal went out to check with the TTE, the halts that the train would make at night. When he returned, he was taken aback to see his fellow passenger fast asleep on the upper berth.

He waited until all the passengers in the other cabins had fallen asleep, and the compartment was in darkness. Then he rose stealthily, and set to work.

He examined the baggage of the shopkeeper, trying open the locks with the implements he carried. But he found only a few clothes and papers. Then he felt carefully under the sleeping man's pillow – no luck! Then he examined the berth inch by inch, gently pushing aside the sleeping man, without actually waking him. The man was sleeping like a log – but where he had put his money away, it was impossible to find. The thief went over the baggage and the upper berth several times. His head began to whirl. Had the man thrown his money out of the window?

Exhausted, he felt into a troubled sleep. He was awakened only next morning by the shopkeeper, who was now fully dressed and ready to get off the train. He was carrying his baggage in his hand, and two burly men had come to receive him. They were introduced to the thief as his partners.

"I'm so sorry to wake you early in the morning" said the shopkeeper apologetically. "But I would like to take my money now".

"Your money? How... what... where?" stammered the criminal, his guilty conscience beginning to trouble him.

"Here it is," said his companion cheerfully, pushing aside the criminal's pillow and retrieving his money. "It was right here, under your pillow, all night."

"But... but... why?" demanded the thief.

"Well my friend," explained the shopkeeper. "You told me to put it in the place which I thought was absolutely safe. I figured that you were the best person to keep it safe for me. But you were out at that time, and so I put it under your pillow and fell asleep. Now it is time for me to go and I cannot thank you enough for taking care of my money. God bless you!"

You would probably think that the shopkeeper's trust was misplaced. But he only saw the good in the criminal – and the criminal's carefully laid plans came to naught!

Look for the good in others – do not consider their faults and failings!

A man was walking along the banks of a river, when he slipped and fell, into the water. "Help! Help!" he cried desperately.

A traveller came along the bank. He saw the man desperately clinging to the steep bank, trying to resist the flowing current. "Shouldn't you have been more careful?" he asked, and walked away.

A rich man passed by, riding in a carriage. He looked out of the window and called, "People like you deserve to drown."

Yet another man came along, and watched the exhausted man struggling pitifully. "You are not even trying hard enough!" he remarked contemptuously, before he too moved away.

Lastly, there came by an old man. When he saw the man in the river, he hurried to his aid. He lay down on the bank of the river and held out a hand to the drowning man. "Come on," he urged, "Take my hand and heave yourself up. I know you will make it!"

With one great heave and tug, the drowning man was out of the water. Before the astonished eyes of the old man, he turned into a mighty God in shining raiment. He rewarded the old man richly and blessed him with good health and good fortune.

The old man had responded spontaneously and only thought of doing his best for the drowning man. He did not criticise or condemn. And so he was rewarded.

I read a story about an Angel who shrank and dwindled when spoken to harshly, but expanded to its full stature and shone with radiance when spoken to kindly and treated lovingly.

"See the good in others!" said the Wise One, reflecting my own thoughts. "Utter kind words and loving thoughts about them. You will find that this has a healing effect on them and on you! Harsh words and criticism cause people to shrink and wither. Kindness beautifies and blesses. Every thought of kindness, every act of love, emits light – and to give light to others is life's greatest privilege and the ultimate joy-bringer to your own life!

"The happy, positive individual does not criticise, he does not find fault with others. Whatever we see in others, we tend to draw to ourselves. If we only consider the faults in others, we are heaping them upon ourselves. If we see the good in others, we will keep on growing better and better and our minds will always be at peace, and the world around us will smile..."

During the Second World War, three different men were shown the same picture and asked to respond to what they saw. The picture showed two stretcher-bearers on the battlefield carrying a wounded comrade.

The first man said, "This picture only goes to show that life is painful and dangerous."

The second man remarked, "It's just another proof to me that life is not worth living! This is what men do to each other – they kill, wound or maim others. How terrible people can be!"

The third studied the picture for sometime and remarked, "To me this picture brings out the heroism inherent in all men. I see the feeling of brotherhood and compassion in these two men which has led them to risk their own lives to save a fellow human being. How beautiful and noble they are!"

"When we look at others with hostility and a judgemental attitude life itself appears hostile and harsh," the Wise One observed. "Let us 'tune into' the good in people – and we shall hear the soft, sweet music of humanity wherever we turn..."

A pious rabbi ordered his assistant to assemble ten men to chant psalms for the recovery of a sick man. When they entered, a friend of the rabbi exclaimed, "Are these the men who are going to pray? Why, I see among them notorious thieves!"

"Excellent," retorted the rabbi. "When all the heavenly gates of mercy are closed to us, we will need experts to open them!"

We emerged out of the wood on to a rocky, hilly terrain. We seemed to have left behind the greenery and fields on the other side of the wood.

We began to climb up a rocky path which went up to a waterfall. As we moved up carefully, my foot slipped, and I would have fallen down the slope if the Wise One had not caught me firmly by the elbow, arresting my fall.

"Thank you!" I gasped. "That was close!"

As I steadied myself, my eyes fell on the message inscribed on a boulder that lay ahead of us:

To Be Truly Happy You Must Be Afraid of Nothing.

The 15th Secret of Happiness

To Be Truly Happy, You Must Be Afraid Of Nothing

"A timely reminder," I remarked to the Wise One.

"Let us climb up to the waterfall and drink some water," said the Wise One. "We can resume our discussion then."

Climbing up carefully, we reached the waterfall and refreshed ourselves with a wash and a drink. To the side of the waterfall was a small cave, and gooseberry trees dotted the entrance to the cave, providing shelter from the midday sun. The trees were laden with delicious bright green berries, which we picked and ate with relish.

"Tell me your views on the newest secret I have found," I requested the Wise One.

"Being afraid is the worst thing that can happen to you," he began. "Let me remind you of the wonderful words of President Franklin Delano Roosevelt: 'The only thing we have to fear is fear itself – nameless, unreasoning terror, which paralyses needed efforts to convert retreat into advance.'

"Fear *limits* your life," he continued. "Fear curbs your spirit; it stifles your potential. When we allow fear to dominate our psyche, we let a vague, shadowy idea darken our horizon. When we set out to actually describe or define what we fear, we realise that these fears are not so terrible after all! In fact, before you try to define your fear, I suggest that you try to look closely at what you are afraid of – and you will find, with Roosevelt, that there is nothing so much to fear, as fear itself!

"It is said that people's most common fears have to do with the following: death of oneself or a loved one; losing a job; illness; losing money; or the break-up of a marriage.

"But there are more subtle and vague fears. There are people who are afraid to take a flight; there are people who are afraid to go out into a crowd; there are people who are afraid to step out of their homes – and sentence themselves to imprisonment within the four walls of their home . . ."

I had read of a woman who suffered from this fear – agoraphobia as it is called. She lived a terribly restricted life – until she developed a severe illness. Then things changed rapidly for her. She was rushed out of her house into an ambulance, rushed into a busy hospital where the Emergency staff surrounded her, and then rushed into an ICU. Fortunately, her condition proved to be completely curable – but the life-threatening incident cured her of her petty, vague phobia. So has it been said, when you really have something to fear, you will drop the 'small stuff'!

The great scientist and Nobel Laureate Madame Curie once observed: "Nothing in life is to be feared. It is only to be understood." How true it is, that when we have understood ourselves and what we are afraid of, fear actually departs!

"Fear strikes at the root of our happiness, sapping our will to live," the Wise One continued. "When we face up to our worst fears and take them on bravely, our fears become very small – sometimes, they actually vanish. Have you heard of the 'worm that turned?' It is about a tiny creature which was chased by something huge and terrible; the faster it ran, the nearer the predator seemed to approach – until the worm stopped short, turned round and actually confronted its tormentor – and there was nothing to flee, nothing to fear! A giant shadow had done all the mischief.

"When you keep on running, you will be chased constantly. Stop and face your fear – and the threatening demon dwindles into an insignificant mosquito!"

The Wise One had, as always, touched the heart of the matter. Fear paralyses us when we visualise failure or an unsuccessful outcome. "I'm going to do badly in the interview," thinks the young man who is setting out in search of his first job. "I'm sure I'm going to feel blank," imagines a student who is about to sit for a crucial exam. "I know it's going to be a malignant tumour," thinks a woman who has come to her doctor to diagnose a little lump on her breast. Fear arrives when you visualise failure.

A well-known psychiatrist offers us this advise: do not visualise your fear as a dragon, a demon or a monster. Think of it as a pathetic, crying infant. What will you do when you see a baby sobbing away? You will pick it up, hold it close and soothe its tears away, won't you? Do the same with your fear – pick it up and hug it close – and the howling infant will soon turn into a bundle of joy!

Confront your fear; face it and accept it – and you will see that it grows smaller! You don't have to wait for a life-threatening illness to conquer your fears!

Like your imagination, your fear also possesses a 'creative power' which draws your worst fears towards you. It is like the negative self-fulfilling prophecy that people speak of – making your worst fears come true.

Many years ago, in the State of Kentucky in the U.S., a little baby girl was born in a wealthy family. From the moment of her birth, her parents were obsessed with the fear that she would be kidnapped. They took extensive, elaborate precautions to guard her and protect her. She was never, ever left alone. They raised the garden walls around their house and put spikes on them. When she was five years old, she was sent to an exclusive, private school to which a chauffeur escorted her daily. She was never ever allowed to go out and play with the other children; she never, ever went to the ice cream parlour to buy herself an ice-candy; she was not allowed to visit parks, gardens or museums.

When she was married, her husband continued with the same elaborate security routine. Electronic alarms and security devices were installed in her new home. She learnt to use a gun so that she could defend herself. A large, fierce, growling dog was brought to guard the house. Three trusted servants – a butler, a security guard and a personal maid – were constantly with her to guard her.

One fine day, she *was* actually kidnapped. The dog was ill; the security guard was out testing the alarms; the butler was making her tea and the maid was tied up by the intruders. What they had feared for her all their lives, actually came to pass!

Do not sow the seeds of fear in your consciousness; you will have to reap the harvest of your past fears and worries! And living in constant fear and anxiety over the possibility of something happening to you is a negative mental attitude, which will greatly increase, strengthen the chances of this nasty fear coming true!

When you feel you are unable to face a certain situation, incapable of handling a particular crisis, you create a mental picture of yourself cornered, up against a wall, powerless to cope. Sure enough, what you visualise will come to pass sooner or later.

On the other hand, if you optimistically and confidently picture yourself succeeding, with good things happening to you, your inner creative power will actually make these good things come true!

In the case of the Kentucky heiress, the intended victim was actually her husband, who was also a millionaire. On the day of the incident, the husband was in his office as usual, and the bungling kidnappers, having arrived in his house at the wrong time, simply decided to kidnap the wife because they did not want to leave empty-handed! Thus the young lady actually found herself in the dangerous situation that she had visualised in her imagination and feared all her life!

Your greatest protection against your fear is your own faith – and your attitude to life. To all my brothers and sisters, who are painting dire pictures of horrible, unspeakable things happening to your near and dear ones, I urge you – stop this negative visualisation here and now! Remember the wise counsellor who tells us: the worst things and events happen in the mind of man before they happen in the world of objective reality.

"People who experience true happiness are those who can face themselves, face reality, and face life bravely," the Wise One resumed. "They are mature people who have learnt from experience; they have learned to strike a balance between their inner and outer selves; they have conquered their emotions and mastered their weaknesses."

"The first step in eliminating fear from your consciousness is to understand and analyse yourself, so that you can control your own emotional reaction to the things you fear most. This will enable you to see clearly, logically, what your reaction should be, ideally. Analyse your state of mind; visualise yourself conquering your fear; paint a picture of yourself courageously facing situations – you will build up a thought structure, a thought pattern that will dispel your fears and make you a much happier person!

"I am told that trainee pilots who experience fear or nervousness in their initial flights, are often sent out on repeated 'sorties'. Taking to the air immediately after a nervous outburst does not worsen the condition of the young pilot; rather, it erases the memory of his earlier unpleasantness and helps him overcome his fears.

"When you realise that your fears and nameless terrors are nothing but groundless fancies, you deal a deathblow to the greatest joy-killer of them all – fear. In fact, you must destroy fear before fear kills your happiness.

"Truly, fear destroys your spirit of joy; it saps your will to live. The Persian poet Hafiz, expresses this in memorable words when he tells us:

Fear is the cheapest room in the house:
I'd like to see you in better living conditions.

"You have to face a tough interview; you have to take a critical medical diagnostic test; you have to undergo a medical procedure; you have to give a public speech; you have to meet your future mother-in-law for the first time; you are going to fly for the first time; you are going to compete in a major sports event...

"Don't be afraid of the outcome! Don't let fear stifle your spirit! Don't visualise failure – and replay a negative mental picture over and over again, before the event actually comes to pass. Shut out those negative thoughts and fears and dwell on the idea that with God's grace, everything will turn out fine!"

I nodded my assent. "Please go on," I begged the Wise One.

"Reflect on what we have discussed," he urged. "You will find your own answers."

A young cub reporter went to his boss, the distinguished journalist Arthur Brisbane, and said, "I have a serious problem. Whenever you send me out to interview a V.I.P. I'm afraid – I'm in awe of the person and I get nervous, and I can't make a success of the interview. What do you suggest? How can I get over this nervousness?"

"I used to have that trouble too, when I was your age," said Brisbane. "I'll tell you how I beat fear.

Whenever you are nervous, in awe of a person, just imagine how he looks in his night clothes."

You can conquer fear by laughing it away!

Fear of death is one of the most dreadful fears that people experience. I would like to share with you the beautiful experience I had when I sat with my mother during the last few hours of her earth-pilgrimage. I held her hands for comfort – hers and mine. I still remember her wonderful words to me. "My child, I'm not afraid to die," she said gently. "Half my friends and relatives are here on the earth. The remaining half are on the other side. Whether I live or die, I'm in good company!"

A wealthy businessman once said that of all the experiences of his life, he treasured one incident that thrilled him to the soul. As he came out of his bank in Mumbai and was about to signal for his chauffeur, a little girl came up to him. Timidly, she looked at his face and put her tiny hand into his great one and said, "Please Sir, I'm frightened of the traffic. Can you please take me safely across to the other side?"

Even as you conquer your own fears, help eliminate fear from the lives of others. This will bring joy into your life – and theirs.

A British publishing house brought out a volume of sermons – not by priests or ministers, but by laymen. The book was entitled: *If I Could Preach Only Once*. One of these sermons was by the distinguished writer, Gilbert Chesterton, who wrote: "If I had only one sermon to preach, it would be a sermon against fear."

Fear is the common enemy of us all. Its physical effects are bad enough: nervousness, acidity, indigestion, sleeplessness, to name only a few. But its mental and emotional effects are even more harmful!

Norman Vincent Peale tells us that fear is not unlike a ghost: it frightens you in the darkness, but you find that there is nothing to it when you get out into the light.

Dr. Peale tells us in one of his books that he was taking an away-from-it-all holiday in a mountain cabin in the North Woods. He found the solitude and silence healing and soothing, and went to bed peacefully on the first evening.

However, he was woken up by strange noises in the porch outside his bedroom window. He strained his ears to listen, and it sounded as if he could hear the scurrying footsteps of not *one* but several intruders. He broke out in a cold sweat. Newspaper accounts of murders and burglaries flashed before his mind's eye. "This is the end," he thought to himself. But he did not want to be attacked or killed! He was not prepared to die! He wanted to get out of there alive.

Unable to put up with the tension any longer, his despair actually lending him courage, he rushed to the door and threw it open, ready to confront whoever it was.

He expected to see a whole band of gangsters, armed with deadly weapons. Instead, all he saw was a little monkey, scurrying away into the darkness over the rustling autumn leaves on the ground.

Dr. Peale says that the incident taught him a great lesson: to confront his fears, and see them for what they really are.

A lot of people today, are afraid of old age. I don't just mean old people, who are afraid to lose their faculties, afraid that they would become a burden on the members of the family. I mean the comparatively 'younger' people, fifty or sixty years old, who rebel against the idea that they cannot eat and live and act as they used to in their youth. I am dismayed when I hear some middle aged people tell me that they would rather die young than live up to face old age.

Young people who feel this way have missed out on the true meaning of life. Their attitude to life is rather shallow and superficial.

To be afraid of old age is to invite misery and unhappiness; it is a refusal to accept the inevitable – nay, it is a stubborn denial of the true joys of life. When we grow old, we are preparing ourselves for old age and what is beyond; we acquire experience and maturity; we grow in wisdom and the capacity to help ourselves and others. How sad it is to wish to throw it all away and regress into the impossible, unattainable desire for permanent youth?

Life is what we make of it, wise men tell us – and this is true of any age. Happiness must be earned – whether you are twenty or seventy years old. Life offers deeper joys and satisfactions as your experience ripens into old age. This will change your whole outlook and your attitude to the future!

"I do not know about other times and other places," I said to the Wise One. "Here in this strange and unknown land with no one but your saintly presence for company, I just don't feel the need to fear anything! I feel I am in the Hands of God – I feel safe!"

The Wise One smiled. "That speaks for your faith and courage!" he said, graciously returning the compliment I paid him.

We ate the last of the gooseberries and got up to move. Walking out of the cave on the other side, I was startled to confront a steep, vertical climb up the hillock.

"Should we turn back?" I enquired anxiously. "Can we make it up this steep upward slope?"

The Wise One smiled and pointed to the side of the cave. "Here is your answer," he said.

My eyes widened in surprise at the next message that awaited me:

Be Assured That With God All Things Are Possible.

The 16th Secret of Happiness

Be Assured That With God All Things Are Possible

After that inspiring message, I needed no further persuasion. Carefully holding on to the rocky ledge and stepping slowly, we negotiated the steep slope, once again emerging out on to a pleasant and shady territory.

"A little patience, a little courage, and life looks much brighter, doesn't it?" I said to the Wise One, as we walked under an avenue of trees. The smell of eucalyptus seemed to waft in the air around us, and the atmosphere was pleasant and balmy. It was just the kind of environment which made one feel that God was in His Heaven – and all was right with the world.

Alas, not many of us feel that way, for the most part. I had met a young college student some time ago. "Life is like a maze, a riddle," he complained. "I feel confused, confounded. I see no way out of the perplexities and problems which baffle me again and again. I feel like a child who has lost his way in a huge fair. What do you think I should do?"

I said to him, "Was there a time in your life when you were really not confused or worried?"

"Yes," he laughed bitterly. "It was probably when I was one-and-a-half years old. And I hardly remember it now, but I know I had a happy, carefree childhood!"

"Exactly," I said to him. "If I become a child, I do not have to worry. The child trusts its mother and knows that the mother will always keep it safe from harm."

"You too, can become a child," I continued. "For that matter, so can all of us. All we need to do is hand ourselves over to the Lord – and He will take care of everything."

Our problems and difficulties begin the moment we cease to be 'children' in spirit – children of God. When I think I have grown up and I am able to look after myself, I am faced with trials and tribulations which overwhelm me again and again, and which rob me of the joy of living.

As we all know, the child is singularly free from worries and cares, for it knows, beyond a shadow of doubt, that the mother is there to provide for all its needs. As for the mother, she anticipates the needs of her children and provides for them well in advance. We who think we are independent only create for ourselves a situation in which we take on our burdens and struggle with them, suffering from accumulated stress and tension. We need to grow in the realisation that we have nothing to fear, when our Divine Mother is near. With God, all things are possible!

I encourage my friends to look upon God as their Mother. Who are we to define and limit God to the masculine form? God is all things to all of us. When we think of God as our Mother, we free ourselves from the pressure and insecurity of imagining that God is someone to fear and keep our distance from. When a child has fallen into a ditch and made himself filthy, he runs to his mother and tells her, "Ma, I've become filthy. Wash me and clean me!" There is no hesitation, no doubt in is mind that his mother will set everything right for him. This is how we must all feel about God.

"The strong alone can shoulder the burden!" sings a well-beloved poet of Sind. Our problem is that we do not realise our strength as children of God. We try to lift heavy loads on our weak shoulders, when we can so easily entrust them to One for whom all the burden of all the universe is as a feather's weight. Weighed down by burdens which we cannot and need not carry, we move through life, groaning in needless agony and pain. All we need to do is go within and make contact with the Mother Divine, and cast our cares at Her Lotus-feet. Then, we may well move along the pathways of life, singing as we go!

Such a child soul I met many years ago, when I was very young, and he was advanced in years: age had written wrinkles on his face – but the smile of God was in his eyes. And he looked fresh and radiant as a child!

I said to him in wonder, "Tell me, what is the secret of your unsullied freshness?"

He answered, "I always feel fresh, for I have no worries, no cares, no anxieties."

In sheer amazement, I asked him, "Do you mean to say you have never had to encounter any unpleasant experiences in your life?"

"Far from it," he answered gently. "The basket of my life has been filled again and again with bitter fruits. Failures and frustrations have come to me in and out of season. But they touch me not. For when I find myself in an unpleasant situation, I close my eyes and gaze at the calm, beauteous countenance of the Mother Divine. I say to her, "Ma! Mother! Here is one more burden for you to bear!" and then, I forget all about it. And all goes well with me – always!"

"The secret of a joyous life is living in contact with God – living in contact with our identity as children of God," the Wise One said.

"How may this contact be established?" I asked him softly.

He replied, "Be still to know God, and develop contact with Him! All around us is the sorry spectacle of restless men rushing in headlong speed, moving mechanically from one task to another, achieving nothing, not knowing where they are going. To such people, I appeal: Be still! Be still! Place your trust in God – with Whom all things are possible!

"To be still is not to be lazy or indolent. To be still is to be relaxed, restful, in the awareness that you are safe in God's hands. Do not take on too much. Do not rush through your daily tasks. Move calmly, slowly, quietly from one duty to another, pausing again and again, for a brief while, to pray and rest at the Mother's feet. Tell her, 'This work, O Mother Beloved, is Thine! May I be but an instrument of Thy Will Divine!'

"This aspiration has the power to transform even the most mundane work into a sacrament. This aspiration keeps the contact alive and makes our work a source of blessing and inspiration to all who cross our path. We will find too, that our efforts are crowned by success, and our lives will become joyous.

"You must remember, it is not the amount of work we do that matters, but the *way* we do it. It is not *what* we do, but *how* we do it that determines our success. There are many people who toil and drudge and slave, day after day, month after month, year after year: their work brings them no joy; it is as a shadow on the wall. It vanishes without leaving a trace. True work, abiding work, the work that may transform lives, is that which flows out of the centre of the heart, the centre of harmony and happiness, peace and joy.

Let God occupy this centre, and you are sure to find your work and life transformed . . ."

Dr. Alexis Carrel, the distinguished biologist and Nobel Laureate, tells us that trustful prayer is not only worship – but an invisible emanation of the faithful spirit, and as such, the most powerful form of energy that we can generate. "If you make a habit of sincere prayer," he tells us, "your life will be very noticeably and profoundly altered."

"Believe that with God, all things are possible!" the Wise One continued. "Many doctors have assured us that they have seen men, after all therapy had failed, lifted out of affliction and disease by the serene effect of faith. Faith, indeed, seems to overcome even the so-called 'laws of nature'. And the occasions on which prayer has dramatically done this have been termed 'miracles.'

"Are you one of those disgruntled people who feel that your life has had no miracles? Let me tell you, a constant, quieter miracle is taking place every day, every hour, every minute in the lives of men who have placed their trust in the Lord, and find His sustaining power flowing into their daily lives . . ."

There was a sister who was under tremendous pressure both at work and on the home front. The company she worked for was passing through a financial crisis, and was severely short-staffed, with each employee doing the work of two or three people. There was no question of complaining, because she knew she was lucky to have a job, while a dozen others like her had lost theirs. At home, she had an old mother to care for and a younger brother and sister to support. Sometimes, she said, she was overwhelmed by the thought of what lay ahead for her when she awoke in the morning.

I taught her a simple prayer. Every morning, as she awoke, I told her to hand her day over to the Lord and tell Him, "Lord, this day is Thine, and all the work I do, I offer to You. I know I cannot carry the load myself. I hand my life over to You. I beg You to get everything done for me."

She found a miraculous change in her life. Everything seemed to fall into place; her burdens seemed to lift of their own accord. Everything seemed – just more manageable!

"Trust in the Lord," the Wise One resumed. "In faith, you achieve harmony of body, mind and spirit which gives unshakeable strength to your weakest efforts. Did not Jesus say, 'Ask and it shall be given to you?' True, prayer cannot bring the dead back to life, or wipe away pain and suffering. But prayer, like radium, is a source of luminous energy that can light up our lives.

"As human beings, we seek to augment our finite energy by linking ourselves to God, who is the source of infinite energy. His power is inexhaustible, and He is ready to give some of it to us so that we may do what we have to do. Just by asking for His help, our deficiencies are set right and we are restored, rejuvenated and strengthened. Here is a story for you..."

A peasant stood at the temple, gazing at the Lord for a long time. Other people came, offered their prayers and went away. But he just stood there, gazing at the beauteous face of the deity.

"Are you waiting for something?" they asked him.

"No," he replied. "I am looking at Him and He is looking at me!"

We should not only pray that God must remember us, but that we should always remember Him. Therefore has it been said that prayer is practising the presence of God.

Prayer is man's attempt to reach out to God, to commune with Him in devotion, in the realisation that He is the source of all wisdom, truth, beauty and strength. He is also the Father and Mother of all of us. When we commune with Him in this awareness, we feel a transformation in our mind, body and soul, which touches our lives for the better. And remember, you cannot pray for a single moment without achieving something good out of it!

By myself, I can do nothing: that is the very first principle of spiritual life. The second principle is – He that is within you is greater than he that is outside. To us, external forces appear to be strong and powerful. But they are nothing compared to that which is within you – the Lord, who is seated in the throne of your heart, for whom everything is possible.

Significant are the words of the great German mystic, Meister Eckhart: "Where creature stops, there God begins. All God wants of thee is to go out of thyself in respect of thy creatureliness and let God be the God-in-thee."

"Let God take over our lives," the Wise One urged, "for He makes the impossible possible!

"All the time, while we are attending to our daily work, let out minds and hearts be fixed on God. Let the ship of the body move hither and thither, attend to its multifarious duties, but let the needle of the heart's compass be ever directed towards God. 'For Thy sake O Lord!' Let this be the *mantra* of our life – and we will see that true happiness fills our lives."

I recalled the words of Voltaire, who had said, "If God did not exist, it would be necessary to invent Him."

Let us invent God in our lives! Let us imagine He is always there for us. But let us not make God our servant or store-keeper, who is supposed to procure everything we want for us. We cannot expect God to carry out *our* will! For it is only when we submit to God's Will that harmony and order will be restored to our lives.

What we need is not this, that or any other thing. What we require is Divine adjustment. When we focus our mind on God, learn to live in His presence and dedicate ourselves and our actions to Him, we break the chains of bondage and make ourselves free!

Absorbed as we are in the pursuit of the shadow-shapes of wealth and pleasure and power, we will do well to pause and ask ourselves the question: "What is the goal of life?" The answer will come to you – the goal is God! Wealth and possessions, pleasure and power, cannot really bring us happiness, unless we rest our hopes in Him.

There are some people who claim that they do not believe in God – however, they do acknowledge that there is a supernatural power that is above us: and "God" is the word that the rest of us use to describe this Supernatural Power.

I often say that everyone prays at one time or another in his life. There is not a soul living on this earth, who at one time or another, finding himself in a difficult situation, at a dead end, as it were, has not cried out, "I am unable to cope with this situation. Is there none to help me?" What is this if not a prayer! It is an appeal to the Power over and above us. We recognise that when all else fails us, He will not fail us.

"God is always with everyone," said the Wise One softly. "but alas, everyone is not always with God..."

During the days of the American Civil War, a woman said to Abraham Lincoln, "I am sure God is on our side!" Lincoln said to her, "What is more important is whether we are on the side of God."

God is always with us – but we are not always with Him. The very fact that we carry our burdens of worry and anxiety on our weak shoulders is testimony to the fact that we are not with God or else, we would gladly hand all our burdens over to Him and rest in the awareness that He will take care of everything for us.

A man of God was walking out with a barber. As they passed through a poor, slum area, the barber protested loudly, "Tell me *swamiji*, where is your God? Look, look at the poverty, misery and suffering all around us. What is He doing? Why does He permit all this? Where is He?"

The man of God remained silent.

Soon thereafter, they passed by a man with dishevelled hair and an unshaven beard. Pointing to him, the holy man asked the barber, "Where were you, my friend? Why are you permitting such people to walk about, unshaven, unkempt? Look at this man's hair and beard!"

"But this man has not gone to a barber," exclaimed the man. "Let him only come to me, and I can do the rest."

And the holy man said to him gently, "So it is with us. It is only if we go to Him that He can do anything for us. The pity of it is, we choose not to go to Him!"

Young people often ask me, "Dada, should we not feel bad to go to God for all our petty needs and problems? Are such prayers really acceptable to Him?"

My answer to them is: all God wants of us is that we go to Him. In the measure in which we think of approaching Him, our level of consciousness rises. This is the elevating power of communion with God. Start with praying for whatever you desire. You will find that a stage will come when you desire nothing but Him!

As for being ashamed to ask God for things – the option is either to ask worldly sources, or to go directly to God, who is our father, mother, our true parent. Why should we hesitate to ask anything from our father or mother? To whom else can a child turn?

"The one lesson we all need to learn is – utter dependence upon God," said the Wise One. "Everything else will follow. We must turn to God for every little thing we need – until, one blessed day, we find that we need nothing: our one and only need is God! Then we make the great discovery that all that we need is already provided for. Before the need arises, it is already fulfilled. Everything comes to pass at the right time, in the right way. One finds that he lives like a king. When a king moves out, everything is prepared for him, well in advance. He does not have to ask for anything. All his needs are anticipated and provided for.

"'Ye are Kings!' we are told. 'Why wander ye like the King's children, who starved and were clothed in rags, because they were unaware of their Royal parentage?'"

"This is indeed, the most inspiring and uplifting idea," I exclaimed. "What could be more powerful than the idea that we are God's children, and that we can always call upon Him for all that we need?"

We had reached the end of the avenue, and we saw the ruin of a great big mansion ahead of us.

"Talk of the ruin wrought by time!" I sighed. "This must have been a magnificient palace once upon a time. Look at it now… crumbled to ruins!"

We walked about the ruins silently. I felt depressed, all of a sudden.

"If this is what our life and work must eventually come to, what is the point of human endeavour?" I asked the Wise One. "What is the point of this entire realm of happiness, which is itself a geographical ruin? If this is what our past is reduced to, what of the future?"

It was the Wise One who pointed out the 17th secret that awaited me, engraved on an archway:

If You Wish To Be Happy, Learn To Walk With God Today And Trust Him For The Morrow!

The 17th Secret of Happiness

If You Wish To Be Happy, Learn To Walk With God Today And Trust Him For The Morrow!

"This time, I'd like to hear what *you* have to say on this concept," the Wise One said.

"Sufficient unto the day is the evil thereof, Jesus Christ says in the Bible," I began. "Instead of taking life one day at a time, people constantly worry about the future. Here are the words of a beautiful song which I heard the other day:

> One day at a time, sweet Jesus,
> Is all I'm asking from you:
> To give me the strength to do every time
> What I have to do.
> Yesterday's gone, sweet Jesus,
> Tomorrow may never be mine:
> Lord love me today, show me the way
> One day at a time.

"One day at a time – that's how we should take life's problems and worries," the Wise One concurred. "Please do understand – I'm not asking people 'to live as if there's no tomorrow' – that is the attitude adopted by hedonistic philosophers who urged their followers to 'seize the day' and enjoy all the pleasures of life, as they might not be alive tomorrow.

"What I advocate is something different, and I'm appealing especially to chronic worriers who ruin their *todays* by regretting their *yesterdays* and being afraid of their *tomorrows*. To them I say, what does worry do for you? It may not solve tomorrow's problems, but it will certainly empty *today* of its energy, strength, joy and zest for living..."

I thought of Charles Kingsley who said, "Be not anxious about tomorrow. Do today's duty, fight today's temptations and do not weaken and distract yourself by looking forward to things which are yet to occur." It is the same advice given to us in the modern song: *Do not trouble trouble, until trouble troubles you!*

A brother once came to me and said, "Teach me the best way to live! Give me a *mantra* that will encapsulate the art of true living."

I said to him, "The art of true living is – walk with God today and trust Him for the morrow!"

A wise man lay on his deathbed, and wished to pass on the benefit of his experience to his sons. "My dear children," he said to them, "During my long life I have fought a great many troubles, most of which never happened!"

The trouble with us is we try to handle *all* of life at once: we think of it as a whole – and we worry about all of it, instead of living one day at a time.

"I am overwhelmed by constant anxiety," a sister said to me.

"What is it that you worry about?" I asked her.

"I'm worried about my daughter, who is expecting a baby," she began. "Also, I'm anxious to find a suitable girl for my only son."

"If that is your......." I began.

"That's not all," she interrupted. "I have only just begun."

"Do go on," I sighed.

"I'm worried about my husband's blood pressure," she continued. "And I'm constantly anxious about my old mother who lives all alone in the village. And I'm on edge at my workplace. I don't think my boss appreciates my work. And I'm dreadfully worried about the future! What will become of our savings with inflation rising so high, and interest rates falling constantly..."

I was reminded of the words of Seneca: "He grieves more than is necessary, who grieves *before* it is necessary."

Many people complain of stress, tension and nervous exhaustion. I am inclined to think that this is seldom the result of present trouble or work, but of trouble or work *anticipated*. It comes with the constant strain of looking ahead and climbing mountains before we ever reach the foothills.

"I'm so unhappy and worried this morning," one woman complained to another.

"What is it?" asked her friend sympathetically.

"I was worrying about something last night," said the woman, "and now I can't, for the life of me, remember what it was."

It is said that the first experimental steam engines actually wasted ninety percent of the energy of the coal they used. When the electric dynamo was designed, it was said to utilise ninety percent of the power, with the wastage just reduced to ten percent. When we worry constantly, we too, fritter away all our energy in fretting, fuming, in scolding and complaining.

It is in *our* hands to convert all our energy into power, vitality and the sunshine of good cheer!

One hundred and fifty years ago, Emerson said, "I question if care and doubt ever wrote their names so legibly on the faces of any other population...old age, in our society, begins in the nursery."

Scientists and medical researchers, who studied the physical effect of worry, have found that worry "works irreparable injury through certain cells of brain life." The insistent habit of worrying is like the constant action of a hammer beating continually upon the brain cells.

"It is not the work that kills men," says a distinguished thinker. "It is worry. Work is healthy; you can hardly put more on a man than he can bear.

But worry is like rust upon the blade. It is not movement that destroys the machinery, but friction."

The Old Testament is full of beautiful poetry; much of it was actually prescribed for study in the Literature Honours classes in the good old days. One of my favourite poetic passages is the 23rd Psalm. I'm sure it is well known to all of you. Let me have the pleasure of going over its inspiring words with you:

> The Lord is my shepherd, I shall not want.
> He brings me to lie down in green pastures
> He leads me beside still waters
> He restores my soul…
> Though I walk through the valley of the shadow of death
> I will fear no evil, for You are with me…
> Surely goodness and mercy shall follow me all the days of my life.
> And I will dwell in the house of the Lord forever.

Many of us take life far too seriously. Aphorisms like *life is a struggle; life is a battle; life is a test*, etc., ideas of struggling, suffering, pain and tears dominate our thinking, and we end up with our own pet dictums: *life is a tragedy; life is a vale of tears* and so on.

While hard work is a virtue, pain and struggle are not necessary to attain happiness and peace. God is Love; God is Mercy; God is Compassion. Why would He want us to suffer and cry and be anxious? I am sure struggle and worry is not what He intended for His children. It was a wise man who said, "God established peace, and fear invented struggle."

We are told that in the days preceding his historic voyage to the new world, Columbus spent a lot of time in prayer. Not content with his own prayers, he decided to go to a convent in Genoa, his native city, to meet the nuns there and request for their support.

A kind and gentle nun answered the door when he rang the bell.

"Sister, I am undertaking a long voyage," Columbus said to her earnestly. "I do not know if God will bless my venture. I have come to ask for your prayers, for I know you must be on good terms with God."

"But Sir," said the nun calmly, "you really do not need me. If you dedicate your venture to God and do your part well, God will surely do His."

Whenever I talk to people I catalogue the ailments that afflict modern man due to his constant tendency to worry; headaches, backaches, insomnia, stress, panic, nervousness, lack of appetite and anxiety neurosis!

People afflicted with these conditions rush to their doctors for help. They swallow antacids, painkillers and tranquilisers by the dozen. But ask them if these drugs have alleviated their worry, and brought them happiness – and you will find them bowing their heads in despair.

The way to seek freedom from worry is not through drugs – but by turning to God in prayer.

Today we have enough scientists, engineers, technicians and executives; but we do not have enough people who can handle life in a relaxed and easy manner. We have enough politicians, bureaucrats and psychoanalysts – but not enough prayer-specialists.

Allow yourself to feel God's greatness and mercy in all that happens to you. Flow along with the current of the Divine Will – and you will be able to conquer your worries, lighten your burdens, and achieve peace and joy in life.

A poor woman appealed to the Sultan of Turkey, asking for compensation for the loss of all her worldly goods.

"How did you lose your money?" the Sultan asked her.

"I was asleep one night, when the robbers looted my house," she replied.

"You fell asleep, and you were looted," said the Sultan. "How then am I responsible?"

"I fell asleep in the secure feeling that *you* were awake," said the woman, "and that you would protect me."

The Sultan was so pleased with her trust that he made sure she was adequately compensated.

The government and its law enforcement agencies are supposed to be on call twenty-four hours a day for the protection of the nation and the people. But we all know they slip up sometimes.

God never fails us. God never sleeps. He never ever lets us down. How blessed we are to have Him always available for us!

God wants us to be happy. True, there are challenges to face and overcome; there is hard work to be put in, before we can achieve success. After all, the world cannot be a happy place if everything is free and easy!

An eminent physician once told a spiritual teacher, "Teach your people not to worry, but to trust God and have faith – and you will keep many of them out of hospitals and away from doctors."

I love to narrate to my friends this significant incident from the life of Lloyd George. He was playing golf with a friend, and they had to go through a pasture gate. The friend, who was following Lloyd George, left the gate open. Seeing this, the Prime Minister went back and closed it himself. He remarked to his friend, "I have always made it a practice to close a gate when I have passed through it."

I think it is an excellent idea for those of us who wish to stop worrying – and reclaim our happiness. Shut the gate! Keep it shut so that your worries do not trail you wherever you go.

There may be some of you facing serious, real problems – economic or social. You may be a businessman who has had to meet a severe financial loss; you may be a salaried worker who suddenly finds himself without a job. Are not these genuine causes for concern, you may ask me.

Yes – they are causes for concern. But let me also add, if you wish to deal with the situation effectively, you must have a clean, calm, uncluttered mind. Only a cool, analytical, objective approach will help you solve the problem and surmount it successfully.

There are other social, situational problems which we face, created by what we often refer to as, "circumstances beyond our control." You have an important business meeting with a valued client – and a *bandh* is declared in the city, and you cannot attend the meeting. You have to fly across the country to finalise a deal – and all flights out of your city are cancelled due to fog. You must realise in such situations, that worry cannot correct these events. Worry will not clear the fog, improve the weather or change the minds of people who are on strike. You will need to tackle the situation with self-control and self-discipline.

Thus far, I have dealt with the first half of my proposition – that worrying is futile; that it only leads to unhappiness. Here is the point at which I offer you the healthy alternative – trust in God.

Trust in God! Leave your cares and worries in His safe hands. Let Him take care of your problems. Why do you have to struggle all alone, when He is with you?

Therefore, I urge my friends to adopt the one line *mantra: I am not alone, God is with me.*

A villager was travelling by train for the very first time in his life. He was told he could carry forty kgs. of luggage with him. But he had baggage, weighing fifty kgs. He decided that he would put forty kgs. of luggage on the floor of the compartment and carry the excess ten kgs. on his head!

As the TTE came along, he was astonished to see the man balancing a suitcase on his head. "Why don't you put that down, my friend?" he asked the villager.

The villager explained that he had excess baggage. "I know I'm not allowed to bring in more than twenty kgs. – so I'm carrying the rest myself!"

We may laugh at his ignorance – but many of us are pretty much like the villager. We try to carry the load ourselves, instead of surrendering ourselves into His care!

If only you consider your situation analytically, you will realise that ultimately, all the burden is borne by the Lord – not merely the burden of our individual lives, the lives of the nations, not merely the burden of the earth or the solar systems, but the burden of all the universes, the galaxies and the nebulae, huge stellar systems in the making – the entire burden is ultimately borne by the Lord. How foolish of us then, to insist on carrying our little burdens on our own weak shoulders!

We pray everyday, uttering the beautiful words:

Tum hi ho Mata,
Pita tum hi ho,
Tum hi ho Bandhu
Sakha tum hi ho.

"Thou art my Father, Thou art my Mother, Thou art my Brother and my Friend!" we proclaim. We claim that we are His children – but do we live as His children? Do we claim our rightful heritage as His children? Do we trust Him as a child would implicitly trust its mother?

Some years ago, a historian called Franklin Baumer, published a book called *Main Currents Of Western Thought*. In this book, he refers to the modern age as an "age of anxiety." Wherever you turn, you find people who are oppressed by worry and anxiety.

The ironic thing, as I said earlier, is that we live in an age in which our material comforts have grown beyond our imagination – but none of this material wealth has given us joy or peace of mind.

The distinguished Swiss psychiatrist, Carl Jung, diagnosed the illness of the present age as alienation from God. Man has cut himself off from God, who is the ultimate source and sustainer of all life. And man cannot live a healthy, happy life – physically, mentally, emotionally, spiritually – until he turns back to God. The more we turn away from God, the more we shall continue to wander in anxiety and unhappiness – and the more restless we shall become.

Trust in God! Turn back to Him! Hand your troubles over to Him in a spirit of complete and utter surrender. Develop faith in His infinite love and mercy.

What is faith? Faith is not blind, as some 'rationalists' would claim. Faith is *seeing* with the eyes of the heart. But alas, with many of us, the eyes of the heart are closed. When we open these eyes, we will see that all that has happened has happened for the best, all that is happening is happening for the best, and all that will happen will happen for the best. There is a meaning of mercy in all that happens. God has a plan for everyone of us, and there is Divine purpose in every little thing that happens to us. The great American poet, Whittier, said, "When faith is lost…the man is dead!"

Sarah Adams had dreamed of becoming a great actress since the days of her childhood. She had worked, studied and struggled to achieve that goal – and she had succeeded too! She was acclaimed as a great actress when she performed as Lady Macbeth, and everyone was certain that a successful career on the stage lay ahead of her.

Alas, her triumph was short-lived. A mysterious, crippling illness afflicted her, and she became invalid, confined to her bed. In her misery, her mind turned Godwards, and she composed the beautiful song, "Nearer my God, to Thee!"

"Nearer my God, to Thee," has today become one of the world's best loved hymns. It gives us the assurance that troubles, worries and sufferings are only meant to take us closer to Him:

> Though like the wanderer
> The sun has gone down,
> Darkness be over me,
> My rest a stone,
> Yet in my dreams I'd be
> Nearer to Thee!

"The sovereign cure for worry is prayer," said William James. "Faith," he asserts, "is one of the forces by which men live, and the total absence of it means collapse."

I had been talking rapidly, sharing my thoughts with the Wise One.

"It's wonderful to hear you," he said. "Do go on!"

"But it's your insights I wish to learn," I demurred.

"You are gathering insights every moment you are here," he said. "Do go on . . ."

The one lesson we all need to learn is – utter dependence on God! Everything else will follow. To surrender is to seek refuge, to trust in the Lord fully, completely, entirely. It is to know that He is the One Light that shines and shines and ever shines. Though the storms howl and the darkness grows deeper, His Light shines on! He is the Creator and the Nourisher of all that is, He is the Deliverer from whom all evils flee. He is nearer to us than our own heartbeats, and closer than our breathing. He is sufficient as a friend, sufficient as a helper. There is not a corner too remote for His help to reach us!

The night was dark and cloudy. Strange howls and eerie noises could be heard in the distance. Every rustle in the undergrowth sent a chill down one's spine. All alone, a weary traveller was crossing a thick forest.

"Keep moving as quickly as you can," he had been warned. "Be on your guard every second. Whatever you do, don't fall asleep, for the forest is full of man-eaters who will be out to get your blood."

The man was near the point of utter exhaustion. He felt he could not take a step further. He sank to the ground and prayed: "Lord, I cannot keep awake any longer. You are awake all the time. Is it necessary for both of us to be awake?"

So saying he fell into a deep slumber.

When he awoke, daylight was bright around him. It was long past dawn, and he saw a man standing guard next to him, armed with a gun.

"Who are you, sir?" asked the traveller in surprise. "How is it that you are here in this obscure corner of the forest, patrolling the clearing where I have slept?"

"I was passing through the forest late last night, when I came upon you, sleeping soundly," the stranger replied. "It seemed to me that you, perhaps, were unaware of the danger of this place. So I decided to stop here and keep watch while you slept!"

"All gratitude to God!" exclaimed the traveller. "How true it is that He guides us and guards us wherever we are, whatever we do!"

There were two poor sisters – humble souls with deep devotion and faith – who regularly attended Sadhu Vaswani's *satsang* in Pune.

Those were the days in the early fifties when many Sindhis in Pune did not have homes of their own. Many of them had left behind everything they possessed, back home in the land of their birth – Sind. The Partition had made them homeless, and many of them were still struggling to lay down new roots in the land of their adoption.

The two sisters lived in a one room tenement rented out to them by a man, who was himself, a tenant of the building. They were sub-tenants, who had no legal rights over their accommodation.

One day, their landlord told them unexpectedly, that they would have to vacate their room within three months. His son, who lived abroad, would be returning home, and the family would need the extra room occupied by the sisters.

"I am giving you three months' notice," the man told them. "Try and find a suitable accommodation within that period."

The brothers and sisters in the *satsang* came to know about this, "Where will you go after three months?" they asked the two sisters anxiously.

"Sadhu Vaswani always tells us that God will provide for us," they replied. "We will go and stay wherever God takes us."

In the meanwhile, they continued to look for alternative accommodation. But nothing suitable could be found! The few places that were available for rent were very expensive – and beyond their means.

The three-month period came to an end. They had to vacate the room – and did not have a place to go to! Their landlord had warned them to pack all their possessions, and a bullock cart had been summoned to take them and their belongings away.

"Where are you going?" the neighbours asked them.

"Wherever God take us," replied the sisters.

The cart was loaded; the driver asked the same question, "Where to?"

Wonderful things happen to people who have faith. Just as they were about to leave, a lady passed by. She was a regular member of the *satsang*, and she recognised her fellow devotees.

"Where will you go now?" she asked them now.

"Wherever God takes us," they replied.

"Supposing God takes you to my house?" asked the lady.

"Gladly shall we come," they said.

The lady took them with her. "I am going abroad," she told them, "I shall be away for two years, I need some reliable persons to stay and look after my house while I'm away. Can you both do it for me?"

This has always been the mark of the faithful – absolute trust in God!

A little girl lived with her grandparents in their huge bungalow. The girl's study was upstairs, while the bedrooms were on the ground floor. Often in the evenings, while the old people were relaxing, the grandchild would ask one of them to go up with her to the study, to fetch a book or a game or her school work.

"Why don't you go up yourself, my dear?" the grandmother would cajole her. "You know Nana and Nani are old and weak."

"But I'm scared to go up the stairs alone," the girl would protest.

One day, the grandmother had a brilliant idea. Taking the child to the foot of the staircase, the lady said to her, 'Now call out to Sri Krishna and ask Him to go up with you. He will go with you, and you will have nothing to fear."

"Will He really come with me if I ask Him?" the child demanded to know.

"I assure you He will," said the grandmother. "Now call Him and go up with Him while I watch you from here."

"Alright," said the little girl, taking a deep breath. "Krishna, please go up the stairs with me, for I'm scared to go up alone."

And she ran up the staircase with determination. From the first landing, she turned back and said to her grandmother, with delight, "See Nani, He is with me, and I'm not scared!"

"I told you so," said the grandmother. "Now go on. Climb the rest of the stairs. He is with you."

The girl reached the top of the stairs in no time and turned round to tell her grandmother, "Nani, I've reached the top!" Then she solemnly turned sideways to say, "All right Krishna, Thank you! You can go now."

We may laugh at the little girl, but we would do well to remember that with or without our call, with or without our dismissal, He is always with us, guarding us, guiding us, ever protecting us.

A Christian pastor has suggested that some of the famous hymns sung by the devout in the church, should actually be rewritten to reflect the truth of how people feel. Thus "Just as I am" should be, "Just as I pretend to be." "Oh how I love Jesus," should become "Oh how I like Jesus" and "He is everything to me," should be, "He is quite a bit to me."

"Let us make the original titles of these hymns come true for us," he urges. "Let us really love the Lord as we are, and surrender to His care."

For those of you who worry constantly, let me repeat Lloyd George's precept: Shut the gate and keep it shut so that worries do not follow you.

There are women who make it a practice to look under their beds every night before they go to sleep – making sure that there are no burglars hidden there. I cannot imagine what they would do if they really found one there!

I often ask my friends to write down their worries in two columns on a piece of paper – those that have happened, and those that are yet to happen. If you do this, you will find that the latter far outnumber the former. In other words, you are worrying about something that exists only in your imagination.

Norman Vincent Peale tells us about his friend who was a very happy man – even though he had met several adversities in his life. This man once wrote a poem which Peale recommends highly to all of us:

> Better never trouble trouble
> Until trouble troubles you,
> For you're sure to make your trouble
> Double trouble when you do.
> And your trouble, like a bubble
> That you're troubling about
> May be nothing but a cipher
> With the rim rubbed out.

What about real, financial problems, you may ask. What about businessmen who face failure and loss?

Yes, you have to face these problems head on – but you must take them on with a clean head, not one that is clouded and flustered with worry. Besides, worry is useless in such circumstances, and cannot really correct the problem. So why waste time worrying?

I realised that I had been talking continuously, and the Wise One had been listening to me, with rapt attention.

"Please share your wisdom with me," I pleaded.

"Walk with God today and trust Him for the morrow!" he began. "This is the priceless secret of true peace and lasting joy. Faith and trust are the twin powers that can banish worry from your life. This is not blind faith that I'm talking about – it is strong, reasoned, well-founded faith in God's goodness and care. It is the positive power that enables you to stand up and fight, and overcome your problems successfully. Remember, I said, '*Walk* with God'; *not* 'Sit back and wait for God to do something'!

"Lazy people do *not* deserve God's help! But if you put in your best efforts and leave the rest to the Lord, I'm sure He will fulfil His part of the deal.

"When you place your trust in the Lord, when you surrender utterly and completely to His Divine Will, you will find wonderful things happen in your life! Here is a Zen story . . ."

There was a disciple, who was asking his master about developing the right attitude to life and work.

"How can I acquire discipline in my search for truth?"

"You must exercise yourself."

"How may I exercise myself?"

"You must eat when you are hungry; you must sleep when you are tired."

"But..." the disciple stammered. "That's what everyone does. Do you mean to say that is sufficient to exercise oneself to acquire discipline?"

"But that is exactly what most people do *not* do!" the master asserted. "When they eat, they are worrying about one hundred things. When they sleep, they dream of one thousand things. This is not at all the kind of exercise I meant!"

"The Zen master in fact, had uttered a great truth," the Wise One continued. "Most of us are unable to engage ourselves fully even in the routine task of everyday life. The reason? *We do not live in the present.* We are drowning in the regrets and disappointments of the past – or losing our balance in vague imaginative anxieties about the future. What we fail to realise is that life would be so much more satisfying and meaningful, and we ourselves would be happier and more peaceful if we learn to live in the present – walking with God today and trusting Him for the morrow.

"As long as we are worrying about the future, we cannot really enjoy the present. Our life may be filled with loving family and friends; we may be blessed with a worthwhile career; our table may be laid with the best food – but if we do not live in the present, we can enjoy none of these things!

"Man can never be happy, he cannot enjoy the great gift that is life, he cannot enjoy the pleasures of the present, the here and the *now*, unless he reposes his faith and trust in the Lord... Here is another story of mine..."

A rich and famous movie star came to say good night to her little daughter who was being tucked in bed by a governess.

The little girl kissed her mother and said brightly, "Mommy, I feel like a queen!"

"You *are* a queen, honey," laughed the mother. "Why, there's nothing in the world that your Mommy will not give you!"

"*That's* not what I meant," said the child. "I meant that God loves me and I love God!"

When God loves us and cares for us, how can we lack anything? When He is there to take care of us and protect us, why should we take worries on our own poor heads?

A tall and strong father was carrying his son on one arm, and a large bag of shopping on the other. His three year old son said to him, "Daddy, you are carrying me *and* the shopping bag. Why don't you let *me* carry the bag? That will relieve you a bit, won't it?"

You may laugh, but you are also like this child, if you insist on carrying your own bag of worries when your Divine Father is actually supporting you and all the universe!

"One mark of the truly happy man," the Wise One remarked, "is that he is *not* worried about tomorrow. He is singularly free from all fear of the future. *Who will look after me when I am old? How will I meet my daily needs when I retire?* Such thoughts do not cloud his mind. For him it is enough that God *is! He* will provide! It is *His* responsibility to take care of us and look after all our needs.

"Have you seen children at play? Do they seem at all worried where their lunch is going to come from? For them it is enough to know that their mother is there – and she will provide for them at the right time."

Of Guru Amardas, we are told that every evening, he gave away all that he had, keeping not a grain of corn for the morrow, not even a copper coin in his purse. Before night fell, he emptied his store of provisions – even drained the pitchers dry!

"The morrow will take care of itself!" he said to his disciples who were amazed by his strange behaviour. And the morrow did take care of itself!

"Ah," you might say, "the Guru was an ascetic. It is easy for the likes of him to live from day to day..."

Let me tell you, the Guru was a family man with wife and children. Each and everyday, he had a *langar* (fellowship meal) at which many pilgrims and passers-by ate their fill. He ran a common kitchen which cooked food for them all! But his faith in the Lord was unshakable. And the Lord never failed him.

Let me remind you of that beautiful passage in the Bible where Jesus exhorts us to walk with God today and trust Him for the morrow.

Once, pointing to a procession of ants, he said to his disciples, "Ye of little faith! Look at the ants: who gives them their daily food?"

And one of the disciples said, "Master, they need so little!"

"Then look at the birds," said Jesus. "They toil not, nor do they save for the morrow. Yet they get their daily food and are happy!"

And the disciple said, "Master, birds have wings with which they fly and pluck fruits from trees!"

"And what about the wild beasts?" Jesus asked. "How fat they are! They have no wings. Yet they too, get their daily food!"

When you feel that He is taking care of your needs, you cease to worry! You do not have to plan in advance for unforeseen eventualities. You do not have to worry about calamities. You simply allow the Divine Plan to unfold. You claim nothing; you ask nothing; you seek nothing; you plan nothing. You simply become a channel for the Divine Plan to flow through.

How many of us are capable of such faith and trust?

Dusk was falling now, and the landscape was tinged with a golden yellow light.

"I sometimes feel that the evening sun is a brilliant alchemist," I said to the Wise One. "See how he is turning everything into gold!"

"Very true," the Wise One agreed. But how many people care to look at the golden sunset and rejoice in its beauty? They are counting their cash instead..."

"There are so many things in life more important than money," I said earnestly. "The list of things that money *can't* buy is virtually endless..."

The Wise One smiled and pointed to a stone seat by the wayside. On the seat were inscribed the words:

Realise That Success Is Not Measured By Material Things Alone.

The 18th Secret of Happiness

Realise That Success Is Not Measured By Material Things Alone

We sat on the stone bench to watch the setting sun – a million dollar sight, offered to us absolutely free!

"Many of us are apt to equate happiness and success with money, material wealth and possessions," the Wise One remarked. "This is sheer ignorance. You cannot be happy just because you live in a mansion or a penthouse apartment. You cannot achieve peace and inner harmony just because you drive a Mercedes or a BMW. You cannot be considered 'successful' just because you are a millionaire.

"Supposing you were told, 'Today is the last day of your life. Make a list of all the things that you feel you have accomplished, all the things that have made you feel truly happy': what are the things you would put down in that list, knowing that you have only hours left to live?

"I'm certain that your car, bungalow and bank account will find no place on the list. What you are sure to put on it would be the most fundamental elements of a truly happy life – your love for God, the love and respect you have earned from your near and dear ones, the sunshine you brought into people's lives by your warmth, affection and compassion, the kindness you have received from your friends and the love and kindness *you* have shown to other people."

I nodded my agreement. I have always thought that happiness is an *inner* quality!

It was Abraham Lincoln who said, "Most folks are about as happy as they make up their minds to be." And since happiness gives meaning and purpose to life, we must know where to find it. All the world's greatest philosophers agree on this point: true happiness stems from *within* us, from a way of thinking about life. This is the most enduring, most agreed upon truth about happiness: if the principles of contentment and satisfaction are not within us, no material success, no pleasure or possession can make us truly happy.

This significant truth is beautifully brought out in a play called *The Blue Bird* written by the distinguished dramatist, Maeterlinck. Tyltyl and Mytyl are the children of a woodcutter. They set out in search of happiness, travelling far and wide to seek it. When they return home, they find it right inside their home. "We went so far," they exclaim, "and it was here all the time!"

Maeterlinck wishes to tell us that it is not necessary to search for happiness in far-off places outside ourselves. Happiness is right within your heart and soul. It is around and about you. Unless you realise this truth, your quest for happiness will be in vain.

Marcus Aurelius, the great Roman thinker, says the same thing. "Very little is needed to make a happy life," he writes in his *Meditations*. "It is all within yourself, in your way of thinking."

William Lyon Phelps was a distinguished writer and critic, as well as a popular Professor at Yale University. He had inspired and guided hundreds of students during his long and distinguished career. When he was asked to write a message of guidance and inspiration for the American people, he asserted: "The principle of happiness is like the principle of virtue: it should not be dependent on things, but be a part of your personality."

When Professor Phelps had been a young student, he had drawn inspiration from the words of President Timothy Dwight who had visited his college and addressed the students. Dwight had told them emphatically: "The happiest person is the person who thinks the most interesting thoughts."

This was what he taught his students too. Real happiness cannot come from external things, he told them. The only lasting happiness that you will experience is that which springs from your inner thoughts and emotions. Therefore, he urged them, cultivate your mind. For an empty mind seeks mere pleasure as a substitute for happiness. It is essential, he said, to "live inside a mind with attractive and interesting pictures on the walls."

The happiest people are not the ones who make money, buy property and own stocks. The happiest people are those who cultivate their minds and think interesting thoughts.

Leela was a hardworking 'go-getting' executive in an advertising company. Barely five years after her MBA she had risen to be a promising young star in her agency. She had received three promotions and five hefty increments and was inching her way to the top of the agency. The salary she received, the perks given to her and the lifestyle she enjoyed were all fantastic – impelling her to work harder and harder. She even went to the office on Sundays, and brought her work home in her laptop every weekday. She had ambitious plans – a flat of her own; a trip round the world; the best clothes that money could buy; and sooner or later, her own advertising agency...

When she was twenty-eight years old, Leela collapsed in the office with nervous exhaustion. She had to be hospitalised for two weeks, and afterwards advised complete rest for three months.

She was forced to re-think about her life, re-examine her priorities. During her convalescence, her parents, brothers and best friends spent a lot of time with her – she *saw* them and *spent time* with them for the first time since she had started working. She realised the little pleasures that she had missed out on – reading good books, talking to her loved ones, watching the sunset from her balcony and just 'pottering' about the house. She decided that she already possessed very many 'things' she valued highly and that she would not drive herself too hard, chasing more increments, perks and promotions.

Driving a Mercedes or a BMW does not make you a better person. Living in a bungalow does not add to your happiness. Diamonds, gold, rubies, stocks, shares and mutual funds do not always guarantee peace and harmony in your life.

Alas, many of us regard these outer 'symbols' as indicators of our happiness and success. These material resources are not as valuable as your inner, personal resources.

One of the biggest 'businesses' in India till recently, was the lottery run by some state governments and other private institutions. If you drove through the High street of any town or city, you would recognise the 'lottery centre' by the hundreds of torn-up tickets littering the pavements – discarded by people who had failed to hit the jackpot. The Government began to take a serious note of the fact that humble workers and poor people were spending over half their daily wages on these lotteries, in the vain hope that they would become *lakhpatis* and *crorepatis* (millionaires) overnight. Many state governments actually banned the sale of lottery tickets.

I read of a man in the U.S. who won $1,00,000 in a lottery several years ago. All that money failed to bring him happiness. His wife filed for a divorce from him six months later, and took away half his winnings with her as a divorce settlement.

"I am told that there is a new movement in the U.S. called the minimalist movement," I said to the Wise One. "They try to live with less – less money, fewer possessions, less comforts. They buy less, spend less. They do not chase after money. Don't you think this is a good trend?"

"Thoreau thought of this two centuries ago," the Wise One remarked, "when he gave up his townhouse and went to live in the lap of nature, in Walden woods. The *mantra* of his life was: Simplify! Simplify! Simplify! Thoreau was a practising minimalist . . ."

As a young writer, Henry David Thoreau had felt stifled and miserable in the city of Concord, where he lived. He was a Harvard graduate, and he had started off as a teacher. But he wanted to lead a peaceful life, to devote his life to study, to thinking and writing. He found the society around him uncongenial for such an aspiration. Everywhere around him men were only in pursuit of one thing – material gains. People were interested only in piling up property and possessions, enslaving themselves to 'things' and 'goods' that really meant nothing to him.

Thoreau realised that the world's greatest thinkers and philosophers of the past had lived lives of Spartan simplicity. He decided to take a leaf from their books – he decided to leave Concord and live alone in the woods, cut off from all the artificial trappings of so-called civilisation; he would concentrate on improving his soul's estate.

In March, 1845, Thoreau set out for Walden Woods with a borrowed axe. He started building a cabin for himself on the edge of Walden Pond on a tract of land belonging to Ralph Waldo Emerson, his mentor. On July 4, the cabin was completed, and a vegetable garden planted. Carrying with him his flute, a few note books and pens and a copy of Homer, Thoreau moved into the cabin in the woods, to launch his experiment in simple living and high thinking.

"He chose to be rich by making his wants few," remarked his friend Emerson.

Thoreau was just twenty-eight years old when he began his remarkable experiment. He was not a misanthropist, nor a hermit. He had many friends in Concord, but he wished to escape from the artifices of civilisation and live a free and independent life.

"The mass of men lead lives of quiet desperation," he wrote. "... Most of the luxuries, and many of the so-called comforts of life, are not only not indispensable, but positive hindrances to the elevation of mankind..."

He lived in Walden woods for a little more than two years. Having completed his experiment successfully, he returned to conventional, social life. From his notes made in the woods, he produced *Walden*, the masterpiece which made him famous, and inspired Mahatma Gandhi.

> I went to the woods because I wished to live deliberately, to front only the essential facts of life, and see if I could not learn what it had to teach, and not, when I came to die, to discover that I had not lived...

The record of an experiment in serene, simple living, *Walden,* is as relevant now, as it was 150 years ago.

"Simplify your life," Thoreau urged his readers again and again. "Don't burden yourself with possessions. Keep your needs and wants simple, and enjoy what you have. Simplify! Don't fritter away your life on non-essentials. Don't enslave yourself for luxuries you can do without..."

What is wrong with earning money? What is wrong in accumulating wealth for the security of our loved ones, you might ask. Nothing – if we are able to be content with what we possess. But unfortunately, we do not stop there. We look at others, we compare ourselves with them, and we are unsatisfied if we have less. We are haunted by the greed for *more, more* and *more!*

It was a wise writer who said, "If money could buy happiness, there would be happiness stores on every street!"

A rich man was told that he had only a few months to live. The chronic cardiac problem which he had ignored all along had now turned critical, and neither surgery, nor treatment was now possible.

His wife persuaded him to leave behind his business so that they could spend their last days together peacefully. Though he was absolutely reluctant to do so at first, he consented to do so. His business empire was entrusted to the care of efficient managers, and the couple moved to a beautiful mountain resort. They bid farewell to their friends, and it was agreed that if the man should meet his end, he would have a quiet funeral in the mountains.

They left – and their friends had no further news from them. Two years later, his best friend picked up the courage to go to the resort to find out what had happened. He was a little hurt that he had not been invited to attend his friend's funeral.

He arrived at the resort and asked to see his friend's wife. Imagine his surprise and delight when the friend came out to meet him!

"John...John..." the visitor stammered, too overwhelmed to speak. "It's so good to see you! I thought you would have...I thought that..."

"Ah well," the rich man smiled. "It's so beautiful and peaceful out here that I forgot to die!"

"There are a hundred things in life which you can enjoy without money," the Wise One remarked. "Money cannot make you happy – but lots of other things can. You can eliminate the negative forces of life that are killing you if you rediscover the joys that money cannot buy. Let me tell you another story..."

There was a best selling author whose earlier books had broken all records and made him a millionaire. His publishing company awarded him a multi-million dollar contract to write three more novels for them in five years. The first novel was produced in eight months; it too created a record.

The publisher presented a beautiful bungalow to the writer, fitted with every imaginable comfort and amenity. There were comfortable spaces in every nook and corner, so that he would sit and write wherever he wanted – actually, he 'wrote' on his computer, so there were half a dozen computers and laptops scattered all over the house, all connected by LAN. If he woke up in the middle of the night, he could use a bedside computer. If an idea occurred to him in the gym, he could use a handy laptop there. The air-conditioning was so adjusted as to remain at an optimum temperature that suited him.

But the second novel was not moving fast. Somehow, the characters proved to be elusive, the incidents were not interesting enough; though he would never, ever admit it to anyone, the novelist feared that he had hit what is called a fallow period in his creative life. He was beginning to suffer from writing fatigue.

One day, a fuse blew up somewhere in the bungalow, and the electricity was cut off. Within minutes, expert electricians were called to set the problem right. They saw that the main circuit breaker was 'popping' all the time, and could not locate the fault.

Evening came, and the writer moved out of the dark house into the tree-shaded avenue outside. A silvery crescent of a moon hung in the sky, as if suspended by invisible strings. A thousand stars seemed to twinkle at him. Fathers and mothers, children, young couples were all out walking, and they waved to him cheerfully.

He returned home after a long walk. His butler had lighted a single tall candle on the table, and left a few fruits for him to eat. He found he was hungry, and he enjoyed the meal thoroughly.

Later that night, he sat down to work on his novel – and he found the book taking shape in a splendid and thoroughly unexpected manner. Everything seemed to fall into place, and he knew, instinctively, that he had another bestseller on his hands!

"When you take a break and look at the world around you, you discover its beauty and joy afresh," said the Wise One. "Darkness can make you appreciate the beauty of candlelight and moonlight.

It is a fact too, that an excess of artificial light creates headache and stress.

"Sometimes, we allow ourselves to be trapped by our routine. We allow ourselves to fall into a rut of our own making, and think that we cannot get out. 'This is my life,' we think; or, 'This is my job... I am stuck with it... I have no options.' We become tired, depressed and cease to pay attention to our own feelings and inner aspirations. We are not listening to our hearts...

"Some years ago, there was a talk in corporate circles of something called a *downshift*. That is, a slowing down of the pace of life, an alternative lifestyle sought by busy young executives who suddenly realised that they did not want to spend the rest of their lives just making money. Thus, strange 'downshifts' came to pass..."

A thirty-year old couple who were high powered financial executives discovered the joys of cooking together. They gave up their lucrative jobs in a London bank and opened a cosy cafeteria in a seaside town. They laughed, played and worked together; they cooked and served tasty meals; they chatted with their customers and charmed everyone with their 'personal touch'. They never ever looked back on their lucrative careers.

A wealthy man from France took a vacation in a Himalayan resort. The peace, tranquillity and the clean mountain air so appealed to him that he decided to live and work there as a ski instructor.

A research scientist from an American University happened to hear an Indian spiritual teacher talking about meditation and silent prayer. The scientist felt his inner being transformed. He accepted the teacher as his Guru and became a devoted volunteer in his *ashram*.

These people listened to their inner voices. They were not carried away by the dazzle of money and by their jet setting executive lifestyles. They thought about what they wanted out of life. They asked themselves what they would *like* to do, what they would *love* to do – and they followed the dictates of their heart. Money, power, position were all secondary.

I can hear some of you saying, "It's alright for millionaires and eccentrics from western countries to 'downshift' and get away with it! What about Mr. and Mrs. Average citizen? What about the Common Man with his multiple responsibilities and commitments?

I am not suggesting friends, that all of you should give up your jobs and open sandwich bars downtown! All I'm saying is that these people discovered that making money was not enough to bring them happiness, and so sought alternate lifestyles and occupations which may not have been as rewarding financially – but offered greater satisfaction and contentment.

"You don't have to quit your job to make a change," the Wise One observed. "Think of the activities you enjoy. Do you like writing? Then begin to write short stories, poems and articles. Do you enjoy singing? Join a music group and take lessons in classical instrumental/vocal/western music. Do you enjoy theatre? Join a drama group. If you love animals, volunteer to serve with Blue Cross, SPCA or a local animal shelter. Do you love reading? Offer to read for the visually disabled or to the inmates of a Home for the Aged. Do you love babies? Volunteer to help out at a Balgram-SOS children's village. Do you love going to the temple? Offer to assist the devotees who throng the local temple during the peak hours. Do what you love – find joy in activities that appeal to your heart, and not merely to your head . . .

"Many of us are trapped by the blaring noise, the glaring lights and the mechanical routine of a demanding society. We are surrounded by the buzzing of alarms, the ringing of telephones, the clatter of the keyboard, the loud volume of the TV, the high decibel levels from the speakers, horns, engines, cars, buses and trucks. The glare of the TV screen and artificial lighting are constantly hurting our eyes. We get up like mechanised robots and go about our daily routine listlessly.

"Exercise your soul! Turn to nature to nurture you. Learn to spend at least a little time everyday in outdoor activities – it can be something as simple as walking, or just sitting in a garden bench. Being in touch with the healing forces of nature helps to restore calm, peace and a sense of harmony to your life..."

"Alas," I sighed "very few of us take time to sit quietly and commune with nature. I know people in Mumbai and Chennai who do not go to the seaside even once a year. I know many Bangaloreans who have never taken a walk in the city's famous Cubbon Park. I know people in Pune who have never explored the green and lovely hill tracks which surround the city..."

"That is indeed a pity," agreed the Wise One. "When you turn to nature, you rediscover yourself. When you turn your back on the noise and commotion of the city life, you are able to capture the beautiful silence of the soul within you.

"The demands and distractions of modern life only take us away from ourselves. This is why Indian philosophy and culture insist on silence, withdrawl, stillness and meditation whereby you can discover the Divine within yourself. Let me tell you about a lady I know..."

Mrs. Ramchand had to have a photograph taken for her passport and visa. Avoiding the 'instant' photograph machines, she went to a studio. Seated before the camera, she presented a stern, severe, reproving look which was always on her face, as she shouted, screamed and bullied the women who worked for her in her garment factory.

The photographer left his camera to cast a critical glance at her. "Smile please, madame," he coaxed her. "Can you brighten your eyes a little? Can you bring a little glow onto your face?"

Mrs. Ramchand tried to arrange her features satisfactorily. But the young man would not give up. "Can you try and look a little more pleasant?" he demanded.

"Look here," said Mrs. Ramchand in her best shop floor voice. "I don't believe in using make-up and such stuff. How can I look bright and shining without all those aids?"

"But madame, I'm not talking about make-up," the photographer exclaimed. "I'm talking about looking bright and cheerful – and that comes from *within*. It's all inside you!"

Something in his words softened the stern lady's heart. She felt her heart open up, she felt her facial muscles relax, and she actually managed to smile.

"Oh, that's perfect!" said the photographer. "Madame, if you don't mind my saying so, you look twenty years younger!"

Mrs. Ramchand was speechless. It was the first time in years that she had actually tried to look pleasant – and it really came from within!

When the passport photographs arrived, she was surprised to see herself smiling and pleasant and relaxed. And she knew it did not come from 'outer' things. She gazed at herself long and hard in the mirror and said to herself: "If I can do it once, I can do it again and again!"

Mrs. Ramchand became a transformed woman. Not only was she happy and pleasant – her workers at the garment factory were ecstatic at the change that had come about in her nature.

One of her personal assistants actually picked up the courage to ask her, "Madame, you're looking different – you look younger, actually! Won't you tell us what is the secret?"

"It all comes from the inside," was all Mrs. Ramchand would say.

Frowning, complaining, worrying and fretting poison us from the inside – and affect the way we look outside. An expert in mental science actually tells us, "The way to be beautiful without, is to be beautiful within!"

"Be good and you will be happy," is an old-fashioned piece of advice. We are now being told, "Be happy, and you will be good." When we allow the true joy of our heart to shine in our life, we are sure to *be* good and *do* good!

"Do not hang dismal pictures on your wall," Emerson tells us. "Do not deal with sables and glooms in your conversation."

William S. Ogdon was a distinguished journalist who had served in the U.S. war effort during the Second World War. After long, lonely months spent on military duty in the Pacific islands, he was ecstatic to get back to New York when the war ended. He had loved the city, and missed it very much all these years. He was sure that he would find New Yorkers happy, cheerful and contented, now that the war was over.

He was astonished to find people angry, bitter and frustrated, instead. Wherever he went, he heard nothing but grumblings and complaints. Their only concern was with money and the things money could buy. This obsession with material wealth, and the people's insistent demand for higher wages and shorter working hours, saddened the writer.

"What is the government doing for us?" people demanded. "What is our future going to be like?"

Ogdon had to write a column called *Topics of the Times* for *The New York Times* newspaper. He decided to write an article entitled 'The Art Of Happiness.' I give below a memorable extract from the article, which appeared on the editorial page of *The New York Times* on Dec.30th 1945:

> The ingredients of happiness are so simple that they can be counted on one hand. Happiness comes from within, and rests most surely on simple goodness and a clear conscience... (Happiness) is quiet, seldom

found in crowds, most easily won in moments of solitude and reflection. It cannot be bought; indeed, money has very little to do with it...

The people's response to the article was profound and powerful. They needed to be told that happiness could not be bought with money; that selfishness and greed actually destroyed their peace of mind. Ogdon had been able to see through the tensions and confusions of the times and point out to people the basic and lasting values of life.

The great Norwegian dramatist Henrik Ibsen wrote:

> Money can buy the husk of things, but not the kernel. It brings you food, but not appetite, medicine but not health, acquaintances but not friends, servants but not faithfulness, days of pleasure – but not peace or happiness.

"Man does not live by bread alone!" the Wise One observed. "Making money, accumulating possessions can never lead to a fulfilling life. Of course it is good to have some of the luxuries that money can buy – but we would be the losers if we miss out on all the wonderful things that money *cannot* buy!"

"The more a man finds his sources of pleasure in himself, the happier he will be," writes the philosopher Schopenhauer. "...The highest, the most varied and lasting pleasures are those of the mind..."

Truly, if we cannot find happiness and contentment within, it is useless to seek it elsewhere!

Socrates was one of those rare breed of men who refused to be trapped by the lure of material possessions. He taught that if men were truly wise, they would not be obsessed with wealth. Determined to practise what he preached, he did not even wear shoes.

However, Socrates loved to visit the market place and gaze contentedly at the vast abundance of all that was on display. When someone asked him what drew him to the marketplace, his reply was, "I love to go there and discover how many things I am perfectly happy without."

I wonder what our modern advertising professionals and marketing executives would have to say to that! These people are constantly persuading us to try this, buy that or use the other so that we can be happy. Millions of dollars are spent on advertising budgets, making commercials which assault our eyes and ears talking about the latest products without which we just cannot be happy – if they are to be believed, that is!

I read of a man who visited a Travel Agent to explore different holiday options. After going through various brochures, he decided that he would take a cruise.

"Right sir, a cruise it shall be," said the sales executive cheerfully. "Now, where would you like to go?"

The man could not make up his mind. The sales executive was a helpful and enthusiastic girl. She told him about Mediterranean cruises, cruises to the South Pacific, or even a luxury crossing from Europe to America. But the customer was difficult. He wanted something different.

"Take a look at the world Sir," said the girl, drawing his attention to the large globe that stood in the corner of the office. "As they say, the world is your oyster. You choose any corner of the globe you like, and we can plan a cruise of your choice."

The man went near the globe. He rotated it and studied it carefully for a while and then turned round and exclaimed, "Is that all you have to offer?"

I suppose disgruntled men like him would now have 'space cruises' to choose from. But the point is, that many of us are disgruntled and dissatisfied with what the world has to offer. No matter how deeply we drink at life's fountain, we are not satisfied. We want more!

Many families who set out on vacation carry an inordinate amount of luggage with them. They pack more clothes, more games, more equipment, more footwear than they will ever need. "We cannot come back home to take what we want," they say.

If only they could ask themselves, "How little stuff can I actually manage on?" or "How much can I do without?" they would travel a lot lighter!

A lady was leaving on a day-trip to attend a friend's wedding reception. She carried a sizeable suitcase with her.

"Why do you need such a big suitcase?" her husband asked her. "You only need one set of change of clothes."

"True, but I always like to have a choice," came the reply, "and so I'm taking four or five sets along with me.'

I know many people who take a lot of stuff with them – and also end up buying more stuff and newer items on vacation. Then they are often forced to leave behind what they brought with them.

Many of us accumulate far too many material possessions on the journey of life. We cannot resist the urge to buy and possess things, which, we feel we "simply cannot do without". So we buy more and more. We end up dragging our possessions with us wherever we go – and we allow ourselves to be dragged down by them.

"Remember that very little is needed to make a happy life," Marcus Aurelius tells us. Alas, we pay no heed to such advice. We want bigger houses, faster cars, more money, more pleasures, more of everything!

"We live in an age of sensation," the Wise One reflected. "We crave, we attain, we are satiated – and we crave for more. And so it is said that modern man is diet-conscious, but spiritually undernourished."

In his book *Seven Pillars Of Wisdom*, Lawrence of Arabia narrates to us an unforgettable event. One day, he rode down with an Arab friend deep into the desert to visit the ruins of an ancient palace, said to be built by a Roman emperor for his queen. It was believed that the mortar to build this palace was kneaded not with water, but with essential oils of flowers, so that each room would smell of a different fragrance.

The Arab took Lawrence to various rooms such as the Rose room, Violet room, Jasmine room etc. In each room, they tried to breathe deeply, sniffing the fragrance of the flowers. But finally, when they looked out of a broken casement and actually smelt the clean, pure air of the desert, Lawrence felt that *that* was the best fragrance in the world!

Lawrence records that the air smelt of the sand – reminding him of the dust that he was made of, and the dust to which he would return one day.

"Like a child who has received several Christmas toys, we play with our possessions happily for a while," the Wise One mused, "and then lose interest in them and start looking for something else, something different. Thus our frustrated search for happiness continues, literally filling our lives and houses with a vast litter of material possessions.

"Money cannot buy happiness, anymore than it can buy love! It can make a contribution to our happiness – we can pay our bills, buy our food and settle our rent with money, and that is indeed a good thing. But money cannot guarantee happiness.

"Did you know, Chesterton points out that simple joy and optimism are to be found more among the poor than among the affluent? Let me tell you a story..."

Mrs. Chand was a wealthy lady who employed a cook, a servant, a driver and a gardener to keep her palatial house in perfect order. But she was not a happy woman – for she was under the impression that she deserved to be richer, more important, more famous.

Her servant set out her lunch on the table and called her to eat one day. In a bad mood, Mrs. Chand criticised the table arrangement, criticised the menu and scolded the servant and cook for not doing their work well.

Sometime later, she chanced to look out through the back door and found the servants sitting together, sharing the lunch that each one had brought with them from home. Obviously, their food was not rich or luxurious; it was the kind of food that thousands of ordinary Indians eat everyday. But the servants were sharing it with kindness and affection, laughing and talking as they ate, and highly appreciative of each other's food. Sitting at her posh table, eating her luxurious fare, Mrs. Chand had never been so appreciative or satisfied – and she realised it herself now!

Here is a poem by Grace Crowell:
I have found joy in simple things:
A plain, clean room, a nut-brown loaf of bread,
A cup of milk, a kettle as it sings,
The shelter of a roof above my head…

There are so many simple, but wonderful things in life that can give us joy. Our trouble is we overlook them, because they do not cost money! We ignore them or underestimate them.

It is always "lack" of something or the other that makes people unhappy. "I don't have a car," they think, "I don't own a house," or "I don't have enough savings."

The problem of "lack" becomes really acute when we begin to add hundreds of things, big and small, to our ever-growing wish list. The question to ask yourself is: are *all* those things truly necessary for your comfort and peace of mind? Will a diamond bracelet make you sleep well? Will the luxury limousine you covet give you peace in the heart within?

Today we live in the age of plastic money, credit card payment and the ever-present 'instalment' culture. A friend showed me an advertisement which said, "Pay just Rs. 100/- and drive away your dream car!"

I am afraid we are falling prey to the danger of mortgaging our future in order to own, possess and acquire an excess of consumer goods that we don't really need.

"I must have that new mixer-cum-grinder!" exclaimed a housewife on seeing an ad in the newspaper. "Shall we buy it today?"

"But you have two mixers in your kitchen," objected her husband. "One large and one small. Why do you need a third?"

"Ah! But I am getting a set of serving bowls free with the new offer," said the housewife. "And these bowls are so attractive!"

When we look at these advertisements, every product seems to promise us happiness, fulfilment and complete satisfaction. Thus we fall into the trap of desiring more, acquiring more, possessing more – and more! We are in bondage to our possessions. And *they* demand more out of us. The bungalow needs to be painted and repaired, it needs security guards; the car needs to be serviced and maintained; the gadgets demand their upkeep. And we carry all these self-imposed burdens for the sake of possessions. But are they truly contributing to our inner happiness?

That is a question which each of one of us has to answer for ourselves.

"I think we are beginning to complicate our lives unnecessarily," sighed the Wise One. "perhaps unintentionally – with excessive acquisitions and unnecessary possessions. But the worst thing is that we tend to ignore, forget or take for granted things that should really matter to us . . ."

I thought of a statement made by the writer Perroux: "The whole value of life comes from things that have no price."

We rose from our comfortable seats and stretched our limbs.

"It's been a long day," the Wise One remarked.

"To my mind, time has been flying," I said warmly. "It seems to me that we stepped into the realm of happiness just minutes ago! I haven't had a dull moment since I got here. My only regret is that we will have to leave this place sooner or later..."

"That should not worry you," remarked the Wise One. "I think you are one of those rare people who create their own happiness, and carry their happiness *with* them . . ."

"Thank you!" I said, touched by his warmth and grace. "That's indeed a great compliment, coming from you. But what I want, above all else, is that people should know that they can also create their own happiness, and carry it with them wherever they go!"

"There's a short cut to happiness that everyone recommends," the Wise One said.

"What's that?" I asked eagerly.

The Wise One pointed to the message inscribed on a road sign:

Develop A Healthy Sense Of Humour.

The 19th Secret of Happiness

Develop A Healthy Sense Of Humour

"This one is really close to my heart!" I said eagerly. "It has been said that humour is to life, what shock absorbers are to automobiles. Those who laugh, surely enjoy a smooth ride on the rough roads of life, don't they?"

We began to ascend the steps that led up to the raised ground.

"Laughter has been described as an important part of the human survival kit," the Wise One said. "It lubricates our inner mechanism when we are worn out by life's cares. It was a doctor who defined laughter as a tranquilliser with no side effects."

I nodded.

Grenville Kleiser goes one step further : he calls good humour " a tonic for mind and body." According to him, "It is the best antidote for anxiety and depression. It is a business asset. It attracts and keeps friends. It lightens human burdens. It is the direct route to serenity and contentment."

"Humour does not just mean cracking a joke now and then," the Wise One added. "As I said, it is one of the basic tools in the survival kit of life. A sense of humour gives us a sense of balance and proportion – we are able to look at people and problems from the right perspective.

"I read somewhere that good humour makes all things tolerable; all problems manageable; and all people likeable. What better aid can we have to make ourselves truly happy?"

It was a philosopher with a great sense of humour, who wrote: "After God created the world, He made man and woman. Then, to keep the whole thing from collapsing, He invented humour."

I am told that some comedy programmes on TV use what is called 'canned laughter' – that is, taped sounds of people's laughter which are mixed into the programme so that people watching TV may also be 'prompted' to join in the laughter. This is not the kind of artificial humour I am talking about. People who laugh at crude, vulgar jokes are not really happy – their laughter cannot bring true release. It can only be hollow, bitter laughter. Vulgarity, rudeness and malice in any form lack the subtlety of true humour. George Santayana tells us: "To be happy is to sing; not to be made to sing, or sing by rote, or as an art or for a purpose, but spontaneously, because something sings within you, and all else for the moment, ceases to matter."

That is true laughter!

Happy are the people who can laugh – especially those who can laugh at themselves!

Thackeray described the world as a looking glass which gives back to us the reflection of our own face: when we frown, the world also frowns sourly upon us. When we laugh, it becomes a jolly companion.

"I have moved house several times in the course of my husband's business," said a bad tempered woman. "Every time I move, I get the most awful neighbours. And they seem to be getting worse and worse."

"Perhaps," said a forthright friend, "you are taking your worst neighbour with you when you move!"

Troubles and difficulties seem to melt away before the man who carries the spirit of cheerfulness with him. If you love peace and joy, good cheer, you will see it wherever you go. If there is a song in your heart, you will hear it everywhere.

The attitude of cheerfulness, the spirit of humour enables us to turn even misfortunes into blessings, and this is the greatest wealth for people who wish to make their life happy. Grumbling and complaining do not require a special talent; everyone can do it. But a sunny, cheerful attitude is a great gift.

The great essayist, Carlyle, exclaimed, "Give us the man who sings at his work!" Worry and anxiety affect our work. Nobody can do his best when he is glum and cheerless. The man of kind disposition and cheerful attitude creates a wonderful working atmosphere for his workers and employees.

In Switzerland, before the days of mechanised, automated cattle farms, milkmaids who could sing were paid higher wages than those who could not sing, for it was found that cows gave more quantities of milk in the warm and cheerful atmosphere generated by singing.

To this day, communities of women who make *papads* in South India, sing as they engage in the difficult task of rolling out thin, delicate *papads* which are highly prized when they are hand made. These women say that *papads* are rounder, thinner and flawless, when they are handled by cheerful workers.

One hundred years ago, visitors to America found the people of this great country singularly cheerless and cold. "In the US," said a distinguished traveller, "there is comfort everywhere, but no joy; the ambition of getting more and fretting over what is lost, seems to absorb the people's life here."

"The Americans are the best-fed, best-clad and the best-housed people in the world," said another visitor, "but they are the most anxious, they seem to hug calamity to their breasts."

In those days, Americans seemed to suffer from exhaustion and burnout. Every American you saw on the street was rushing in haste – everyone seemed to be late for a pressing appointment. Hurry was stamped on the national face of Uncle Sam! Americans wanted to live fast, work fast, move fast.

"In other countries people live to enjoy life," said a European prince who visited the U.S. "Here they seem to exist only for business."

"It is not work that kills men," says Beecher. "Work is healthy; it is not movement that destroys the machinery, but friction."

The power to laugh, to relax and make merry is indeed the greatest gift bestowed upon man. Man has been called a social animal, a rational animal, a thinking animal and a political animal. My favourite term for man was the one given to us by Bernard Shaw: "Man is the only animal who has the gift of laughter."

"Humour will help you finish," says best selling author Bernie S. Siegel, "no matter what race you enter."

When we were little children, laughter came to us naturally, spontaneously. Thus grandmothers who see infants smiling in their sleep, remark, "God is talking to His little ones!" Alas, we loose this childlike capacity to smile as the years advance.

"Nobody is allowed to enter here," said a signboard at the entrance to the cricket stadium. A little boy walked up to the entrance and tried to push the door open.

"I'm nobody!" he said cheerfully to a sentry who looked at him with narrowing eyes.

The sentry smiled in spite of himself. With tongue in cheek, he said to the boy, "Well, we shall make you *somebody*, and lead you out of here with an escort." Both the boy and the sentry were grinning as they marched.

The queue at the post-office counter was long, and people's tempers were fraying at the edges. "I'll give that man at the counter a piece of my mind when I get there," muttered one man. "These people are slow, inefficient and dull," cursed another. At last, when one of them managed to reach the window, he was taken aback to see a physically disabled clerk who was handling the counter. The young man was cheerful and smiling, and cracked jokes as he wrote receipts, issued notes and filled endless forms.

"I'll tell you what," the man who had been grumbling said to him, "I'm going to come here everyday and stand in this queue just to hear your jokes."

Laughter lifts the clouds and brings back the sunshine into our lives. When we laugh, we transcend our troubles, cares and worries.

I have always been inspired by the story of Norman Cousins, who cured himself of a serious illness just by watching cartoons and funny movies.

There was a man I knew, who cut out funny pictures, cartoons and jokes and took scrapbooks filled with these funny bits to circulate amongst hospital patients. It is not without reason that they call laughter, "the best medicine"!

A physician explains that laugher begins in the lungs and diaphragm, setting the internal organs into a quick jelly-like vibration, which causes a pleasant sensation. He adds that frequent laughter sets the stomach dancing, thus hastening the digestive process.

And this is not all. The heart beats faster, and blood circulation improves throughout the body. Laughter also accelerates respiration and gives warmth to the whole system. It improves the eyesight, expands the chest, sends air out from the least-used lung cells, and stimulates the heart.

"There is not," says Dr. Green, "one remotest corner or little inlet of the minute blood vessels of the human body, that does not feel some wavelet from the convulsions occasioned by a good hearty laugh."

'Laughter Therapy' is now well recognised by the medical profession, making true the wisdom of the ancient Hebrew proverb, "A merry heart doeth good like a medicine."

"Mirth is God's medicine," said Dr. Holmes. "Everybody ought to bathe in it." In fact he goes so far as to say that if ever we have to make a choice between two physicians, we must be sure to choose the one with a cheerful, smiling countenance!

"A joyous spirit not only relieves pain, but increases the momentum of life in the body," says a research article published in *The Lancet*, which is one of the most eminent medical journals in the world.

There are several tendencies in the human personality which restrict our capacity for happiness – such as grief, fear, worry and anxiety. The best way to fight these negative tendencies is to take up the powerful weapon of laugher. The delicate balance of mental harmony and peace can be destroyed even by such things as a sleepless night, a piece of bad news or a nagging worry. A good hearty laughter session will restore the balance in no time!

Alas, 'fashion' or 'propriety' or 'custom' often forbids people to indulge in hearty, body-shaking laughter. However, I always tell my friends we must do much more than merely cultivate a cheerful spirit – we must cultivate the spirit of mirth that allows us to laugh heartily – at least three times a day!

Laughter is also an excellent aid to beauty. To quote another Hebrew proverb, "A merry heart maketh a cheerful countenance." It keeps mind, body and spirit young.

Lycurgus, an eminent man of medicine in ancient Greece, set up pictures of the God of Laughter in the eating-halls of Sparta. The Kings of Prussia always had jesters cracking jokes and quips as dinner was served at the table. Now, we have discovered that laughter can cure indigestion and dyspepsia.

"Laughter is the brush that sweeps away the cobwebs of the heart," writes Mort Walker.

"Shall we try and sweep away a few of those cobwebs here and now?" said the Wise One. "Why don't you make me laugh…?"

Having moved to a new house, Mrs. Joshi filled up an application to open a savings account at the local co-operative bank. A couple of days later, her phone rang. A girl from the bank had called to tell her that her application was not complete.

"I'm so sorry," said Mrs. Joshi. "Have I left out something important?"

"Don't worry," the young lady assured her. "I'm only ringing you to ask for your phone number."

A mother was driving her eight-year old daughter to her first summer camp. The little girl was told to be kind, considerate and courteous to all the other children.

"And if you see any girl feeling left out, lonely and sad, be sure to go and talk to her and cheer her up."

The little girl swallowed hard, and asked in a small voice, "What if *I* am the one who is feeling sad and lonely and left out?"

A friend who lived in a remote hilly area, had written a letter to Mr. and Mrs. Smith, inviting them to come and spend a weekend in his idyllic cottage.

The Smiths were very excited and set out early on the Friday evening, hoping to reach the cottage in time for dinner. Mrs. Smith carried in her hand their host's letter, with his detailed instructions on how to reach his house.

They seemed to be driving on and on, and not getting anywhere. Tempers began to fray, and the couple snapped at each other. They stopped at a filling station and Mrs. Smith began to re-read the letter carefully to see if she had missed out any of the directions.

"Oh no!" she exclaimed after a while. "We've been driving for so long and we've only got to the end of the first paragraph!"

An eighty-nine-year old man was asked to reveal the secret of his long and happy married life. He cleared his throat and said, "My formula consists in two simple words with which I end all conversations, discussions and arguments with my wife: the words are *Yes Dear!*"

Ever since Mrs. Patel was given a book on numerology, she became obsessed with numbers and alphabets. She wanted to change the car number; she wanted the house to have 3 doors instead of just two; she even wanted to spell her name P – E – T – A – I – L.

Mr. Patel suffered her newfound enthusiasm patiently, and was highly relieved when she said to him one evening, "According to the numbers of our first names, we are both supposed to get on well with each other."

"That's great!" exclaimed her husband.

"Yes, isn't it?" continued Mrs. Patel, "But according to the spelling of my name, I ought to have married someone else whose name adds up to eight."

Gina visited her old grandfather, and found him laying out old magazines and Sunday newspapers in his garden, between the neat rows of his newly planted flowers and vegetables.

"What are you doing grandpa?" asked Gina, perplexed.

"Well, the man at the gardening centre told me that my plants will grow well if I talk to them," grandfather explained. "But I can't stand here chatting to them all day. So I thought let them *read* something instead."

Mrs. Jones, a morose and strict lady, was attending Sunday service with her grandson. When the collection tray came to them, little Jim was mortified to see his grandmother put just fifty cents in.

"It was not at all a good service," Mrs. Jones remarked sourly, as they left the church.

"What do you expect for fifty cents?" said her grandson.

Mrs. Murphy was ninety years old, and had always been healthy, cheerful and fit as a fiddle. Her daughter who was only sixty-five, was suffering from constant back ache. Mrs. Murphy forced her to visit their family doctor and go in for a complete medical check up.

All the tests were completed, and the daughter was pronounced to be fine. "You will live to be one hundred and ten years old," the doctor remarked, smiling.

Mrs. Murphy was, however, not happy. "Oh dear," she sighed. "What on earth will I do with a one hundred and ten year old daughter?"

A young and enthusiastic teacher was teaching her eight-year old students a lesson on patriotism. She talked about the Statue of Liberty, what it signified and how it had been given to the Americans by the people of France.

Becoming more and more enthusiastic, she longed to recite the inspiring message on the base of the Statue, "Give me your tired, your poor..."

Clearing her throat, she asked, "And who can tell me what is written on the base of the statue?"

There was silence. And then one hesitant little hand shot up. Little Naomi ventured, cautiously, "Made in France?"

A young man had become prone to severe depression after several girls had turned down his marriage proposals. He was put under psychiatric care.

The treatment did him good, and he improved considerably.

"I'm getting married," he said to the psychiatrist one day.

"Excellent!" exclaimed the good doctor. "Congratulations! And who is the lucky young girl?"

"It's an octopus, actually," the man replied.

"But you can't possibly marry an octopus," said the doctor, alarmed.

"What do you expect me to do with eight engagement rings?" the man shot back.

Leena had had offers of marriage from three young men – a doctor, a lawyer and a solider. She consulted her friend about her choice.

"Marry the solider," said the friend thoughtfully. "He can make beds, sew and cook. Above all, he is accustomed to obeying orders."

As Suresh was driving home from the University one wet afternoon, he saw his Professor of Philosophy waiting at the bus stop. He stopped the car and offered the Professor a lift, which was gratefully and quickly accepted. The Professor got into the car with alacrity, and gave Suresh directions to reach his home.

At the door of the house, Suresh dropped him off and enquired politely after the Professor's wife.

"How is Madame these days sir?"

The Professor gave a start. "She must be very wet by now. I've just remembered I left her at the bus stop."

Every evening in the summer, a bird with a very different call would whistle from Mr. Lal's garden. Mr. Lal was so intrigued by the unusual whistle that he soon began to whistle back to the bird. To his amazement, the bird responded, and quite a 'conversation' was set up between the two.

This happened day after day, until Mr. Lal proudly told his friends that he now understood bird language and spoke to birds regularly.

One day, his nephew happened to be present at one of the sessions. Out of curiosity, he looked over the wall into the neighbour's garden – and saw the neighbour standing attentively on the lawn, whistling answers to Mr. Lal's calls.

The two men had been whistling to each other every day, blithely assuming that a bird was 'talking' to them!

By now, both of us were laughing heartily.

"Let us learn to laugh at ourselves!" said the Wise One. "It has rightly been said that the person who can laugh at himself is a delight to be with: he applies to life's problems, ills and errors the most soothing balm that the human spirit needs – **laughter!**"

Gandhiji often remarked that his sense of humour helped him to keep his blood-pressure down. An American lady once asked him, "Do you suffer from nerves?"

"You must ask Mrs. Gandhi," said the Mahatma. "She will tell you that I am on my best behaviour with the world, but not with her."

"Well," said the lady, with some aspersion, *"My husband is always on his best behaviour with me!"*

"In that case" retorted Gandhi, "I am sure your husband has bribed you heavily!"

A sense of humour enables us to see the absurdity of the situation, the lighter side of things.

A bitterly controversial case was being argued in court. The lawyers on both sides were getting more and more heated. One of them turned upon the other and shouted, "Of all the unmitigated, absolute asses that ever lived, you are the worst!"

"As for you," roared the other. "You must be the one with the smallest, puniest brain in the world!"

The judge heard this unseemly quarrel and decided to ease the tension with his inimitable sense of humour. "Gentlemen, gentlemen," he warned, rapping his gavel, "You forget that I am present here!"

Bernard Shaw and Churchill had witty sparring matches. Once Shaw sent two complimentary tickets to Churchill for one of his plays, adding a note: "For you and your friend – that is, if you have one."

Churchill sent a polite reply, "Thank you for the tickets. I am afraid I have another appointment for the evening. But I would certainly like to see your play – that is, if there is another performance."

Humour is a vital ingredient in our process of social adjustment. It helps us to understand, tolerate, laugh away and even overlook or forgive others' foibles and errors. Truly has it been said that laughter is contagious: for when you laugh and smile, you make every one around you happy!

"Laugh and grow fat,' says the old proverb. I would change that slightly and urge you to laugh and be healthy – laugh and be happy! For laughter is hostile to pain and disease; it is the best cure for depression and melancholy; it is the perfect antidote to anxiety and worry. You can also be certain that laughter enhances your 'face value' – for it makes your countenance sparkle, and does away with frowns and wrinkles.

"There are so many friends and acquaintances who never smile at me," I heard someone say the other day. "Now give me one good reason why *I* should smile at them?"

My answer to that person was, "There is nobody who needs your smile as badly as one who has none to give. So give them a smile!"

John Haggai tells us that there are two kinds of people in the world – the first type is the 'thermometer personality' – these people only register the temperature of the environment, the second type is the 'thermostat personality' – these people *set* the temperature, control the temperature of the environment. They create an environment which is happy and joyous.

"Who do you think is the happiest man on earth?" a sage asked his disciples.

"The perfectionist, who achieves the perfection he seeks," they answered.

"Unfortunately, no one has yet found him," smiled the sage. "But luckily, all of us can be reasonably happy if we develop a sense of humour and learn to adjust with our problems and troubles."

Laugh your blues away! Stop worrying and frowning! Learn to laugh at your problems. Tolerate others' weaknesses with a smile. Laugh at yourself – and it will make you a wonderful person to be with. This is what Ella Wheeler Wilcox tells us in a memorable poem:

> Laugh and the world laughs with you.
> Weep and you weep alone.
> Rejoice and men will seek you,
> Grieve, and they turn and go,
> They want full measure of your pleasure,
> But they do not want your woe.

We had reached the top of the steps, and my eyes widened in wonder as we saw before us a beautiful little temple. Like everywhere else in the realm of happiness, the temple too was deserted. But the stars twinkling overhead, and the full moon which shone like a silver lamp, seemed to be offering their own *aarti* to the smiling form of Lord Krishna, enshrined in the temple. And the bells suspended from the temple roof tinkled melodiously in the evening breeze...

"I'm sorry, I was mistaken," I said softly to the Wise One. "We were not alone here, after all. God was with us, God is with us all the time."

The Wise One nodded smilingly and drew my attention to the message carved over the temple entrance:

If You Would Be Happy, Keep On Thanking God All The Time.

The 20th Secret of Happiness

If You Would Be Happy, Keep On Thanking God All The Time

"Thank you God, Thank you God, Thank you God!" I exclaimed, repeating my favourite slogan.

I have always said to my friends: *In all conditions and circumstances of life, keep thanking God: let the words, "Thank you God!" be on your lips all the time.*

It is easy enough to thank God when you are having a good time; when you get everything you want; when you are healthy and strong; when you are climbing the ladder of success; when you are enjoying the ride; when things work according to your plan; when everything turns out to be fine.

But I'm talking about difficult times, when the going gets hard; when we lose something we value; when a relationship breaks up; when illness strikes us; when failure dogs our footsteps; when the world seems to collapse all around us.

A sister came to me and with tears in her eyes; she said, "I cannot take it any more. I have reached the limit of suffering. I feel completely crushed."

I said to her, "Now is the time to start thanking God!"

"Thank God – for what?" she cried.

And I replied, "Thank God who continues to give you the strength to get through your suffering!"

Just consider this – when you were a child, it didn't take much to make you cry. If someone took away your toys, if another child snatched your crayon or picture book from you, you would howl in anger. If the teacher scolded you, if your father spoke a harsh word, or a friend pinched you, your eyes would overflow with tears. But as you grow older, you learn to handle problems and face difficulties in your own stride. You are not crushed even when you are overwhelmed by troubles. Doubts assail you: you set them aside and get on with what you are doing. You take a few knocks: but you refuse to give up. You stumble and fall; you pick yourself up and keep going.

Is this not true of you as it is for all of us?

Have you ever stopped to salute the indomitable human spirit that God has blessed you with? Should you not keep on thanking Him for this marvellous gift? Should you not feel grateful to God for never, ever abandoning us, for being with us all the time, guiding us, guarding us, protecting us, leading us on?

"Keep on thanking God all the time!" said the Wise One, and his words fell on my ears like soft music. "In joy and sorrow, in loss and gain, in pleasure and pain, in praise and censure, come storm or sunshine – let the words 'Thank you God! Thank you God! Thank you God!' be upon your lips constantly!

"Consider the lives of the great ones of east and west. None of them escaped pain and suffering. Christ was crucified; Prophet Mohammed was persecuted; Christian saints were burnt alive at the stake during the horrible days of the Inquisition; Guru Gobind Singh and Guru Arjan Dev became martyrs for the cause…where there is love and faith, there has been suffering. But the witness of the great ones teaches us that suffering strengthens faith, even as faith bestows on us the strength to endure suffering! Therefore, thank God even in adversity…"

I thought of the great poet of my native Sind, Shah Abdul Latif, who sang:

> It is never heard
> God is realised without suffering.

"Buddhists scriptures point to us that the world is full of suffering," said the Wise One. "Birth is suffering; sickness is suffering; to meet people we do not like is suffering; to be separated from someone we love is suffering. Inasmuch as life is never free from desire and passion, it is necessarily inclusive of distress and suffering.

"Perhaps it is not surprising that people begin to think and act selfishly in this world of sorrow and suffering! But this attitude will not solve our problems. In fact, selfishness will only lead to more suffering and unhappiness.

"Earlier, I spoke to you about the need to appreciate people. Let me add now, appreciation of God and His gifts is the best form of prayer. Truly has it been said, 'Gratitude paves the shortest route to happiness.'

"When you are thankful to God for His infinite kindness and mercy, you are focussing on all that is best in your life, and the Law of Attraction will draw more of the same into your life. But let me also warn you, if you complain about unpleasant things, you will draw more of those negative forces into your physical experience..."

I thought of the best selling author Alan Cohen, who says, "Curse what you see and you will live in a world of pain; give thanks, and you will find more to be thankful about. The choice is yours!"

I read an old parable in which God invited all human virtues to attend a banquet in heaven. It was an all-ladies event, for virtues are personified as women – let men take note!

Hundreds of virtues, great and small, attended the banquet, and they were all on the most cordial terms with each other. Cheerfulness went round, talking to everyone; Friendship was busy bringing the guests close together; Hospitality saw to it that everyone helped themselves to the food they liked; Goodness beamed on everyone present.

Suddenly, God noticed that there were two ladies among his guests who appeared to be total strangers to each other.

He took it upon Himself to introduce them. He took one lady by the hand and went towards the other. "Charity," He said turning towards the first lady, "I'd like you to meet Gratitude."

The two virtues, we are told, shook hands in astonishment, for this was the very first time that they had met each other!

This parable only shows that a lot of things go unrecognised, unacknowledged in this world of ours. We take a lot of things for granted – we fail to appreciate them, or return good for good.

I always think of the good things of life like the sunshine and the air we breathe – we know they are there and we take them for granted.

I would say that gratitude is like sunshine – we can do without it, as when the sun hides behind the clouds; but when it is there, its warmth and light add life and joy to the world.

There was a man who started from humble origins. Through his hard work and enterprising spirit, he built up a flourishing business. However, the vagaries of the stock market brought bad times upon him, and one day, he became bankrupt.

Amidst the ruins of his fortunes, the man did something very few of us can do. He took a piece of paper and wrote down all the things he still had with him: a loving, caring family; a strong, healthy body; an active, intelligent mind; friends and genuine well-wishers who would always stand by him; contacts and associations which he had built up over the years; the business acumen and valuable experience he had gained in the past...

The man realised that he still had a great deal to be thankful for! With gratitude to God in his heart, he decided that he would start anew.

His optimism was well founded. In a few years' time, he had built up a still larger business than his previous venture.

When we count our blessings and thank the Lord even in adversity, we will find that our sufferings recede into the background.

There was a woman whose husband fell seriously ill. The doctors who were treating him began to despair of his condition. "Your husband does not have long to live," they informed the woman.

She was a lady with tremendous faith. From that day, from that very moment, she began to thank the Lord a thousand times everyday.

"Thank you God! Thank you God! Thank you God!" she prayed again and again. "Thank you God, for taking care of my husband! Thank you God, for healing him and making him whole again. Thank you God, for being my support and comfort!"

She continued to offer these prayers of thanksgiving even though there were no signs of improvement in her ailing husband.

Strangely enough, a few weeks later, when her husband was put through a series of tests, the doctors were amazed at the results. He seemed to have turned the corner, and was actually making an amazing recovery.

"A power above and beyond us has been at work," they exclaimed. "This man will live!"

The woman's happiness knew no bounds. "Thank you God! Thank you God! Thank you God!" she repeated, for it had now become the *mantra* of her life.

"Whatever be the conditions in which we find ourselves, whatever be the sufferings through which we pass, let us thank the Lord all the time," the Wise One repeated, and his words sounded like a scriptural recitation to my ears. "When we do so, our hearts expand, and we become receptive to the helpful and healing forces of the Lord…"

"Here is a song I read sometime ago," he said and recited it in his melodious voice:

> Thanks be to God for His love and mercy.
> Thanks be to God for His boundless grace.
> Thanks be to God for the hearts that love us.
> Thanks be to God for each friendly face.
> Thanks be to God for strength in suffering.
> Thanks be to God for joys we've known.
> Thanks be to God for the hope He gives us.
> Of rest eternal by His throne.

I reflected, rather sadly, that ingratitude is becoming the mark of our age. Children, young people, workers and family members take everything for granted. Worse still, some of them have even developed a critical and rebellious spirit. They are more prone to criticise and complain and blame, rather than express thanks.

Today, people complain about the government; they complain about the state of the roads; they complain about prices; they complain about their working conditions.

In a book called *Virtues for our Times*, William Doty writes:

> There is a serious lack of the spirit of thanksgiving between the employers and the employees, between citizens and public officials, and between the community and those who, through their artistic efforts, make a contribution to the common cultural heritage…

The mutual lack of gratitude between employers and employees is becoming so common that there is no sense of belonging or loyalty any more, even among the educated and cultured classes. The employee does not appreciate the facilities provided to him; he feels unappreciated, taken for granted; he feels he is overworked and underpaid.

As for the employer, he feels he has done a favour by hiring people to work; he regards his workers as shirkers and slackers who will try to get away by doing as little as possible…

I would urge all employees to thank the Lord that you have been blessed with a livelihood. Thank God, that your needs are being taken care of at a time when unemployment is rampant. Thank God that you have a job which makes your life worthwhile.

By the same token, I urge the employers: be grateful to God that you are in a position to give rather than receive. Thank the Lord that He has given you the wherewithal to employ people and offer them means of livelihood.

"Ungrateful people describe this world as a vale of tears," the Wise One said. "But I believe that God intended it to be a Vale of Content, a Vale of Sweetness and Joy. However, there are two types of people who live here. The first group live on Thanksgiving Road: they are healthy, happy and peaceful. The sun shines on them, they hear the birds singing, they know that God is in His heaven and all is right with the world. And, there are plenty of houses 'to let' in their part of the world.

"As for the second group, they live in Ingratitude Street. They complain constantly of stress, tension and ill-health; the atmosphere is itself polluted, they claim; the water is bad; the weather is harsh, and life is just not worth living. Conditions are crowded here, yet more and more people are moving into the area.

"Ask yourselves, where would you rather live – Thanksgiving Road or Ingratitude Street?"

I thought of Iceland, a country in which it is almost perpetual winter. The landscape seems to be harsh and rocky, without much greenery. Yet the Icelanders exclaim: "Iceland is the best land that the sun shines upon."

I was reminded too, of an incident from the life of Abu Usman. He was walking one day on the street, when someone threw ashes from the terrace of a house. The ashes fell on the head of the man of God.

His companions who were with him, felt infuriated and were about to abuse the offender, when Abu Usman said to them, "Keep your peace, my friends. Let us thank the Lord that one who merits fire has been let off with ashes."

A friend of mine lost one of his eyes in an accident. He was admitted to the hospital, where several people visited him to sympathise with his family, and commiserate with him in his great loss. They were surprised to find him warm and cheerful as ever.

One of them actually expressed his surprise in words. "How is it that you have taken this tragic accident so cheerfully?" he asked my friend. "I thought that I would find you depressed and gloomy."

My friend smiled. "I thank the Lord that one eye still remains," he said. "It will take sometime for me to get used to it, but I can see with it as well as I did when I had two eyes. The accident could have easily robbed me of both my eyes – but God chose to protect one of them. Blessed be His Name!"

My friend had the greatest gift that adversity could have brought – the gift of gratitude even in tough times. The accident which would have plunged another man into the slough of despondency, did not seem to touch him.

There was a king who was in the habit of feeding the poor and the underprivileged every day, in the courtyard of his palace. Hundreds of beggars and destitutes would line up in the yard to receive their food. When their meals were set before them, they simply pounced on the food, for they were so hungry. They often pushed and jostled one another, grabbed whatever they could, helped themselves to more food so that they could take some of it away – and left without a word after they had eaten.

"His Majesty should stop this habit," his courtiers complained to one another. "These people are so thankless – their behaviour is utterly disgusting."

The king overheard them. "What is it that troubles you, my friends?" he asked them mildly.

"Oh Sire," they complained volubly. "We are shocked by the ingratitude of these barbaric, uncivilised hordes! Not a word of thanks do they offer to their king who feeds them day after day."

The king smiled, but said nothing by way of reply.

A few days later, the courtiers were invited to a banquet at the royal palace. The courtiers arrived in all their splendour, and took their seats at the royal table. When the food and the wine were served, they began to eat merrily.

"Just a minute," said the king holding up his hand. "Everyday, the King of kings offers us food as sustenance for the body. How many of you have paused to thank the Lord for His kind gifts to us? Is He not the Provider of our food? Are we any better than those whom you have called barbaric and uncivilised?"

The nobles bowed down their heads in shame.

Our journey through life has been perfectly planned by Infinite love and Infinite wisdom: let us realise therefore, that there can be no mistake. Every experience that comes to us is just the right experience occurring at the right time to train us in the right way. So let us accept God's Will in the spirit of gratitude and cheerful acceptance. Let us not complain, nor attempt to circumvent anything. Let us thank God for everything that happens to us.

"Our unhappiness arises from the fact that we try to avoid and resist what we regard as unpleasant experiences and difficult situations," the Wise One said. "We must realise that they are essential to our spiritual growth. God means us to face them, learn from them and thus to develop our moral and spiritual muscles. The best way then is to accept them and cooperate with their inner purpose, all the while fixing our mind and hearts on Him who has planned it all for us.

"In all conditions of life, thank the Lord. Let us make it a habit to praise the Lord at every step, in every round of life. Even in the midst of fear and frustration, worry and anxiety, depression and disappointment, let these words come out of the very depths of our hearts: "Thank you God! Thank you God! Thank you God!" And we will be filled with joy and peace that amazes us. When we thank the Lord all the time, we ensure the basis of our own happiness…"

The words seemed familiar; even the voice was well known to me; surely I had heard them earlier – in this birth or the previous one?

The moment was magical; I felt transported, I felt that a light was descending on me…

"It's time for us to leave," the Wise One said softly. "You have been told twenty secrets that can help you lead a happy life; share them with people; show them the way; tell them that happiness is their birthright…

"Tell them, above all, that the realm of happiness awaits them; they only have to wish to live here, and this beautiful land will receive them with all its warmth and charm…

"Shall we go?"

I looked at the Wise One intently, wordlessly… his features seemed to me very familiar, well beloved… his loving form was the same one that had been enshrined in my heart ever since I could remember…

"Master!" I called out, as realisation dawned on me. It was my beloved Gurudev who had accompanied me on this momentous, memorable spiritual quest!

... I awoke, as from a vision, Sadhu Vaswani's book still clutched in my hand.

Had it been just a dream? Or was it a waking vision?

Twenty ways to lead a happy life: I have passed them all on to you. In conclusion, let me say to you: forget the other nineteen, if you will. But do not forget the twentieth secret. Keep on thanking God all the time! Repeat the three magic words, "Thank you God! Thank you God! Thank you God!" and see for yourself the difference it makes!

May God continue to bless you, take care of you, and lead you from height to height, from success to greater success, from happiness to vaster happiness!